Swee' Pea
AND OTHER PLAYGROUND LEGENDS

by John Valenti
with Ron Naclerio

The door opened and, as the two basketball junkies stood in the runway just outside the visiting Boston Celtics locker room at the Meadowlands Arena, out stepped a gray-haired man. "Hey," one of the bystanders said, making sure he spoke loud enough for the gray-haired gentleman to hear, "there goes the second-best player ever to come out of Andrew Jackson High School." With that, Bob Cousy, former Celtic and member of the National Basketball Association Hall of Fame, turned. "Second best?" Cousy asked, an incredulous look on his face. "Who's first?"

"What d'ya mean who's first?" the bystander said, making no effort at all to hide a sly chuckle. "You must've heard of Lloyd Daniels."

Swee' Pea
AND OTHER PLAYGROUND LEGENDS

Tales of Drugs, Violence
and Basketball

by John Valenti
with Ron Naclerio

Michael Kesend Publishing, Ltd.
New York

Book and cover design by Kim Llewellyn

FIRST EDITION

Library of Congress Cataloging-in-Publication Data

Valenti, John 1960-
   Swee'pea and other playground legends: tales of drugs, violence, and basketball/by John Valenti with Ron Naclerio.
     p. cm.
   Includes index.
       ISBN 0-935576-38-X: $26.95.—ISBN 0-935576-39-8 (pbk.) $13.95
   1. Daniels, Lloyd. 2. Basketball players—United States—Biography. 3. Tarkanian, Jerry, 1930-
       4. Basketball—United States—Coaches—Biography. 5. University of Nevada, Las Vegas—Basketball. I. Naclerio, Ron, 1958-   . II. Title.
GV884.D36V35 1990
796.323'092—dc20
[B]   90-45321

For my wife, Judy Lee, who endured life with me as I wrote this book, and for my son, Jarek, who was born on the day I began this work. For Mom and Dad, who, no matter what he thinks, is much more than what he once termed "a backwater generation." And for my brothers, Jim and Rob, who from now on will have to give me some respect. They'll call me "Mr." Butthead.

For Randy and Rafer and Stephon and the players of a new generation. There is nothing so sad as a generation that does not learn from the mistakes of the ones previous. Learn, then, and stay strong. Become all that you can.

Contents

Illustrations follow page 130

Acknowledgments

This is my first book. And, though hopefully not my last, it is thankfully done. That may sound strange, since my business is writing. I am a reporter for a major daily newspaper. I write every day. But, though I still live with some of those stories—I probably will keep some of them with me forever—I have never lived with one in the process of being born for as long as I lived with this book. I began to gather information for this work as long as six years ago, saving it, thinking one day it might make a worthwhile story. After years of talking about doing so, I began to write it in mid-September, 1989, and it was mid-May, 1990, before I had finished. During that time I learned a lot about life. And, I learned a lot about myself.

I learned that some days I did my job well. I learned that some days I did it not so well. And, I learned that other days I didn't do it at all.

What I also learned was something about people. This is, after all, a book about people. I learned that when I grew cocky, friends and relatives—and, usually, my wife—were there to force me back down to earth. I learned that when I was vulnerable, those folks were there to lift my spirits. I learned that most people aren't as fortunate. For that, then, I am grateful.

I am grateful, also, for those who went the extra mile during this process. Those who made themselves available, submitting to my incessant requests and demands. Those who endured the incessant babbling about "my book." And, those who extended themselves. I can only hope what you find herein made all that inconvenience worthwhile and necessary.

That having been said, I thank my wife, who spent many lonely days and nights while I sat in "my cave" with my computer and wrote. She listened to me rant and rave when things didn't go well. She listened to me complain and yell when I was confronted by my own shortcomings. And, yet, she endured and rarely, if ever, said a word about my foul state—all this while taking care of our newborn son. For that, I am eternally grateful.

I am grateful, too, for the assistance I have received during the writing of this book. I am grateful for the efforts of Ron Naclerio, the main contributor to this work, who despite being a pain in the ass at times, provided too many funny, sad and strange stories—all of which made this book the best it could be. It is impossible to tell how many times I placed calls answered by his mother, Gloria, who was always ready to offer a word of encouragement. I am also grateful for the time spent with Lulia Hendly, a wonderful, strong woman who has endured much pain and sorrow in her life and still manages to smile at it. She invited me into her home, poured out her heart and shared memories that must have hurt to recollect. She gave of herself.

Others, too, gave of their time and of themselves, among them, John Lucas, Roy Tarpley and David Thompson—marvelous athletes who spoke about their own vulnerability. They did not have to share their stories. Yet they did, without complaint, and I believe this book is richer for it.

It is richer, also, for the time given by Flora Adams and Carmellita Boatwright, who spoke of their families and of their pain and suffering. It is richer for the time given by all those who spoke with candor and honesty: Tom Konchalski, Saul Lerner, Kevin Barry, Stan Dinner, Arnie Hershkowitz, Lou d'Almeida, Thomas Rome, Esq., Howie Garfinkel, JoJo White, Alvis Brown, Steve Smith, Bernie Glannon, John Killilea, Cedric Hunter, Ron Kellogg, Chip Engelland, Al Quakenbush, Steve Cropper, Dave MacCalman, Bob McCullough, Sr., Sonny Johnson, Butch Beard, Jack Curran, Vincent Smith, Joan Anderson, Boo Harvey, Moses Scurry, Ron Matthias, Ronnie Arrow, Scott Gernander, Howard Reynolds, Brien Crowder, Donald J. Martin, Esq., Dr. Walter F. Pizzi, Dr. Daniel L. Picard, Robert Czaplicki, Abraham Bruin, Ron Brown, David Daye, "Billy Bang" Thomas, Rynell Calloway, Vernon Harton, John Cirillo, Dennis D'Agostino, Colleen Roche, Happy Fine, Joe Queen, Annie Sargeant Stephens and Barbara Stephens. You'll never know how much you helped.

Even more special thanks go to several athletes who gave their valuable time to share some special insights. They did not have to spend the time they spent. They received no compensation other than knowing that their words would help tell the story of the streets and failure, of the streets and success. These folks include John (The Spider) Salley, who managed a few serious stories to go with his jokes—Jerry Salley and Johnny B. can attest to that—Mark Jackson, J.R. Reid, Kenny Anderson

Thanks to Tony Chiles, Orlando Antigua, Maurice (Mo Diamond) Johnson, Chris Brooks and Gary Springer, who shared their time. Thanks to Tony (Red) Bruin, who has suffered much self-inflicted pain, but who stood up to his past and is beating it. I wish him the best in his new job and hope he, his girl, Tracey, and son will always be able to enjoy life for what it is.

Thanks to Earl Manigault, one of those who fell the hardest, but whose goal is to make sure others never suffer his fate. He spoke words of wisdom. We can only hope future generations decide to listen.

Thanks, too, to Jerry Tarkanian, his daughter, Jodie, and his family. I have no doubt created many difficult moments for them and still they were more than courteous with me and we shared some laughs. The same is true with Mark Warkentien, who is a gentleman despite the names I've called him.

As with any book, there are also those whose input goes unnoticed by everyone—everyone, that is, except the author. Therefore, thanks go to: Michael Kesend, who believed in this project. Though he was wary of my inexperience in the world of books and did bust on me numerous times—"We're pushing deadline, John!"—he was always there to calm my fears and listen to sob stories; Kent Oswald, who edited this book. I would like to think Kent made many good suggestions and some not so good ones and that I was smart enough to chose the right ones to incorporate. That probably isn't totally true. But I think that all of his green pencil marks and red flags were not in vain. This would not be half the book it is—it would still be a series of unrelated newspaper stories, a scary thought, really—without his advice and skill; and, Neil F. Best, a reporter and friend at *New York Newsday*. He proofread this book as a favor and then issued many valuable opinions on its contents. As for his assessment of the work, he said, "It was good." For Neil, that was the ultimate praise. And, it meant a lot. Really.

To John Quinn, my immediate editor at *New York Newsday*, who overlooked a few of my shortcomings during the writing of this book. Thanks for not hitting me that day and thanks, too, for keeping me from hitting you. It saved a sometimes strained, though irreplaceable, friendship.

Thanks to Michael Dobie of *New York Newsday* and Joe Hawk of the *Las Vegas Review-Journal*, who provided me with information. Thanks to Mike George of *The New York Post*, who spent time talking about structure and street slang. Eternal gratitude to the late Dick Sandler, the former executive sports editor at *New York Newsday*, who walked through permission for this project just weeks before he succumbed to cancer.

An incredible amount of thanks to John Henderson, formerly of the *Las Vegas Review-Journal*, who graciously passed along notes and quotes about Richie Adams and Lloyd and who talked about this book for hours and was never too busy to field a few questions—or tell a few stories about piranhas, the kind that swim in the Amazon and the kind that navigate the basketball world. Thanks to the nth degree to Danny Robbins, now of the *Los Angeles Times,* who taught me an awful lot about reporting when I worked with him on the *New York Newsday* investigation of the basketball program at Nevada-Las Vegas. He showed me the ropes—and how to spot the loopholes—and refined my skills. I couldn't have had a better teacher. Honest.

And last, though surely not least, thanks to all those friends who listened to my tales of woe and still offered advice—yes, Dave D'Allesandro, Joe Tintle, Jim O'Connell, Al Cohen, et al [everyone, that is, who asked, "How's the book?"]—all of which was very greatly appreciated.

To all my relatives, including Mom and Dad and my in-laws, Red and Audrey Edwards, who dealt with eight months of horror and hell and still lent their support. To Dennis and Carol O'Donnell, who taught me how to write. And, to Jack Salzman and Peter Koper, two professors at Hofstra who taught me what was good and interesting.

Most of all, to Lloyd Daniels. He lived the life described herein and still, with a laugh—and, sometimes, a con—took the time to talk about it. There were too many times he made me laugh and cry in the same moment. But, he really did play the game like no one you've ever seen and he may be the best there ever was. If there's anything I learned in writing this book, it's that it's never too late to save yourself. I hope that if Lloyd can't find a way to do that, others will at least learn from his mistakes. I'm cynical enough to believe that neither will ever happen. But, there's always hope.

Or, so I've been told.

"It's one thing to tell a man he must lift himself by his bootstraps. It's another thing to tell a bootless man he must lift himself by his bootstraps."

—MARTIN LUTHER KING, JR.

"A man got to survive. When you ain't got no money and you need clothes and food to eat, you don't think about it. You got to survive. Got to survive, got to eat, got to have sneakers."

—LLOYD DANIELS JR.

Swee'Pea

AND OTHER PLAYGROUND LEGENDS

1•Three-Shot Barrage

Blood was everywhere. It had drained, crimson, into the most intimate corners of the torn and tattered shirt, almost as if it were trying to forever change the complexion of the fabric it had soaked through and through. Matted on the cloth and on the skin, it caked and congealed, gummy to the touch, and gave an eerie, almost surrealistic aura to the patient stretched out on the hospital gurney in the white-washed emergency room.

It was two-thirty in the morning and, by now, Dr. Daniel L. Picard had long been up to his elbows in one mess or another. Director of Surgery at Mary Immaculate Hospital in Jamaica, Queens, he had been the primary surgeon on call for an indecent part of the night. And, based in an area of New York City where witnessing the results of early-morning, drug-related street violence had long ago become as normal as the band-aging of minor scrapes and cuts, nights were seldom quiet at Mary Immaculate.

Called to emergency fresh from working on another patient, Picard took little time disrobing from his sweat-drenched, blood-stained outfit and getting scrubbed and changed into a clean gown. Here was yet one more serious problem on his hands. On a stretcher lay the victim: Size-thirteen feet dangled over one end of the cart as if hovering at the edge of a precipice, his eyes wide like a mortally-wounded fawn in a futile search for a last-second reprieve from death. Darkened blood stained his coffee-chocolate skin.

There was a bullet hole in the left side of his neck just shy of the jugular. There were two bullet wounds in his chest, one, just wide of his heart, the force of the other so sure, so brutal, that it had ripped its way across the distance of the cavity, exiting through a nasty opening in his back. In their wake, the spent lead had left damage untold.

Picard caught his breath, drawing it hard as he considered the situation. "A major thoracic wound," he thought to himself, as the fresh droplets of blood began to spatter his gown. Tenuous red streams flowed across his rubber gloves. He had no idea who the patient was. Nor, did he care. He knew just one thing. "It's extensive." When you get shot, it always is.

1

On the table, the six-foot, eight-inch body of twenty-one-year-old Lloyd Daniels—the person countless basketball scouts had once called the best professional prospect from New York City since Kareem Abdul-Jabbar was known simply as Lew Alcindor—clung to life by a thread ever so much thinner than the strand of a well-worn playground net. Already, he had lost six pints of blood. He was almost dead.

The night had begun in rather unceremonious fashion. It had rained, poured actually, and Lloyd, bored and with nothing to do, had called one of his longtime friends, Ron Naclerio. A recovering addict, Lloyd was struggling with himself to stay out of trouble, stay clean.

Already, he had been through in-patient and out-patient rehabilitation three times in an effort to beat an alcohol and cocaine addiction that had cost him a possible basketball scholarship at Nevada-Las Vegas and jobs as a pro with the Topeka Sizzlers in the Continental Basketball Association and with a team called Waitemata in Auckland, New Zealand.

And it was widely known that those problems and a troubled academic past—he had attended four high schools in three states before quitting his junior year at Andrew Jackson High School in Cambria Heights, Queens, without a diploma and without having learned to read—had caused him to be bypassed in the 1988 National Basketball Association Draft despite not-so-subtle hints from several general managers that he might be a first-round selection. Although word suggested Lloyd had been blackballed by the league, people who had seen him play understood that if he could only prove he could be responsible for his actions, if only he could stay clean long enough to at least earn an invitation to a rookie-free agent camp, well, a job was all but his. Rules, after all, were often bent for stars.

"Yo, Ron," Lloyd asked. "Want to play some ball?"

Ronnie thought for a second. A junior high school teacher, as well as the basketball coach at Cardozo High School in Bayside, Queens, Ronnie had known Lloyd for more than five years. He was almost a guardian, someone who would spend time with Lloyd, go to games with him. They'd play ball, talk the talk, Ronnie, a basketball junkie who was barely in his thirties, being tuned in to the streets and to their kids. He had been an athlete, an all-America baseball player at St. John's University—once, in college, he had led the nation in stolen bases—and later was a minor league outfielder in the White Sox organization. He could be raw, coarse. But he understood an athlete's mentality. He knew how to deal with them and with their problems. Lloyd's relatives had grown so accustomed to him and respected him so much, in fact, they'd even nicknamed him "Lloyd's white brother."

"Nah, I'm watchin' the game," Ronnie told Lloyd. "I don't want to go."

"C'mon, Ron," Lloyd said, prodding. "Let's go work out."

Another time, Ronnie would have gone. But he suspected Lloyd was again using drugs. They had fought just two days before, during a confrontation over those suspicions. Ronnie had screamed at Lloyd. He had come very close to punching him out, nearly throwing a combination. He wanted to make the point that he would not tolerate such failure. Like so many others before him, he had reached the breaking point. If Lloyd really wanted to succeed, really wanted to prove to the world he could turn his life around, he'd have to take the first step. He would have to prove he could stand on his own.

"Nah. I'm tired," Ronnie said. "I'm stayin' home."

A while later, then, Lloyd left his house, alone, to work out in a gym on Long Island. It was Wednesday, May 10, 1989. The NBA Draft was two months away, rookie camps little more than three.

Lloyd had probably stopped thinking about the NBA by the time he returned home to the green, single-family row-house his grandmother owned on 203rd Street in the Hollis-St. Albans section of Queens. His workout against a few of the locals had been relaxed—they hadn't offered much competition—and, bored after his return from the gym, Lloyd was still looking for something to do. It really didn't matter what.

On the surface, it was a quiet, residential neighborhood, the neighborhood that had given life to the dreams of people such as Mark Jackson, who had come out of there to become an all-America point guard at St. John's and the 1987-88 NBA Rookie of the Year with the New York Knicks. But it also was a neighborhood with a darker, much less visible side.

For years, it had been a neighborhood in transition, one which, day-by-day and block-by-block, was falling prey to drugs and to the drug-related violence that skewed community and disembodied lives. It was a crack neighborhood. A place where dealers sometimes dealt from street corners down near Francis Lewis Boulevard. A place where the dealers sometimes dealt from the house next door. A place where the quiet of any given night might be shattered at the most unlikely moment, the sound of gunfire erupting in the street.

And Lloyd Daniels was going to be the next victim.

Outside, it continued to rain. For a while, Lloyd and his aunt, Sherry, herself only in her twenties, settled down in the kitchen with a deck of cards, a bottle of champagne and a few quart cans of "O.E."—Olde English. It was hardly a good start on a long night for a man with an alcohol problem. For about an hour, the game went on. Hands were dealt, jokes were told, laughs were exchanged, alcohol was consumed. Soon Lloyd, feeling good, feeling that old feel, walked into the living room. It was almost midnight.

"Gran'ma," he said. "Let me have one of them posters you got."

His grandmother, a hard-working woman in her late fifties, looked at him.

The posters, made when Lloyd was in Topeka, pictured him in a Sizzlers uniform. At the bottom, in an ad for Gaines Cycle Dog Foods, Lloyd was stretched out with some sad-eyed puppies and their dog-food bowls. Around the neighborhood, where Lloyd was considered a folk hero because of his ability, they were like gold. "I'm not giving you any posters," Lulia Hendley said. "You're gonna sell them to buy crack, you are."

"No, gran'ma. Gran'ma, I'm not."

"Don't con me," she said. "I know what you're doin'."

"I ain't, gran'ma. I just want one."

"Junior," she said sharply, a warning to the grandchild named after her eldest son. "If you don't stop it, stop doin' those drugs, you're gonna get busted in the ass, you know that? You'll get busted in the ass, the cops will pick you up, put you in Rikers Island and you know you can't deal with no Rikers Island. And you know you're gonna be dead if you get shot."

"Gran'ma, gran'ma," Lloyd said. "I ain't doin' that stuff no more."

"You'd better not be," she said, though Lloyd, not interested in her advice, had already turned his back on her and returned to the kitchen.

Lloyd still had the hunger. And, facing the temptation and feeling weak as any recovering addict can surrounded by a neighborhood filled with the bad stuff, he picked up the phone around midnight and called his friend, "Moe." The next day, the newspapers and police were rampant in their speculation about Moe, whose name and beeper number were found on a slip of paper in Lloyd's bedroom after the shooting. Doctors carried beepers. So did cops. But in areas like Hollis, most folks who carried beepers were drug dealers. It was their business lifeline.

In reality, the number belonged to Kevin Barry, a man as far-removed from the bad thing as could be. Barry was almost forty. Still, it often seemed like he was from another time, back when life was simple. He believed in people. He believed they owed something to each other.

He believed in lending a helping hand. And, like others before him, he believed in Lloyd.

He had met Lloyd not a month before. Ronnie had introduced them. Immediately, Barry offered support. He ran a small, independent school bus company. Lloyd called his ride, his bus, "the yellow stretch." A man who had been friends with Cus D'Amato, having met Mike Tyson when the boxer was just thirteen and having seen what D'Amato had done with him, Barry had also founded a non-profit organization called the Give a Kid a Chance Foundation. He ran neighborhood basketball games, took underprivileged kids to the movies. He taught them there was a way other than what they saw on the streets of New York. He taught them that they had a future.

Barry took Lloyd to his house in Brooklyn. He moved out of his room, hung a sign on the door that said "Lloyd's Room." He slept on the couch. He bought clothes for Lloyd. He found him a trainer to get him in shape. He and his sons shared meals with Lloyd. They shared their lives. Their hearts.

He was teaching Lloyd to read. He was teaching him responsibility. Lloyd called him "Moe," mainly because he liked to watch the Three Stooges. Then, one night, Lloyd showed up at a club game at St. John's. He was high.

"He was with a drug dealer," Barry said. "He was zonked out of his mind. Ron read him the riot act. I told him, 'You're fucked up. You're an asshole.' I cursed him out. We had a big fight. I went home, put a poster of Len Bias on the wall. When Lloyd got home, I pointed at that picture. I said, 'Am I gonna be coming to visit you in a casket? Is that how this ends?'

"He said, 'No, Kev. I'm goin' to make it.' "

Barry didn't believe him. He threw him out of the house. That was Monday, May 8th.

When Lloyd called the beeper number that Wednesday, Kevin Barry was out of the house. But he was in a forgiving mood and, deep down, he knew Lloyd needed him. So, when he got the message, he called Lloyd.

"C'mon an' get me," Lloyd said. "I got to get out of here."

"But, I'm in Albany," Kevin told him, trying to sound serious.

"How far's that?" Lloyd asked.

"About four hours."

"Okay," Lloyd said. "Can you come by and pick me up in twenty minutes?"

Kevin laughed. Even if he did believe Kevin was in Albany, Lloyd never did have a conception of time. And, even though it was somewhere around 1 a.m., Kevin knew Lloyd needed him. So, without complaint, he hopped in the yellow stretch and headed from Manhattan to Queens. For a while, Lloyd waited. But he had the urge. And so, when Kevin arrived little more than an hour later, Lloyd was gone. Kevin searched the neighborhood in vain.

Lloyd was nowhere to be found.

As best as anyone could tell, Lloyd had remained in the house and continued to fight his temptation until near 2 a.m., when finally he decided to give in and wandered down to the corner of Hollis Avenue. There, according to relatives, he visited a local businessman who worked the corner. From him, relatives later told police, Lloyd picked up a little rock, the street name for crack, the smokable derivative of cocaine.

For years, friends told Lloyd that drugs might someday be his downfall. But as one acquaintance said, "With him it always seemed to be a case of where the spirit is willing, but the flesh is weak." So, when Lloyd returned to the house owned by his grandmother, he had the rock as well as the kind of company no man wants for friends, let alone enemies.

No sooner had he closed the door of the house than a white sedan arrived out front. Two men got out of the car and stood at the gate. Seeing them, Lloyd, who had run inside to hide the vials he had on him, stepped outside to talk.

"Yo," one man yelled as soon as Lloyd walked out the door and onto the front lawn. "Gimme my stuff."

"Ain't got your stuff," Lloyd said. "Get out of here."

"Yo," the man said, again. "Gimme my stuff or the money. Don't play."

"I told you, man," Lloyd said. "Ain't got your stuff."

Unsure of what caused the confrontation, relatives described to police a scenario that would later prove somewhat incorrect. They said that Lloyd, streetwise and king of the street con, had slipped the man, described as a black male in his late-teens, early-twenties, two dollar bills instead of the two fives required for payment for the rock, sold on the streets by the vial. Now the dealer, finding he'd been ripped off, wanted his money. Getting no satisfaction, he signaled for his friend, who had gone back to the car.

With accuracy, though, witnesses told police how the second man pulled a gun and pointed it at Lloyd, probably as a threat. But with no money on him and too far from the door to make a run for it, Lloyd made yet another bad decision in a life filled with bad decisions. He reached for the gun.

"Bam!" And his body recoiled with the shot.

"Bam!" And, again, his body recoiled with the shot.

Four or five times, no one seems sure which, the gun went off.

Three times, for certain, bullets hit Lloyd.

Have you ever seen a man get shot? It is almost mystical. Fire spews out the gun barrel. Skin tears, lead explodes. Shrapnel splinters and punctures organs as surely as spilled acid eats its way through metal. Powder residue hangs in the air—moist and warm, yet chilling—its smell like that of rotten eggs, its stench powerful, spectacular.

Everything moves in slow motion. The body tumbles as if in instant replay. Blood shoots forth as if to replicate the motion of an oversized rock dropped into a pool of water; first, droplets splatter outward to reach escape velocity, then follows a steady stream. Screams, if there be, echo inside your brain until, finally, in agony, they register.

And then the man falls, his innermost possessions most likely no longer locked away in secrecy. Body and earth, momentarily one.

It all takes little more than a second.

"I looked out the window and I said, 'This joker's gonna shoot Junior,'" Lulia Hendley recalled. "I gets to the door, I heard the shooting. And Junior grabs him, grabs the guy. One shot hit Junior, then two more."

"I was getting in the shower and my mother said, 'Lloyd, there are two people out there for you,'" recalled Gary Hendley, an uncle who lived in the house. By the time he reached the lawn after the shots, Lloyd, whose street name was "Swee'pea," was sprawled out, writhing, his lean, lanky body folded and contorted, the two men and the car, going. Gone. "I heard four shots," he said. "I ran outside and saw Swee'pea lying on the ground. I didn't even see the bullet holes at first. I said, 'Swee'pea, they ruined you.'"

With all the strength he could muster, Hendley, with shoulders like a linebacker, pulled Lloyd, already a bloody mess, down the driveway and into a side door. He laid his broken body down in the hallway. "My mom and my sister called the police and an ambulance," he said.

"I was like, 'Oh God, he's shot,'" Lulia Hendley said. "'He's gonna die. Junior's gonna die.'"

As they loaded him onto the stretcher, Lloyd, still conscious, the $100 sweatsuit Barry bought him already having been torn apart, its turquoise fabric soaked almost pure scarlet red, looked at anxious relatives and then at another uncle, J.C. Daniels. "I don't want to die, J.C." he pleaded. "Don't let me die."

New York City is well known for the strange twists and turns it puts on life, the awkward, sometimes bizarre angles it brings to the fates, and this day was certainly no different. By the following nightfall, across the river in Manhattan, the crowd would be letting loose with a deafening roar as Mark Jackson and the New York Knicks met Michael Jordan and the Chicago Bulls in a playoff game at Madison Square Garden.

But now, back in the operating room at Mary Immaculate, where the trauma team had assembled, Dr. Picard and his crew worked in virtual silence, save for the clattering of instruments and tools, as they fought to rescue the life of Lloyd Daniels. There was a chance. But honestly, Picard figured, it was a miracle his patient was still alive at all.

The average body has ten pints of blood and, already, Lloyd had lost sixty percent of that. His pulse was weakening, his breathing erratic. A bullet had punctured and collapsed his right lung. Another had barely missed his heart and embedded itself in his posterior chest wall. All around, blood spurted and seeped into the chest cavity. This would be touch and go.

Around 6 a.m., as people in the neighborhood awoke, Lulia Hendley went outside to tear down the yellow police lines that had been drawn taut across her lawn from fence to house. She was angry. She couldn't stand to see them any longer. When she finally regained her composure, she went back inside and called Ronnie. It was bad news, she said. Momentarily, Ronnie wrestled with his emotions, fought back his tears. Then he called Kevin Barry and made a call to Tom Rome, the Manhattan attorney who represented Lloyd.

Just the night before, the two had talked about Lloyd's future. They had joked about the career that waited out there for him, waiting to be grabbed like a brass ring on some childhood merry-go-'round. They joked about the movie that could be made about Lloyd's life. A soap opera, they'd called it.

"All we need is one of two things to happen," Ronnie had told Tom that night, laughing. "All he has to do is get killed or make the NBA."

When Tom Rome answered the phone that morning, Ronnie tried to salve his guilt by putting the best face he could on what had happened. "Well, Tom," he said. "It looks like we can finally make the movie."

2 · The Legend of Swee'pea

Lloyd seemed to be unconscious and, as far as anyone could tell, had been for the better part of the past half-hour. Around him uniformed bodies raced with a ridiculous sense of urgency, their actions spasmodic and haphazard and brought forth with random precision; the result of their motions, in reality, little more than energy wasted.

He had viewed the scenario as if at half-speed, watched it and visualized it slow as sap runs from the cut bark. This was the biggest game of his life, he thought. He couldn't give someone else a chance to screw things up. Not after he had fought so hard. Maybe it was heart; maybe just his survival instinct. But something inside told him he couldn't go down without more of a fight. So he yelled, yelled like only a man who has an understanding of such a grave nature can yell, calling hard and loud to be heard above the din, but trying his best not to sound like a man of desperation.

"Yo, c'mon!" he screamed. For emphasis, he clapped his hands twice in quick succession. "Ain't I said, 'C'mon'? Get me the motherfuckin' ball!"

The game was close, on the line. That Andrew Jackson still led was, in itself, a miracle. A late run by Wyandanch had trimmed a 57-44 lead—what had seemed like a nice, safe cushion—to 59-58. In that span, Lloyd had actually missed two straight shots from the field and a jam off an offensive rebound. Now, with little more than five minutes left, the crowd of about 8,500 that had gathered at the Nassau (L.I.) Coliseum on January 12, 1986, to watch eight teams meet in four games in the Martin Luther King Classic, had grown anxious, frenetic. Many stood, awaiting the next move.

For so long, it seemed, these people had read accounts of his ability in the four New York daily newspapers and had heard what sounded to be tall tales of the skill possessed by this teenaged player from the streets of New York. Stories, they thought, that surely were pure exaggeration. Yet, here before their very eyes was Lloyd Daniels, the player known simply as "Swee'pea," his vast ability mocking the best efforts of the players around him.

A hush settled over the crowd as the pass came to Lloyd. He had never played in front of so many people before. And, there were more than a few college scouts in the stands. Still, Lloyd took the ball near the top of the key, faked a pass, juked his man, spun off him and posted up. From eight feet, he let it ride with the smoothness of a seasoned con man putting the touch on an easy mark. He even laughed at his man, too, talking trash to him. It was pure playground. "Real fine," someone in the stands yelled from a few rows back, as it went in, banking off the backboard and in. Jackson led, 61-58.

Over the course of the next few minutes, when the game was won and lost, when his inexperienced teammates appeared on the verge of panic before the crowd at this, the most prestigious of all local regular-season high school tournaments, Lloyd took control. He seemed oblivious to everything going on around him, except what was important. The game. He zeroed in, focused on his mission. He never once lost his poise, never once let his concentration wander. He laid passes on all the right fingertips. He made all his shots.

Double-teamed—no, triple-teamed—he buried a pull-up twelve-footer in traffic to make it 66-60. He hit a clutch ten-foot banker to keep Jackson ahead, 68-65, after the lead had been cut to one. He sent home a short-range jumper—child's play, really, for him—with fifty-one seconds left to give Jackson a 70-67 advantage, and followed it with passes that put teammates Anthony Johnson and David Savage in position to be fouled in the final seconds, all of which gave the Hickories a 72-71 victory made close only on an insignificant basket at the buzzer by Wyandanch.

"We knew we wouldn't be able to stop him," said Wyandanch coach Carl Gainey, when it was over. "He had too much size, too much ability. We just tried to slow him down a little. But, we couldn't even do that."

Unconscious? By the time he was done, Lloyd had gone 17-for-26 from the field, scored a tournament-high 36 points, grabbed a tournament-high 17 rebounds, blocked two shots and left those in the crowd, as well as several opponents, shaking their heads in amazement. It was estimated he had totaled at least 10 assists, though no one had thought to keep track. He had also been named recipient of a two-foot-high trophy as the tournament's outstanding player, all while playing the highly unlikely combination of center on defense and point guard on offense.

"One hell of a player," Wyandanch point guard Sean Ramos said.

"That's why," Jackson coach Chuck Granby said of his junior all-America candidate after the game, "he's Lloyd Daniels."

The ironic part was that those who had watched Lloyd in the parks and in the playgrounds and on the courts of the band-box gymnasiums throughout the city understood one thing: The game had hardly been his best.

There are those TV commercials. Spike Lee, the bill of his hat flipped up to reveal the word "Brooklyn," is talking about legends. "Yo," Lee says, "Mars Blackmon in the house talkin' 'bout my main man 'Money.' Here's action photos of 'Money' slammin' in Detroit." All you see is a rim and sneaker-clad feet. "In L.A." More feet. "Boston." More feet. "Hmm. Must be Bird's eye view," Mars says. "Denver." Feet and mountains. "Some serious hang time. Must be the mountain air." The other L.A. Paris. *"Oui, oui!"* Walla Walla. Budapest. The Sea of Tranquility. Yeah, the moon.

Or, here's a parkie sitting on the stoop of a brownstone, talking to some kids 'bout Lamarr Mondane, an old-time park legend—a man who could rain thirty-footers all day. Throwing them in from every conceivable angle, hitting all net. Like some god. A playground basketball god.

These are mythical figures, made-for-television legends used to sell sneakers, products, nothing more. But they still represent something more, because you know "Money" could be any real street legend if he only got a chance at the big-time, the NBA. Because you know Lamarr Mondane is the reality of the streets; to be talked about only by the few who remember.

They represent the basic premise of what a playground legend like Lloyd is all about. The idea that people are remembered, honored and talked about on the streets and the playgrounds the way kids once talked about Old West gunfighters like "Billy the Kid" and Jesse James. The way folks used to talk about the old Apache medicine man, Geronimo; told stories of the demise of Indian scouts, like in the tale of "Deadshot, Skippy and Dandy Jim."

Talked about the way most folks around the country, folks in those NBA cities, talk about their stars. About Bird. About Magic. About Patrick. About Isiah. About Dominique. About the guys they watch all the time on TV. About the exploits of Bill Russell and "Pistol" Pete Maravich and Bob Cousy and "The Big O," Oscar Robertson. About Wilt Chamberlain, who more than a million people "remember" seeing score a hundred, though in reality almost no one went to the game in Hershey, Pennsylvania, that night in 1962.

But something about those legends is never explained, something about the real playground basketball legends that even a guy like Mars Blackmon never tells us. It is the part about why they never escaped the playgrounds, despite their vast abilities. Why they never made it to the big time, too.

It is the part about how they were, and are, real men in the real world. Real men with real problems. Real men, not heroes. Humans, not gods.

In legend, they are "Swee'pea," "The Goat," "Red" and "The Animal." They are folks like "88 James," so-called because he had just eight fingers—four on each hand. They are "Bullethead," "The Terminator," "Razor," "Predator," "Jim Ice" and his homeboy, "Dido." They are a cast of characters. Folks like "Fly," "Helicopter," "Pee Wee" and "The Destroyer"—a/k/a Joe Hammond; a/k/a some little-known identification number in a police file somewhere in New York City.

Often, no one is quite sure how they came to be legends—whether it was a move, or just a moment. It doesn't matter. Just that they are remembered, that their names alone seem to evoke respect and regard, is enough.

They are folks who talked trash while they took you to town. Folks who had an ability that made them stand out from the rest on the playgrounds, a place where a basketball reputation can lift a man above the din.

In reality, though, they were folks like Lloyd Daniels and Earl Manigault, Tony Bruin and Richie Adams —men whose frailties meant they could never quite live up to their street status. Men who, in some cases, despite some brief, shining moment of stardom, might not have been as good as the folks who made the NBA. Men who, in some cases, despite their down side, might have been better than the best who ever played. Anytime, anywhere.

They were, and remain, men who became legends because, despite their talents, they weren't much different from the folks who came to watch them: the locals and the parkies, the addicts and the small-time entrepreneurs.

They were just like them. They were them.

Joe Hammond once scored twenty-five in a half against Julius Erving and, once, had seventy-three on cable television in a game in the Rucker Pros, the summer tournament in Harlem. But later he turned down a contract offer from the Los Angeles Lakers because it lacked a no-cut clause and, when a pro scout came to see him on the streets, told him to wait a few minutes because he was busy shooting craps. He blew his chance, turned to drugs and turned up in Rikers Island—the New York City jail on an island in the East River near LaGuardia Airport—before he moved on to the state prison at Dannemora.

Pee Wee Kirkland's head-to-head battles with Tiny Archibald remain the stuff of legend in New York. "Pee Wee was a guard, Norfolk State. Got drafted by the Chicago Bulls," recalled Archibald, who came out of a Bronx housing project to star fourteen seasons in the NBA with the Boston Celtics, Cincinnati Royals, Kansas City-Omaha Kings, New Jersey

Nets and Milwaukee Bucks. "I used to go against him on the streets and in the playgrounds. He was one of the best there ever was. His problem was he wasn't just an educated guy, but a street person, too. When Chicago offered him a contract, he laughed in their face and said, 'Hey, I could make more money in a couple of days out on the street.' He ended up in the federal pen."

James (Fly) Williams, the man from the "Ville," Brownsville, once set the NCAA scoring mark for freshmen, averaging 29.4 per game at Austin Peay—a mark which stood from 1973 until the 1988-89 season, when it was broken by Chris Jackson of Louisiana State University. Once, his game was so spectacular and so full of flash, that he sparked the creation of perhaps the most memorable of all college cheers, the one which went: "Fly is Open, Let's Go Peay." Fly would take you down and have the gall to tell you about it while he was doing it. One game, he even cut on Erving. Dr. J dunked on him and, legend has it, just about everyone in the neighborhood has a picture to prove it. Usually, though, Fly more than held his own.

Now, when he isn't in Rikers, Fly, the man who once dropped sixty-three on Moses Malone at the Dapper Dan Tournament, a high school all-star game, hangs around the Noble Drew Ali Plaza in Brownsville with half his lungs and a massive scar on the left side of his back—the result of an ill-fated robbery attempt that ended with a shotgun blast that nearly killed him.

And still, despite the folks they really were, they were also men who, on the court and in the playgrounds, brought pride to their neighborhoods. Men who played for honor and self-respect. Men who often played because they had nothing better to do. Because they loved the game, nothing more. That they eventually fell through the cracks in the concrete dream—failing in life, failing in their quest for success, failing to live up to others' expectations, failing themselves—was immaterial to what they accomplished.

After all, they couldn't do well in everything. They were only human. Which is, despite what you think, usually all folks who become legends ever really are. Men who start life, live life, and sometimes—actually, more than just sometimes—end life like Lloyd Daniels. Losing it all.

Sheets of tin and aluminum covered the building where its windows had once been, their glass having long ago been knocked clean away in the name of burglary, vandalism and simple, honest, old age. It was as if bandages had been placed on the running sores of a wound, and—for all the protection afforded against the elements, both natural and man-made—had allowed it to become gangrenous nevertheless. Just a shell now, the structure that remains serves as a soulful, if tired, reminder of what had once been, standing among a line of ancient, beaten and battered sentinels on this long-ago discarded block in East New York known as New Jersey Avenue.

Looking around, it is difficult to imagine that this place has ever been beautiful, has ever been new or even clean. Everything about it, about this section of Brooklyn, in fact, paints a harsh picture of abject poverty.

Just a block north of here, in the abandoned, weeded lot at the corner of Belmont and Jersey, old tires form a mountain, almost one-story high, and bags of uncollected garbage sit, decaying, on the sidewalk outside the long-silenced doorways. On the streets walk the living dead, corpses who don't know they are corpses, searchers for salvation in the form of needles and nods and schemer's dreams. Reality here comes in the form of rat-infested hallways, roach-infested kitchens and lice-infested bedrooms. Here, families are often forced to sit huddled in winter coats in heat-starved buildings in the dead of winter; are forced to broil in undershirts in congested, sweat-filled brick row apartments in the humid heat of summer—unable even to slip onto their fire escapes for relief, so powerful is the fear that they, too, might become the innocent victims of stray bullets from the random, often unsolicited shootings on the street below.

Even the honorable folks—folks who, for the lack of a better way, but not for a lack of pride, work dead-end honest jobs and sweep their streets and clean their cars—remain stuck here, as if by fate, in the middle of what has become a god-forsaken hell on earth.

It is here, on the first floor of a dilapidated walk-up that stands among the boarded-up buildings that line this stretch of Jersey Avenue between Belmont and Sutter, that Lloyd first came to be introduced to the world and to its nuances. It was a difficult way to start life. From here, things almost never got better. And usually, it seemed, they only got worse.

Judy Stephens was a woman of considerable good looks, light-skinned—"almost white," her mother-in-law recalled—and fine-featured. She had been born into Brooklyn in a different time, before Brownsville and East New York had gone to crack; back when those still were places where people like her could live and work and go about their business in relative safety.

She had met Lloyd Daniels while in high school. He was lean, a little bit over six-foot tall, with a rich, even-toned, coffee complexion; a handsome man with a knack for a good line. Even the gap between his front teeth lent to his appearance. She found herself attracted. And the two soon fell in love, became an item in the neighborhood.

Lloyd had come to Brooklyn just a few years earlier with his mother, Lulia, who had been born in Cordele, Georgia, a back-roads town about sixty miles or so south of Macon. He had been sheltered by family, his mother one of sixteen children—eleven of them girls—on a farm where they picked cotton, shucked corn, raised hogs and chickens and milked cows.

In her teens, Lulia had met a man named Walter Daniels. And in 1948, when she was just eighteen, the two had Lloyd, the first of six children. Lulia was a strong-headed woman, who, as she said, "had ambition." And she soon grew tired of that farm in Cordele. "I wanted to better myself, make a better life for myself," she said. So, in 1959, Lulia took her children and moved North. When Walter declined to go, she said, "I walked." As she said, "I'm a survivor." Nothing would stand in her way, not even a man.

Lulia arrived in New York on a Sunday afternoon. By nightfall, she had a job as a housemaid for an invalid woman. Years later, she divorced Walter Daniels, married a man named James Hendley and had five more children, the first three of them boys. Her second husband, she said, had a penchant for chasing women. "So," she said, "I threw him out of the house."

Though on her own, Lulia worked hard to instill good values in her kids. She worked six days a week. And, seven days a week she showered them with love and affection. She tried to understand their problems. All she ever asked in return was respect. When she heard that Judy Stephens, then just sixteen, had become pregnant by her son, she went to see her. "One day, I went to her work," Lulia said. "I said, 'You're pregnant, aren't you?' She said, 'How do you know? How do you know I'm pregnant?' I said, 'I know these things. I'm a mother. I can tell.' She said, 'Please don't tell my mother.' She was eight-and-a-half months pregnant when she and Lloyd got married."

Still, Lulia allowed the teenaged couple to hold the wedding reception at her home in Brooklyn. She loved them. What else could she do?

Theirs was not the best life, Lloyd's and Judy's. Like many in the neighborhood, they lacked money. But they were young and had their son, also named Lloyd and otherwise known as "Junior," who had been born on September 4, 1967. Lulia liked to tell folks how, when she went to the hospital, the nurses didn't even have to tell her which child was her grandson. "The big, big baby," she said. "The one who got some good looks from his mother and that sweet face from his father."

But Junior was born into an accident waiting to happen. Not long after his birth, Judy was diagnosed with uterine cancer. He was almost three when she died. It nearly destroyed his father, who, in an effort to kill the pain, turned his attentions to alcohol, his mother said. See, Lulia said, her son had wanted to be strong, too. But like the rest of her children—who, despite Lulia's best efforts, all seemed to be finding problems of their own on the streets of New York—he just didn't know how.

"My son tried to commit suicide," she said. "He started drinkin', he started pickin' fights and stuff. It was rough. He wanted to die with the mother. My son, Junior's father, stayed drunk for two-and-a-half years. I'm talkin' about he started drinkin' big. Then one day he fell out, right there on the avenue. I guess his blood pressure, whatever, it got so bad, that they had to put him in a strait-jacket, because of the drinkin', the seizures he was havin'. Junior used to say when he see his father, that he was embarrassed. That's why I figured Junior would never do drugs or drink. He was embarrassed to see his father. He'd say to me, 'Ooh, if I ever do that stuff like that, grandma, I'll kill myself. I'll commit suicide. I won't never do no drugs or drink.' "

It was the first of many promises Junior wouldn't keep.

It is said a hungry tiger gives no indication of impending strike, that it stalks its prey with an illusive, elusive touch, that it insinuates itself on a situation with purposeful stealth in order to gain best advantage and then, and only then, does it make its move, bold and impudent.

Watch footage of Lloyd Daniels on a basketball court and you will see such presence, such purpose. There is self-assurance in his game, a certain awareness, perception, instinct that seems to let him know when the time is right. Almost never does he attempt to force a situation. Almost never does he tip his hand too soon.

His passes all seem to have that touch. He looks off the man, sends the ball in the opposite direction, as if he knew, felt, where his man would be. You can see how they are timed, so that his man is in a position of advantage, ready to strike. All his shots, whether they come from two feet or twenty-five, seem to be released with a precision that cannot be taught—but rather with the kind that is felt deep within a man's bones, in his soul.

Even his rebounds all seem to be grabbed with just the right amount of authority. There is no wasted motion or effort, just what is needed to get the job done and get his message across.

This is a man who understands the game the way Mozart understood music, the way Michelangelo understood painting. A feel, a magic that cannot accurately be described because, in reality, it is the stuff of legend.

Saul Lerner claimed he saw that magic the first time he ever watched Lloyd, in the fall of 1983, when Lloyd was an eighth-grader at Intermediate School 218 in Brooklyn. Lerner was a high school basketball coach who had spent three years as a pro player in Israel. He also headed the school's special education program. Lloyd was a special ed student who played ball and sometimes attended class. "He had one thing in his life," Lerner recalled. "Basketball. I remember the first time that I watched him on the court. He was only about sixteen. But you could see that he had a certain brilliance on the court, one that he shouldn't have had because it was contradictory to everything he did in the classroom.

"Here was a kid who was on the pre-primer level in class—we're talking stuff like C-A-T—who was on the major-college or professional level on the court. You don't see kids graduating from college with the kind of on-court knowledge he had then. At that age, you're happy when a kid can put it in the basket. But he had vision. He knew how to balance out the floor. He knew how to find a kid cutting through the middle. He was something else."

Then again, Lloyd always seemed to be something else on the streets and playgrounds of New York. A place where the best often are known only by their calling card—a nickname, a move, a moment—Lloyd became known simply as Swee'pea. It was a nickname he acquired comin' up on the streets of Brownsville-East New York, where the local folks—in particular, a guy named "Yodel"—noticed that his peculiar shaped oval head, skipping-stone flat cheeks, high, receding hairline and skin-tight hair gave him a curious resemblance to the baby-faced character from "Popeye."

He was something else on New Jersey Avenue, where, after his mother died, he lived with his maternal grandmother, Annie Sargeant Stephens, in that apartment a block from Thomas Jefferson High School and not far from where former heavyweight boxing champion Mike Tyson was born.

And, he was something else at "Jeff," where, as a ninth-grader, he broke his ankle playing ball and missed most of the regular season, then returned for the last seven games to lead a seven-man team into the playoffs and, after scoring 29 points in a first-round win over Tilden High School, netted thirty to almost single-handedly beat Abraham Lincoln.

Swee'pea owned Lafayette Gardens, a park which often showcased some of the best talent in Brooklyn. There, he once scored 54 points to win a head-to-head battle with the brother of former Utah Jazz forward Carey Scurry; Moses Scurry later went on to Nevada-Las Vegas. And Swee'pea owned Five-Star Camp, where, back in 1985 he deftly handled J.R. Reid, who became an all-American at the University of North Carolina and the fifth overall pick in the 1989 NBA Draft, selected by the Charlotte Hornets.

Swee'pea was slick, refined. He was confident, but not cocky. In an era when, and in a neighborhood where, taking it to the hoop and jamming it home with thunder was considered to be the real deal—it was once written that a city guard will "give up his gold and his girl before he'll give up his dribble"—he was secure enough and knowledgeable enough to lay off a pass or lay it in when the moment called for it. One game, he might control things with his passing, making no-look feeds or simple bounce passes—something rarely seen in an age of glitter and flash. Another, he might dominate with his scoring, firing jumpers with consistency from twenty-five feet.

"He was born to play basketball," said Tom Konchalski, an East Coast recruiting expert who evaluates high school talent for many of the nation's college coaches and who said he first saw Lloyd play ball in junior high school. "He just had a special gift, almost a mystical grasp of the game. I don't think it was anything he was even taught. He had a great instinctive feel for the game, such sophistication, such pedigree. Maybe the best way to describe it is to compare it to the Socratic ideal of knowledge as remembrance, almost as if he had inherited it as knowledge learned in a previous life. His biggest problem on the court was that he was such a sophisticate, had such an understanding of the game, that he had little tolerance for others who were not as sophisticated and so he easily became querulous with others who could not do what he could. But, aside from that, not many have ever possessed his ability to read the game, had his understanding of how to let the game come to him and of how to let the game dictate what he should do. He understood you could not predetermine what to do with the ball. No one saw the floor like Lloyd. No one." The closest comparison?

"Maybe, Magic Johnson," Konchalski said. "Maybe." And, as Konchalski pointed out, not really being facetious, that was being kind to Magic.

As Larry Davis, who in 1984 briefly coached Lloyd at Oak Hill Academy in Mouth of Wilson, Virginia, said: "God just said one day, 'I'm going to laugh at the rest of the basketball world,' and he made this kid."

Swee'pea was not, of course, without flaws. He didn't like to play defense, didn't like to hit the weights, didn't like to work to get in shape. He could be lackadaisical, sometimes so bored with the competition that he didn't give his best effort. But those deficiencies were minor in comparison to his skills.

"Talent is our narcotic," said Al Menendez, the Indiana Pacers scout, who watched Lloyd all the time when he scouted for the New Jersey Nets. "We are addicted to basketball. I've watched Lloyd play since he was a sophomore in high school. He's as good as there is."

"He is a tremendous talent," Pacers general manager Donnie Walsh said. "No doubt, he has the talent to play in our league."

That ability made Lloyd a *Parade Magazine* All-American his junior year at Jackson, when he averaged 31.2 points, 12.3 rebounds and 10 assists. It made him a much-sought-after player by college coaches, who were more than willing to overlook his well-documented academic deficiencies—which included undiagnosed dyslexia, a third grade reading level and frequent truancy—just to get him into their school's uniform. And, it later made him a hot commodity in Topeka, Kansas, where he averaged 16 points, 3.5 rebounds and 4.7 assists as a twenty-year-old rookie in the CBA.

It also made him a playground legend on the streets of New York City, one often mentioned in the same breath as a pantheon of basketball gods.

"Sometimes, people talk a lot of shit," said Chris Brooks, an all-America candidate as a forward at West Virginia University who played with Lloyd on the Gauchos, an Amateur Athletic Union club team in the Bronx. "But I seen him play. He can shoot, he can dribble, he can play defense when he wants to, and he's 6-foot-8. They say he is the next Magic Johnson and I tell you what, I think he is. Is he the best I've ever seen? I don't know. I like Michael Jordan. But, next to him, it's Lloyd. Hands down."

"He's the best," Tiny Archibald said. "As far as entertainment, he's gonna do some shit you've never seen before. He's gonna make a pass you've never seen, hit a shot you've never seen, make a play you've never seen. He's a crowd pleaser. My generation it was Earl Manigault and Joe Hammond and guys like that who were the best. But guys like that aren't goin' nowhere because they have no direction, except when they're on the playgrounds. There, they know what they want. They know how to handle it. But, take them away from that and they're lost.

"Now, take Lloyd. He's good. But there's a lot of guys in New York who are good. Not as good as him. But they're hungry, willin' to sacrifice. There's a need to prove it every game. It's hard. Some guys do it, some don't.

"See, Lloyd could be a George Gervin. He's that type player. He can score. He can do things like George Gervin. But then again, he's not like him, because George Gervin was in the NBA and Swee'pea isn't and don't might never be. He has the ability to play on the pro level. He has the talent to be great. But management—coaches and general managers—want someone who's reliable, who will show up for practice and work, who will show up at a game and do his best. There are a bunch of guys in the NBA who are not as good as Lloyd. But they're reliable.

"Swee'pea, meanwhile, is in the mold of Joe Hammond. Joe had the talent, but wanted the street life. Lloyd is like that. He could be in the NBA gettin' a little money. But he doesn't want that disciplined role. He doesn't want to pay the price. And, if you ain't payin' the price, then you ain't gonna get there. There's got to be someone to push you. No one ain't givin' you nothin'. Somethin' has to motivate him. You can't baby-sit him twenty-four hours a day, because as soon as he goes back on the streets he's in the same mold. I seen him once and he told me, 'I'm goin' to get in shape.' He never did.

"His problem is that he'll bust you for fifty one night and the next night he'll be hangin' with his boys gettin' high. He wants the cake, the icin', the frostin'—he wants to eat it all."

In his day Howie Garfinkel, the basketball super-scout who also serves as the director of Five-Star Basketball Camps, probably has seen too many basketball players come and go. He has liked some, disliked others. Precious few has he held in as high regard as he holds Lloyd Daniels.

Garfinkel first saw Lloyd back in 1985, when he broke onto the national scene as only the second high school junior-to-be in fifteen years to be named outstanding player at the week-long camp in Pittsburgh. Lloyd might as well have been a magician. Garfinkel was hypnotized by his talent.

So enamored was he that, after the camp ended, Garfinkel proclaimed to Al McGuire, "Lloyd Daniels is the best junior alive, dead or yet unborn."

"The first time I saw him, I nearly fell out of my seat," Garfinkel said. "He was just incredible back then. He was great. I remember one time where he was on a three-on-two break and, as he came down I thought, 'Is he going to shoot, going to pass?' He went to shoot, drew the defender. No one was free. At least, I didn't see anyone. Then, all of a sudden, *bingo!*, while he was in mid-air he hit someone for an easy lay-up. I was like, 'How did he find that man?' *I hadn't seen him.* After a while, every time he touched the ball you would lean forward in your seat in anticipation of a great play."

And seldom did Swee'pea fail to deliver.

"Calvin Murphy, inch-for-inch, pound-for-pound, shot-for-shot, was the greatest high school player I ever saw," Garfinkel recalled. "I saw him get thirty-four at the Dapper Dan on a Friday night, then score sixty-two in twenty-nine minutes the next at the Allentown (Pa.) Classic. After that, you can choose between Connie Hawkins, Lew Alcindor and Lloyd Daniels. It's a pick 'em for second. I call Lloyd 'Magic Johnson with a jumpshot.' "

As Stan Dinner, an associate of Lloyd who once coached now-closed Benjamin Franklin High School in Harlem, a team that fielded five NCAA Division I college stars in Kenny Hutchinson, Richie Adams, Gary Springer, Walter Berry and Watkins (Boo) Singletary, said: "He is Magic Johnson with a jumpshot, all right. Larry Bird's jumpshot. Lloyd Daniels can do everything with a basketball except one thing. Autograph it."

And that was a problem.

3 · School Daze

I.S. 218 sat on the corner of Fountain and Blake about twenty blocks from Lloyd's home in the heart of East New York. It was a hazardous walk for a kid, even one as street-smart as Lloyd. It was even more hazardous for the ones who weren't as streetwise, for the kids who had to walk past the Cypress Houses, the Pink Houses and Linden Plaza—housing projects once built in an effort to provide shelter for the poor and underprivileged, but now all but forgotten worlds, seen but unseen. Left to the drug dealers and to their clientele. Left to the wind and the rain. To the elements.

The neighborhood was so bad that it had the highest murder rate in the city, one of the highest in the nation. Over a span of little more than two years, the area, which measured just over five square miles, saw more than a hundred murders, most of them drug-related. As a takeoff from the local all-news radio station, 1010 WINS, whose motto was "Give us twenty-two minutes, we'll give you the world," the police officers from the embattled 75th Precinct often told their visitors, "Give us twenty-two minutes, we'll give you a homicide." Real-world humor, they called it.

The school provided a sort of safe haven in this turbulent world. It was one of the few places local residents could attain the skills that would help them escape this environment. Unlike some public schools in the city, where students had to walk through metal detectors and be searched for weapons by the school security guards just to enter the building for class each morning, I.S. 218 wasn't quite so bad. It didn't have a principal like Matthew Barnwell, who, while head of a public school in the Bronx, would be arrested for possession of crack. It didn't have a substantial amount of hardcore, violent, students—mainly because those kids almost never came to class.

"The school, I would say—considering its neighborhood, where it was—was not as bad a school as you might think," said Saul Lerner, head of the special education department at I.S. 218. "It was clean. It was relatively new. In many senses it was not a bad place. It was a shelter from the problems that surrounded the school."

Trouble was, those problems almost seemed to overwhelm and undermine everything accomplished inside the school.

22

"There are working parents in East New York," Lerner said. "People do work. They do have jobs. But sometimes, you just can't escape. Now, I'm a big believer in environment. And, that environment breeds failure because by the time a kid is in the third grade there, he knows he's probably not going to escape. He knows he can't read. He knows he can't write. He knows he's a failure. He knows he's doomed for life. I'm not a sociologist. But the point is, these kids don't have a book in the house, most of them don't have a father or maybe don't have a mother or, at least, don't have a family the way you and I had a family. They're not the same. They're not coming out of middle class homes. And, as teachers, we can't handle the social issue, only the academic and so, right off the bat, we start off failing these kids. It only gets worse from there. The kids who do get out, who simply do make it through school and get out, are the ones who beat the system. They got out of school more than it could offer them. It's a shame it has to be like that."

The streets are no place for a kid. But by the age of seven, Lloyd knew them, inside and out. He knew East New York. He knew Brownsville. He knew how to panhandle money and how to take the train to the amusement park at Coney Island, where he would spend an afternoon alone by himself on the rides. He knew how to take the subways and buses to the Hollis-St. Albans section of Queens, where Lulia had moved when he was still an infant.

He also knew how to sneak out at night from the first-floor apartment on New Jersey Avenue, where he lived with Annie Sargeant.

Back then, Lloyd would leave at midnight, basketball in hand, and head down the block to the local park. And after he slipped through a cut in the chain-link fence—"Soul in the hole," he called it—he would stand in the darkness, stand amid the broken bottles and shavings of glass, amid the rocks and debris that would coat a man's hands black with dirt just from dribbling the ball. He would shoot baskets for hours. Just a kid, alone in the world, an island unto himself, trying to make sense of his situation.

Some afternoons, he took time to watch the older kids on the playgrounds, where they'd go five-on-five, three-on-three or just one-on-one, sometimes playing "H-O-R-S-E," sometimes just getting in runs. But, the rule in New York is that every player—no matter how good—has his age, his time. And, unless you own the only ball on the block, you don't get to play ball with the big boys until you've paid your dues, grown a little.

And so, being just a kid, Lloyd almost always practiced by himself out in the park at night, stopping only to run for cover when he heard gunfire on the surrounding blocks.

He taught himself how to dribble on those darkened, glass-strewn courts. Taught himself how to pass, bouncing the ball off the fences. He learned to shoot banked jumpers in the park, which had no lights. He said it developed not only his eye for the basket, but his feel for it. He'd take a hundred shots. After a while, despite the darkness he could make ninety-eight, ninety-nine.

"Nobody helped me," Lloyd said. "I practiced myself. Shootin', dribblin', passin' off the gate or the fence. Sometimes, twelve, one o'clock in the mornin', I'd be out playin' ball down the block. If I was lucky, I'd get to the lighted park on 33rd Street in Manhattan right next to the mouth of the Queens-Midtown Tunnel. Usually, I stayed right in the neighborhood."

"Lloyd would disappear for hours on end and just play basketball," said Annie Sargeant, who'd let him go. "At first, I'd worry about him. But then I always figured I could find him down the block, shooting. About the only time I saw him was the weekends when we'd go shopping on Pitkin Avenue."

Lloyd was, in effect, on his own. Annie Sargeant worked. When she left the house in the morning no one was around to watch Lloyd, who then went off and did what he wanted to do. Because of the trauma he had experienced, Annie was reluctant to punish him when he did do something wrong—like cut school or hang out with a crew that was headed for trouble. "What he found out," said one childhood friend, "was that, when he got older, he had to take care of hisself. He didn't have no choice. It was like people pushed him out into the world and said, 'Okay, take care of "biz." Take care of yourself.' It was like he didn't have no chance. He was on his own."

When Lloyd needed new sneakers, he had to get them for himself. When he needed clothes, he had to find a way to come up with the cash. When he wanted to eat, he had to figure out how to get food. It was a simple fact of life. Annie didn't have much money. She had her own kids to support. She had her own life to manage, first and foremost. She did what she could for Lloyd, but she couldn't do much. Lulia, knowing her own son had abandoned Lloyd, left him with Annie. She didn't want to interfere and Lloyd didn't want to be a burden. So he took care of himself. No questions asked.

"I had to support my own self," he said. "That's just the way it was. I had to buy my own clothes comin' up, so some days I had to go to the grocery store and pack bags to make money. I'd go to Waldbaums and Key Food. I had to survive, man. My grandmother had it rough. My father wasn't around, my mother died. I had to go there to pack bags. I had to buy me sneakers and some fancy clothes. The boy didn't want to go to school with the same shit on every day. Some days, I had to work. Some days, I had to survive.

" 'Cause I was an only child, my grandmother, she tried to spoil me. I didn't have no mother, so she let me get over. I'd get a little hittin', a little spankin'. But she'd punish me and I still would go out—sneak out the back door, walk out the front door. As soon as she'd go to sleep, I'm gone. Swee'pea down the block somewhere shootin' ball. She'd let it slide."

Annie let it slide and Lloyd soon learned that he could do as he pleased. When he didn't know the rules of the game, when no one bothered to tell him what the rules were, he improvised and made his own. If something was beneficial to him—be it legal or illegal, moral or immoral—he did it. As one observer said, "People tell kids, 'You should know better.' But how? Children are born blank. How are they supposed to know if they are not told?"

Like his grandmother before him, Lloyd was a survivor, doing what it took to survive. Except, unlike her, he didn't always play by the rules. "I never stole shit," Lloyd said. "I never stole shit. I never robbed, never stole." But one relative said that wasn't quite true. She said Lloyd was taught by other family members to shoplift. They would take him to the local stores and, while one family member occupied the cashier, Lloyd, in an oversized jacket, would tuck away the merchandise. It all made for quick cash.

Asked about that, Lloyd admitted, "I did what I could. I got into trouble, a lot of trouble." But he also said he often seemed to have luck on his side. He seldom got caught, and, even if he did, unlike his friends, he was able to talk his way out of a situation. He had style. He had a rap. He was sweetness, a smooth operator. He made people laugh. He made people like him. Even folks he did wrong by. After all, he was just a troubled kid trying to make it. So they'd give him the benefit of the doubt. They felt he deserved it.

Now, give a kid, any kid, an inch and he'll take a mile. It's the nature of the beast, the nature of growing up. Except, when you have responsible role models, they'll put you in line when you step out. But Lloyd had no one. As he grew, Lloyd mastered an old trick: How to get over on folks.

He became lord of the street con, begging money, talking folks into "lending" him things. He learned to play on sympathies and, due to his situation, he found those were many. What Lloyd also learned was that

packing bags did not earn him much. If he was going to get by, he needed
to find another way. And, in the neighborhood, what he saw was drugs.

It is a lesson learned early on in the inner city. Take all you feel
you're entitled to, expect nothing in return. Do what you can to survive.
Figure you'll have to look out for yourself, because everyone has their
problems. No one has time to waste worrying about yours. Everyone
knows only the strong survive. It's the law of the urban jungle, where
tomorrow morning you may wake up to find you're in a body bag. Maybe
that's why the ultimate put-down on the streets and in the playgrounds
is the phrase that goes, "You're weak." As in no muscle, no power. No
survival instincts.

Power, on the streets they call it "juice," is what separates new jacker
dopeboys—hip-hop culture's description of trendy, but lethal, new-wave,
new-money drug dealers—from the burger boys working the golden arch
grills at Mickey D's. McDonald's. It's what separates cools who got a nice
ride—as in BM's, Benz's, Samurai's, Jeep's and Maxima's—from the
bummy-boys who hop the bus, take the subways and walk. If it means
going illegal, then that's what a man's got to do.

Power equals success on the urban streets and, in turn, it equals
survival, because the strong get to dictate the rules, get to feel invincible,
even if it isn't for long. Power is what separates class from mass on the
playgrounds, where a 360-degree tomahawk dunk often means more
than a lay-in, where a rejection is viewed as the ultimate insult to mas-
culinity.

It is why dis'in' someone—showing them disrespect—often calls for
retaliation. It is about macho, machismo. Reputation and regard. In a
societal setting where wearing finger-thick gold—being able to hang it all
out front where you can dare someone to snatch it from you—is the
ultimate sign of success and prowess, it is the reason you always have to
show how much juice you have. It is the same reason why, when you're
on the playground and make a move that isn't strong—a move not geared
toward declaration of your manhood, not geared toward survival—the
chant will come down on you. "Runnin' low on Tropicana," they might
yell. Or, worse. "Word up!" they'll scream. The truth. "You're motherfuckin' weak."

Except, when you're not strong on the streets, when you don't look
out for Number One, you don't hear put-downs. Often, you just end up
dead.

What a kid has to do for self-preservation and self-protection, then, is steel himself to the world. Steel himself to the elements. Which, of course, only begins to explain a kid like Lloyd. Only begins to explain a host of inner-city kids, including an acquaintance of Lloyd's named Cool Mo D.

Maurice Johnson, known on the street as Mo Diamond, was taking the official ghetto stand: Arms crossed and pulled up tight into his chest, hands covered by black leather gloves with the fingers cut off, head cocked downward with dark, cold eyes staring out from under the low-raked, slightly off-center bill of his grey leather cap. He was sizing up the crowd. Searching for weaknesses, playing enforcer.

But Mo Diamond looked a bit out of place. He was almost sixteen and hardly tough. You could tell. He had grown up in the infamous Forties Projects in Jamaica, Queens, a place where crime is a common occurrence, where drugs and drug-gangs rule with an iron fist and a handful of Uzis. But he wasn't yet tough like most of the projects' homeboys or the boys uptown Manhattan, the ones whose faces, if they were lucky enough to still be around, that is, reflected a full lifetime by the time they reached his age.

Diamond bore no marks of untold battles, no scars marking his rites of passage. He still had that soft skin, just another young buck trying to best the field. A kid feigning a look for survival, faking his toughness like many of the B-Boys—the bad boys, the banji boys; the ones who intimidate the public at large by wearing banji shit like kangol hats and Mr. T Cadillac gold emblems on counterfeit gold chains, stuff that makes them look mean, look tough, hard.

"Want to know how tough Mo is?" Ron Naclerio said, as Mo stood his ground nearby. "Here's how tough."

Mo Diamond was a member of Ronnie's team at Cardozo, a place far removed from the midnight streets of the Bronx, where this war of vanities was being waged courtside during a battle between local club teams. He was a decent player and, as an acquaintance of Lloyd's, had come with Ronnie to watch the game.

"Mo," Ronnie said. "Tell him about Teddy." Diamond looked hard and pretended not to hear. "C'mon, Mo," Ronnie chided. "Tell him." Still, Diamond stood firm.

"Mo brings Teddy everywhere," Ronnie said. "Brings him to games, brings him to school, brings him to class. He once brought Teddy to class

and gave him his own seat so he could hear the teacher and set him up
with a paper and pen to take notes. The teacher had different ideas. She
told Mo that Teddy couldn't stay in class, so she took him and sat him by
the desk in the front of the room. But that didn't work, either. Teddy
was a distraction. So she finally took Teddy and put him in a closet and
locked the door.

"You know what Mo did? Mo, tell him." Diamond didn't move. "He
jumps up, runs over to the teacher yelling, 'No, no. Teddy's afraid of the
dark.' Can you believe it? Teddy's a god damned stuffed bear."

Everyone broke up, laughing. Still, Diamond was a rock, trying to
intimidate the field, make them think the tale was little more than some
"gip," some talk, aimed at dismantling his rep. He stared. Hard. His look
cut through the crowd, cut through Ronnie until, finally, he could take
no more.

"Man, you dis'ed Teddy," he said. "You shouldn't a done that. Now,
I'm gonna hafta kill you." His response, that of a kid and not of the thug
he pretended to be, was futile. Again, everyone laughed.

But everyone also knew this: Honor was at stake. And, had Ronnie
dis'ed anyone other than Mo, who was still an innocent despite trying not
to be, he might've been dead within the hour.

For some, using an act as a method of self-protection works. For
some, it only works for a while. For some, it doesn't work at all. Instead,
those kids often fall victim to their own routine. They get hardened,
become entangled in that netherworld. They get sidetracked, become lost
in the mist.

Ronnie, who had become friends with Lloyd through an acquaintance, a teacher named Arnie Hershkowitz, understands how that happens. He knows how lost some of these kids are, knows how many of the
basic survival skills—not the ones for the street, but the ones for the job
market—they lack, because he works with such kids every day.

Teaching a special ed class one afternoon at J.H.S. 8, a junior high
school in Jamaica, Queens, formerly known as I.S. 8, Ronnie saw kids
who were having trouble answering all but the most basic questions re-
garding a range of subjects—from geography to math—and so, finally,
he decided to give a few of them a chance to get some questions right.

"I figured it might give them a boost," he said. "Build some self-
esteem. So I look at this kid in the back of the room. I go, 'Name a state
in the South that begins with an "F".' The kid looks at me a second and

goes, 'France?' Now, everyone in the room starts laughing hard, a few kids falling out of their chairs, rolling around. What am I supposed to do? I sit there a few minutes and finally, I go, 'Ah, no. Good try. But that's not it.'

"Another kid looks at me, raises his hand and so I call on him. I go, 'You know the answer?' He goes, 'Sure. Everybody knows it's Philadelphia.'

"What can I say? I go, 'No. Let's move on.' So I ask another kid, 'What's the "D.C." in Washington, D.C., stand for?' The kid goes, 'Duh Capital?'

"What can you do?" Ronnie said. "These kids are gone. They're all gone. They just don't know it yet. Most of them have no chance. Most of them don't care. Most of them don't have anyone at home who cares. And the ones, the few, who do care usually get caught up with the ones who don't and they get dragged down, too. The thing is, there isn't much you can do about it."

As Ronnie said, "There was this other time, when I had to teach this class on hygiene, you know, sex ed. I was nervous as it was, you know, trying to figure out how to tell these kids—they were like eighth-graders—about stuff like 'safe sex' and 'how to use a condom' and like 'planned parenthood.' So I started off with a story. I was like, 'You know, you're hanging out with some friends and talking to some girl or some guy and the subject starts to change from like sports to sex and so what do you do?'

"I'm going on and, all of a sudden, this kid in the back yells out, 'Yo, Mr. Naclerio. Kill the noise. I don't want to hear none of this shit. All I want to do is get laid.' See what I mean? These kids are gone. They grow up in some of these places and they just don't have a chance."

Kids who attend school have some chance, however small, to find success through education. Lloyd didn't even have that. Because, as Saul Lerner said, "If I'm not mistaken, Lloyd did four years at our two-year school. The first year, he was just a kid on my no-show list. I had never seen him, never heard of him. After that, he paid an occasional visit."

There are 184 days in an average school year in New York City. And, though no records were available for his first year at I.S. 218, which Lloyd entered as a thirteen-year-old seventh-grade student in September, 1980, records for his subsequent years there paint the picture of a chronic truant. For the 1981-82 school year, Board of Education records indicate that Lloyd was present just sixty-two days, absent 122. "And I don't think he was there that often," Lerner said, "because, what happens is you have your attendance taken in the mornings and, after that, you could not attend any of your classes and still be considered in attendance. If I remember, we were lucky to see Lloyd two times a week, if at all. And that was good weeks."

The records also showed that Lloyd was marked present just thirty-two times during the 1982-83 school year, when he was absent a staggering 152 days. Nevertheless, the next October, when Lloyd was a sixteen-year-old in eighth-grade, he was "promoted" to Thomas Jefferson.

"Maybe promoted is a bad word," Lerner said. "Because he never really graduated, *per se*, but instead was kind of pushed on despite the fact that he probably was present fewer than a hundred days, in my opinion, over the course of three full school years. He was 'pushed on' because there was nothing else we could do with him. Here he was, sixteen years old, 6-foot-7 and almost too big for the desks, he could not read and he was in classes with twelve-year-old kids. What else were we supposed to do?"

It was a situation that seemed to summarize the problems that plague an ancient, under-budgeted, over-burdened school system. "This isn't just Lloyd," Lerner said. "There must be thousands of no-show truants in the city. Thousands and thousands. And, there are something like four attendance teachers in each district to keep track of hundreds and hundreds of kids and, even if they can keep track of them, in reality they are powerless to do anything to make sure they get to school.

"You can't babysit them. You can't call up ten times a day. When Lloyd stopped showing up, when he did not come to school for a couple of days, we'd make a call. But, really, that was all you could do."

Reasons vary why kids don't go to school. Some, because of problems with their home lives, turn to the streets. To drugs, to prostitution, to crimes that cause them to be sent away. Some, because they lack educational skills, leave school to pursue legitimate, though low-paying, dead-end jobs. And some, for whatever reason, simply don't like to go.

For Lloyd, the reason was partially laziness and partially embarrassment. Due to what would, years later, be diagnosed as dyslexia, he had fallen behind in school, which threw a label at him—he was classifed, Lerner said, as "Neurologically Impaired, Emotionally Handicapped"—but could not find a method by which to help him learn. He was thrown into remedial classes. Frustrated, he avoided the work. Later, that frustration with his inability to do the work grew into boredom with school and then embarrassment. By the time he reached the eighth grade he still could not read, could not handle the most basic school work. As he said, "I didn't have no mother at home to help me with my schoolin' when I got home. I had no one to ask, 'Is this right?' How was I supposed to have felt? What was I supposed to have did?"

"He was in with special ed kids, kids who were two, three years behind in reading level and those kids were calling him dumb," Lerner said. "How was he supposed to react? He was, and please forgive the scientific explanation, labeled 'dumb.' So, he got so frustrated he would not go to class."

Most mornings, Lloyd would pull stunts on Annie Sargeant. He'd sleep late and not go to school or he'd cut the backstreets and not go to school. He'd pretend he was getting washed and dressed, run the water in the bathroom, and, when she left for work, he'd go back to bed and not go to school.

"Some days I would sleep 'til nine o'clock and I wouldn't go," Lloyd said. "There was days she'd wake me and I would act like I'm sick and I wouldn't go. She would baby me. She'd say, 'You don't have to go to school today.' And so, I wouldn't go. Then there was days when she say, 'Hey, you can't pull none of that sick shit on me.' Then I would go, but maybe when I got there I would cut class. The big thing was you had to get me out the house. You didn't do that often. I would be sleepy from shootin' ball late at night. See, there was days I wanted to go to school, days I didn't. Some days I felt good goin' to school, like I should try to do well. Then there were some days I just didn't want to go to school 'cause, you know, there was a lot of frustration. Whenever I sat there and put my head to it, when I wanted to learn, I felt I could learn. When I wanted to catch on, I felt like I could catch on. Like that." He snapped his fingers. "But there was times when I didn't try."

Instead, Lloyd acted like a kid. He looked for the easy way out. He'd try to get into trouble—maybe disrupt a class, take someone's jacket, maybe just get caught roaming the halls—because he knew it would get him out of class. He would be sent to the guidance office, where he'd sit around most of the afternoon talking or just hanging out. If he was lucky, Lerner would get called away and he'd have a chance to escape school for yet another day.

"I ran with the wrong crew," Lloyd said. "Got caught up in the wrong crew. Like the old gangs, we went around school takin' kids' jackets, runnin' around school. I used to go to school and look for trouble, so I could go home. It was like, 'Send me home.' 'Cause when they put me in that office, I could cut out. 'Cause you know, Lerner'd have another kid fightin' in another class and the second he walked out to go there, I would walk right out the side door. And I'm gone. Once I hit the streets, I'm gone. You don't see me for weeks."

"He was a kid without supervision, who grew up on his own," Lerner said. "And when that happens, you fall into things. I would call one grandmother and she would say, 'He's with his other grandmother.' I'd call the other grandmother and she'd say, 'He's with the other grand-mother.' What that meant to me was he was on the streets by himself. This was not your Harvard-bound scholar. Just a kid who grew up without guidance."

"It's a shame, right?" Lloyd said. "For a little kid like Lloyd, it's a shame 'cause everybody in the world I had around me then, there was a lot that wanted to see me make it for me. They didn't want nothin' from me back then. They just wanted to see me do well. I had teachers that used to beg me to come to school. I mean teachers that, when I was in junior high school, wanted to pick me up from my house to make sure I got there. But I denied them. I would not let them pick me up. I'd tell them, 'I'll be all right. I'll be there.' I had teachers drop me home after school and talk to me, give me lectures. They would tell me, 'Lloyd, they is nothin' in the streets. Come to class. Be a good athlete. Try to do your work. All you got to do is come to class and learn a little bit 'bout edu-cation.' But I wouldn't.

"See, I'm an easy catch on, man. If I had went to class like any other student, I'd be smart. If I went to class. But I never would. And there was teachers used to begged me, man. They'd come get me, but I'd say, 'No, I'm all right.' You know, I used that con. I'd be that con artist, 'cause I felt bad. I knew the teachers was doin' it for me—they wouldn't do it for every kid—'cause eveybody else got they parents and I ain't got my parents. I'd feel ashamed, a lot of times, I'd feel ashamed. Teachers used to look out for me. I had teachers buy me a couple of clothes. I used to feel embarrassed 'bout that 'cause a couple of kids tried to jump on me 'bout that, man. You know, fights would break out 'cause they got jealous. They would go, 'You know, Lloyd, you got your teacher buyin' you clothes. What's the deal?' They'd go, like, 'What 'bout your parents?' I ain't goin' to lie. I felt embarrassed by that. That made me feel embarrassed. A kid told me that and I didn't come to school for 'bout three weeks. Three weeks I didn't come."

"He was a strange kid," Lerner said. "He just didn't communicate well with the other kids. He had a short attention span, which wasn't really surprising. A kid who is dyslexic, who can't read, is not going to try to do the work. He is going to become bored and go on to something else. The general impression was that he was turned off by school. That he didn't belong there. And his hatred of school was completely justified, because the system did not serve this kid. The system was just not capable of helping this kid. There was not a whole lot of learning going on. How many times can you ask the same kid to do his ABCs? From the first to the eighth grade, this kid had learned nothing. Somewhere along the line, he had to say 'I'm not going to do it.' How does a kid go through six years of reading pre-primer books? What can you do? Hold him over in kindergarten? Then what, first grade? Second? The kid would be twenty-two in the first grade. Instead, you put him in special ed. But that's not the answer either. What we have then are addicts, muggers, rapists, murderers and kids just hanging out on the corner with nowhere to go, nothing to do. What you end up with is kids with no direction."

The Jamaicans down the block had cornered the market on marijuana. Business was sweet, the clientele ever-expanding. They could always use extra hands to distribute their product. Young boys preferred, the man told Lloyd. No complications, he said. No problems for juveniles.

Now, Lloyd had made a promise never to use drugs. He did not want to sell them, either. But he was now ten years old. And promises did not begin to fill the holes that burned in his unfilled stomach. Promises did not begin to clothe a kid who had no clothes to wear, or begin to ease the burden of a child who felt embarrassed over his impoverishment. Besides, Lloyd said, almost all his relatives used drugs. He had watched them smoke marijuana, snort cocaine. It didn't seem so terrible, didn't seem to hurt anyone.

So Lloyd put aside his promise to his grandma and became a businessman. "I would sell a little marijuana, sold a little cocaine," he said. "When you doin' it and you ain't got no money and you need clothes and food to eat, you don't think about it. You got to survive. A man got to survive. Got to survive, got to eat, got to have sneakers. I didn't believe in takin' from my grandmother. She had it rough, too. She had to support her kids. She did her best with me. But a lot of times, I needed my own money in my own pocket.

"That's how I got caught in that shit, smokin', sellin' drugs. That's when I first started smokin' weed. I was smokin' weed when I was ten years old. Bein' around that shit, man, you say, 'I'll try a joint.'

"I ain't goin' to lie. I just started smokin' a joint. Next thing I know, I caught myself every day smokin' weed, weed, weed, weed. You know how it feel. You just feelin' nice. I just got caught up in the game. It made me feel good. I could have did a lot of things. I could have gone to school. But I just liked to get high. It was easy to do. I'm goin' to tell you the honest truth. I grew up in that type of environment with all of my family. You know, everybody in my family do drugs. There's only 'bout three people in my family that don't do drugs—and I ain't countin' my grandmothers, 'cause you know they don't do it. I got two aunts and an uncle that don't do drugs. Everybody else do drugs, so it was growin' all up in the family. I ain't goin' to lie, I started 'cause I first saw my uncles smokin' weed. I saw them smokin' weed. I said, 'I'm goin' to get me a bag. It must be good for them, they enjoy it. Let me catch a buzz. I should get contacts with my own boys.' Next thing I know, I was smokin' weed every day, dealin' it. I wake up in the mornin', I smoked. I thought it was okay. I said, 'I'm young. I could smoke weed. It ain't goin' to hurt me.' I didn't have nobody to tell me not to do it."

Like everything else, he just figured it was all right. "It was almost like," Lloyd said later, "it was in my genes. Like I let it be in my genes."

The kid had it in his genes, too. He knew it, understood it. The college scouts could tell that, too, even though he was just twelve, playing in a Catholic Youth Organization game at a local gymnasium.

It was apparent in the way he dribbled the ball, apparent in the way he saw the court, apparent in the way he handled himself under pressure. He had innate talent. He had the potential for greatness. "He was," scout Tom Konchalski recalled of the moment, "amazing. Just amazing."

Even the kid, himself, would later concede that he was in the process of "gettin' a little name." But the question was, where would that recognition, where would the game of basketball, lead Kenny Anderson?

A handful of years earlier, when Anderson was still just a baby, basketball had captured the imagination of his uncle, James McLaughlin. He had thrown himself into the game, had earned a little name, too, in some of the local parks. But that name, the reputation, had also attracted the hangers-on, folks looking to see what they could get from a man who might be headed for success. They were folks of not so fine moral stature. But James McLaughlin was really just a kid and, in them, he saw the easy life. Besides, he was a star and they had befriended him. Before he knew it, James McLaughlin was cutting school to hang out. Before he knew it, he was a man going nowhere fast, another kid who had fallen for the old routine and gotten sidetracked. It also happened to his nephew, Ricky Anderson, Kenny's older brother.

Though no one will talk about just what happened—"He got turned around the wrong way, that's what happened," Kenny's mother, Joan Anderson, once said—those associations left Jimmy Mac a lost, broken man, dead at the age of twenty-seven, left Ricky Anderson the next best thing to it, having dropped out of school to pursue other interests.

And now, here was Kenny Anderson, a little lefthanded guard with a game that bordered on brilliant for one so young, seemingly headed down the same path. He was in sixth grade, struggling in intermediate school in South Jamaica, where he lived not far from the Forties Projects. He was throwing himself into basketball, passing on his academics, which he said he didn't like. As he said, "There were temptations out there in the world. I saw them and I can't say that I hadn't thought about them, because I did."

All of which worried his mother, as well as a host of others who saw his potential and did not want to see it go to waste. "My brother had some troubles," Joan Anderson said. "He played for Jamaica High, but he never pursued it. He had a bad heart. He didn't do what he should have done. My other son, Ricky, he didn't do the right thing, either."

Luckily, Joan Anderson did. With the assistance of some acquaintances who were also concerned about her son's future, she moved from South Jamaica, which had already claimed two members of her family. The idea, she said, was to give her son a chance for a future. So she moved with Kenny to Lefrak City, a huge apartment complex near the Long Island Expressway in Rego Park, Queens.

The tenants at Lefrak often were a bit short on income. But the apartments sat amid a middle-class neighborhood thriving in its ethnic diversity. That proved to be a good influence on her son, as did a man he met at Lefrak; a man named Vincent Smith.

Smith, like those college basketball scouts, first saw Kenny in a youth game at Lost Battalion Hall on Queens Boulevard in Rego Park. Smith knew a bit about basketball. His brother, Kenny, was then an all-America guard at Archbishop Molloy High School in Queens and was leaning toward attending the University of North Carolina. He understood that Kenny Anderson needed guidance if he was going to find success, too. So, he lent a helping hand.

First, he talked to Joan Anderson. "She told me about [Jimmy Mac and Ricky]," Smith said. "How they played and how they didn't do as well as they should have. I told her Kenny would be different."

As Smith recalled, "Kenny had a lazy attitude. You could tell that he knew he was good. I always told Kenny, 'You have to be a student first, ballplayer second.' I stressed that if he didn't keep working, he'd slip and then all he'd have left were people talking about what he could have been."

Kenny Anderson, just a kid, could have done what Lloyd seemed to be doing, could have done what Jimmy Mac and Ricky had done before him. He could have nodded in agreement and gone about his business.

After all, he was good. He knew that. He saw the way people fawned over him when he worked on his game on the court at Lefrak, or on the one at Lost Battalion. He saw the admiration for him, a kid, as if he was something special. But he also remembered what happened to Jimmy Mac and Ricky.

"My brother was real good," said Kenny, nine years younger than Ricky Anderson. "He had a lot of talent. He was like, you know, a legend in the parks. He had a reputation. I heard stories about my uncle Jimmy, too. A lot of people said he was real good, that I reminded them a lot of him, you know, of the way he was in the playgrounds. My moms told me stories about him all the time. She said that he and my brother, they got sidetracked. She said that they didn't want it bad enough." They couldn't see the future.

The people who were beginning to hang around Kenny Anderson now could see the future. They knew what it would take to find success and they told him so. They said it wouldn't be easy. They said it would take a lot of work. But, Kenny Anderson wanted it. Badly. So, he decided to listen.

Some people tried to point Lloyd in a new direction, too. They tried to lead him down a new path. Tried to start him on the road to success. And, if it wasn't teachers trying to convince him that if he only did a marginal amount of work he could be a success, it was coaches.

The teachers did it because they wanted to see him get an education. The coaches did it because they wanted to see him play ball. In some way, though, both groups were doing it for him, as well as for themselves. There was ego involved. They wanted to be the one who saved Lloyd.

One person who tried was Arnie Hershkowitz. Hersh was a special ed teacher at Westinghouse High School, a vocational school in Brooklyn, and was a basketball fanatic who ran a summer-league team called Albie's Trimmings. He also recruited players for Westinghouse, mainly because he liked to associate with the up-and-coming stars—rub elbows with them, feel he had some control over what happened to them. He did it because, though married, he had no kids of his own. The players were his surrogate children. He also did it because he liked his school to win, so much so that he often went to games—usually, he sat in the first row of stands on the side opposite the team bench—and shouted instructions to "his" players; instructions often in direct opposition to orders from the coach, Irv Turk.

It is difficult to tell if there was more to it than that, especially since many street-level recruiters also befriend kids in order to eventually steer them to certain colleges, which then pay the recruiters what are known as "finder's fees"—kickbacks which can range from a few hundred dollars to several thousands, depending on how good a player the school receives.

Hersh didn't seem to be about that, though it was difficult to tell exactly what he was about. He was in his forties, a small-time horse player, strictly dollar, two-dollar stuff. He was balding, had a full beard and was one of the most hyperactive people around. He had braces on his teeth. Some fashioned him an outlaw and he liked the image. Often, he gave players money for food, taxis or the subway. Sometimes, he gave them as much as fifty dollars, mainly, he said, just because he knew them. It was his entertainment, like a night out on the town, like taking in a movie. Unlike most known street recruiters, he seemed to have no ties to specific colleges. He seemed, instead, to be more like a groupie, someone who did it to be liked, to be respected.

Hersh also knew Ronnie, whom he had met at a high school game. Between them, they knew almost every legitimate big-time player in New York City. Players knew them, seemed to listen to them.

"I would attend a game, see a youngster play and try to corral him one way or another," Hersh said. "It's a simple procedure—you're dealing with kids on the junior high school level. You give them a little attention, they feel obligated to you, feel closer to you. Most of the time, they had never been recruited before. The first impression is lasting.

"The kids didn't know anything. You could do anything you wanted with them. If I took a kid to McDonald's or said, 'Here's twenty dollars,' or bought him a pair of sneakers, that was it, what else could they have wanted? If you pay a kid attention or take him to a game, that's all you have to do. It doesn't take that much. It's not like recruiting a kid for college. Say I give him fifty dollars—he learns to have money in his pocket. When he gets to college, he's going to be around kids with money in their pockets. At least I'm giving him a sense of how to spend money, what it's like to have money. One thing you learn, you never ask for anything in return. If you're looking for monetary value in return, you shouldn't be in it in the first place."

Among the players Hersh befriended were Mark Jackson of Bishop Loughlin High School in Brooklyn, who would later play for St. John's and the New York Knicks, and John Salley, who played for Canarsie High School in Brooklyn, as well as Georgia Tech, and later won two NBA titles with the Detroit Pistons. Hersh claims he once "lent" Salley over five-hundred dollars—"Just to help him out," he said—while Salley was in college.

For all the players he knew, though, Hersh had met Lloyd by accident. He was eating at a restaurant in Brooklyn one afternoon. Lloyd walked by wearing a jacket from Bishop Loughlin, a jacket given to him by someone he said tried to recruit him. "Hey, I know you don't go to Loughlin," Hersh yelled to him. Lloyd stopped. "We talked for a while," Hersh said. He found out that Lloyd was Swee'pea. He knew the name. "I took down his phone number." A week later, Hersh took Lloyd to see the Philadelphia 76ers—in Philadelphia. And, then, he recruited him for Albie's Trimmings.

Hersh also tried to convince Lloyd to attend Westinghouse. As he said, "I just went out and recruited five kids to come to the school and, if they had all been in the school at the same time, we probably would've had the Number One team in the country." One of those players was Lloyd. Another was Jamal Faulkner, who became an all-American at Christ the King.

Eventually, though, Hersh realized that Lloyd could be more trouble than he was worth to have to deal with every day at Westinghouse. So, while he remained an advisor to Lloyd, as did Ronnie, he quit trying to recruit him. Instead, Lloyd enrolled in his zoned school, Thomas Jefferson.

That Lloyd was even able to be "pushed on," as Saul Lerner put it, was because he finally decided to come to school beginning in September, 1983. Not that he really had a choice. Lerner knew how badly Lloyd wanted to play high school basketball. So he lied to him. He told Lloyd the school would hold him there forever—not promote him to high school—unless he came to school on a regular basis. Where talks about education and the future had failed, using basketball as the carrot to entice Lloyd seemed to work.

For the better part of a month, Lloyd came to school. Every day. And, in October, he was sent on to Thomas Jefferson.

"The only reason we ever saw Lloyd was because he wanted to play basketball and he had been told that, if he didn't get out, he was not going to ever play," Lerner said. "Otherwise, it would have been impossible to reach a kid like this." As Lloyd said, "They knew how good my talent was, they knew I was a good ballplayer. Teachers told me, coaches told me, 'All you got to do is come to school and we'll make sure you get a passin' grade, even if it ain't nothin' but a seventy.' They told me that in junior high school. Teachers said to me, 'I'll pass you if you just come to class.' That's the system."

But, placed in Jefferson, Lloyd again rarely went to school—even though it was just a hundred yards from his house, across the vacant lot from New Jersey Avenue to Pennsylvania. Worse, Lloyd broke an ankle that fall and missed the first half of the season. Still, because of the way the marking periods fell and because he had a medical excuse, after Lloyd recovered he became eligible for the final seven games of the regular season. His high school debut was against Wingate, a team coached by Saul Lerner.

Wingate had a senior forward named Dexter Campbell, who would go on to play at Xavier University in Cincinnati. Lloyd weighed 150 pounds, but he used his basketball knowledge to exploit the weaknesses in Campbell's game, used his finesse to negate Campbell's strength. "He did not start," Lerner said. "But once he got in, he ate Campbell for lunch. It was a complete domination of the game. And this was against a kid who played for what was a Top Twenty program. It was impressive." So were his performances against Tilden and Lincoln in the Public Schools Athletic League Playoffs.

But the problems were again catching up. "I would just wake up in the mornin' smokin' weed, goin' to practice, smokin' weed every day," Lloyd said. "It wasn't a day I didn't miss smokin' weed. It was like that was the only way I'd get through practice, like by feelin' good, goin' through the motions. At one point, I thought nobody could stop me if I smoke a joint before I play. I thought nobody could hold me. I'm sure I ain't the only guy who thought like that. Like, soon I just got tired of all that school stuff, though. After basketball season, I was history anyhow. I didn't like that place. I called it 'Baby Rikers Island.' A kid came up to me once in the halls, showed me a gun and said, 'This is my school. This ain't your school. So what you play ball? You could still get killed here.' I was like, 'Get me out of here.' I wanted to get out."

And so, he stopped going to school.

4 · Miles to Go

Even as the crow flies, Mouth of Wilson, Virginia, seems to be more than a hundred miles from even the faintest hint of civilization. A one-horse town in an almost literal sense, it lends new definition to the word "isolation."

There are no traffic lights in Mouth of Wilson. A run-down mill, a general store, a car dealership and a post office form the entire "business district." There are but three pages in the local telephone book.

"There are," one writer once wrote, "only a hundred stories in this naked city." And, perhaps, even that number is slight exaggeration.

Here, along a deserted stretch of road known as Highway 58 in the foothills of the Iron Mountains—somewhere between the Appalachian and Blue Ridge Mountains on the Virginia border near North Carolina and Tennessee—stands Oak Hill Academy. Some refer to this place as "The End of the Earth." And, after one look around, you can tell it isn't with affection. But Mouth of Wilson—known as such because the locals used to tell each other, "Meet me at the mouth of Wilson Creek"—and its school serve as a refuge of sorts; a place where a student can salvage his faltering academic career, as well as salvage his future before it becomes his past.

"Most of these kids are at the end of their rope," basketball coach Larry Davis once said of his players at Oak Hill. "It's their last stop. If they don't make it here, they're going to junior college or not at all." As assistant coach Steve Smith said, "This is the last road out." The court of last resort.

It was here that Lloyd, entering his sophomore year of high school after having quit Jefferson, found himself in September, 1984.

The task at hand would be difficult, especially for someone with his track record. Lloyd had shown that, due to his lack of family structure and his lack of self-discipline, left to his own devices, he was not capable of doing what was necessary to ensure his own success. Enrolling at Oak Hill might eliminate some of the variables and increase the odds of him making the grade. It had to. Without improvement, and with the National Collegiate Athletic Association tightening entrance requirements for student-athletes, Lloyd might never become eligible to play college basketball.

Once, enrolling in preparatory school to improve weak academic skills had been a practice reserved for the financially well-to-do. It gave those students another year of refinement, gave them a chance to gain maturity and discipline in the classroom. It gave them an opportunity to bolster their averages and enhance their chances of gaining admittance to Ivy League universities, service academies and other prestigious academic institutions.

A few schools specialized in dealing with more troubled students from less suitable economic backgrounds, kids who needed to improve basic academic skills. Fewer still, most notably Laurinburg Institute—a traditional black prep school in Laurinburg, North Carolina, which in the 1960s produced future college and pro stars Jimmy Walker and Charlie Scott, among others—even gained a reputation for working to keep troubled athletes on the road to college. But, in reality, those opportunities for success were few and far between.

It is only in the past ten years or so since college basketball exploded into the national consciousness, moving from a provincial extra-curricular activity to a national obsession in the wake of the 1979 NCAA Championship Game between Michigan State and Indiana State, that the attraction with prep schools has blossomed in inner-city environs. With that game, the first of many memorable meetings between Magic Johnson and Larry Bird and the single most viewed college basketball game in television history, college basketball became big business in the United States.

It led to cable broadcasts of games, a call to expand the tournament field from forty-eight teams to sixty-four, and an increase in tournament revenue—which by 1990 was almost $1.4 million for teams making the Final Four.

It also meant that, to ensure success on the court and remain in the run for the gold, schools had to find athletes able to meet entrance requirements and remain eligible. Coaches of high school, college and club teams understood that new NCAA legislation such as Proposition 48—a rule which became an NCAA bylaw in 1986—meant they needed to guarantee the best players the best possible chance for academic success. After all, the NCAA, conscious of the beating its image was taking because of the questionable enrollments and eligibilities of under-qualified athletes—athletes such as Kevin Ross, who played basketball at Creighton University and then went back to grammar school to learn to read—was now setting firmer academic standards for entering college freshmen. A recruit had to achieve a 2.0 scholastic grade-point average and a minimum score of 700 out of 1,600 on the Scholastic Aptitude Test to "predict," to be eligible for competition. That didn't bode well for the futures of many inner-city athletes, who often had educational backgrounds not much different from Kevin Ross or Lloyd.

Cheating to get players eligible—using stand-ins to take an aptitude test or actually cheating on the tests, the way the NCAA would declare University of Kentucky recruit Eric Manuel did on his test in June, 1987—was the last resort for desperate schools. The first choice was simply to identify the right kids and get them immediate help. Suddenly, anyone with an academic problem who could shoot, dribble or score was becoming a preppie.

Brian Shorter, who was headed to the University of Pittsburgh, passed on his senior season at Simon Gratz High School in Philadelphia, where he was just 384 points shy of the all-time city scoring record of 2,252 set by Wilt Chamberlain, to attend Oak Hill. Dennis Scott, who would take Georgia Tech to the 1990 NCAA Final Four, left his home in Reston, Virginia, to attend Flint Hill in Oakton, Virginia And, that only touched on the number of big-time players who were making their way to previously unheard of places like Fork Union (Va.) Military Academy, Solebury (Pa.) Prep and Maine Central Institute.

Lloyd, of course, never chose to attend Oak Hill. That was the idea of Lou d'Almeida, who coached the Gauchos. A wealthy real estate developer who was born in Paris, raised in Buenos Aires, Argentina, and educated at Yale University, d'Almeida once worked as an actor in off-Broadway productions as well as on television in "Playhouse 90" and "The Dinah Shore Show." He said that he first became involved in youth basketball by accident, when a friend with whom he was playing squash asked him to purchase a few T-shirts for a team run by another friend. That was 1967. One thing led to another and soon d'Almeida had laid the foundation for a program that would become the Gauchos.

D'Almeida is a slightly built man with short hair almost as white as his Jaguar, which is adorned with vanity license plates that read "GAU-CHO." He is a good dresser, and always well-groomed. Congenial, sometimes to a fault, he seems to have a genuine interest in his kids. His gym, an ultra-modern facility not far from Yankee Stadium in the Bronx, sports a massive orange and brown logo of a snorting bull with the word "Gauchos" that is visible from the Major Deegan Expressway. Inside, it features a deluxe all-wood floor and a wall covered in imported African mahogany. A bachelor, he has lived in the same two-bedroom penthouse apartment at 57th Street and Seventh Avenue in Manhattan almost all his adult life.

He likes to tell folks how he has given away "more sneakers than Imelda Marcos has," and said the purpose of his club is, through basketball, to offer hope to those who because of their environment and because of their lot in life have been raised without it. He said he gives kids a chance.

"A gaucho," he once said, "could build his house, catch or hunt his food, cook his meals, tame horses. The connotation is of an outlaw, but the reality is not. A gaucho is a peaceful person, a conqueror of nature. These kids should look up to gauchos. They are the ultimate survivors." Which is why, he said, he chose to work with these kids in the first place.

Some critics allege the purpose of his program is ego gratification, claiming that the club insulates players, demands their prime concern be basketball and winning games, not education. Some allege that the driving force behind the program is not a concern for those players, but for kickbacks from colleges who sign those players. After all, like college basketball, club teams throughout the nation have become big business, often receiving funding from sneaker companies, as well as alleged behind-the-scenes financial support from colleges who covet their best players.

D'Almeida, who declines to discuss his financial background or real estate holdings and investments, admits he spends about $100,000 in tuition each year for players. But he denies his program receives "kickbacks" or other outside funding, just as he denies he pays players—except to give them team jackets, sneakers or meal money—in an attempt to lure them to his program. He also denies allegations—to the best knowledge, none proven—that his players have been caught using drugs, shoplifting and trashing hotel rooms at various tournament sites. He calls such allegations "bullshit."

Still, in New York, where almost every elite player belongs to one of four basketball organizations—Madison Square Boys Club, Elmcor, the Gauchos and Riverside Church, which, built in the 1920s by John D. Rockefeller, Jr., runs its program out of community service, as well as to enhance its image among minorities in the bordering neighborhood of Harlem—his program often attracts the most talented among them. Former members include Dwayne (Pearl) Washington, Sidney Green, Ed Pinckney, Rod Strickland, Jerry (Ice) Reynolds and John (The Spider) Salley, all of whom made the NBA. Greg (Boo) Harvey, who played at St. John's, was a Gaucho. So was Roosevelt Chapman, who went to Dayton University, Tony (Red) Bruin, who went to Syracuse University, and Richie Adams, who went on to Nevada-Las Vegas. Salley, who went from the Gauchos to Georgia Tech to the Pistons, said d'Almeida was an important factor in his success.

"We talked about business, we talked about life and the future," Salley said. "When we went to dinner on trips, he'd even sit the players down and teach them how to eat properly —you know, what eating utensils to use, how to hold your knife, how to hold your fork. He cared."

As d'Almeida said, "I care about the lowliest and the worst kid. I never give up on a kid. Never. I get them launched into the real world and teach them how to take hold of the advantages."

It was a lesson that was not lost on a kid like Lloyd, who always seemed cognizant of taking whatever advantages he could. Lloyd had joined the club sometime back in 1983, after, he said, he had gone to one of the other local clubs and first promised to play for them. "Everybody wanted me," Lloyd said. "I knew that everybody wanted me. So, I went to [one team] and said, 'The only way I'll play for you is if you pay me.' They gave me a couple of crispy hundreds. But I never showed again."

Instead, Lloyd went to the Gauchos. Arnie Hershkowitz claims, "Lloyd was always getting money from the Gauchos. Lou would give him money all the time." Rumors had it at least $250 a game, often more. Possibly more than $2,500 for an out-of-state tournament, which may not be as absurd as it sounds. After all, AAU tournaments around the country —tournaments like the Las Vegas Invitational, as well as others, including the Basketball Congress International in Phoenix—guarantee appearance money for teams. And, if you win or make a good showing in those tournaments, your team gets invited back. So good players, it would seem, do get paid.

D'Almeida said none of his players, even Lloyd, ever got paid to perform. In fact, d'Almeida said he didn't even know who Lloyd was when he first arrived at the club, which was then run at P.S. 197 in Harlem. "He came into the gym while I was there," d'Almeida recalled. "I didn't know who he was. I had no idea. I asked one of my assistants, 'Who's that?' He said, 'His name's Lloyd Daniels.' But even then he looked like he was better than a lot of the kids. He must have been for me to notice. I'm not a basketball genius, but even I could tell he was better than the other kids."

D'Almeida soon realized Lloyd also had more problems than the other kids, especially when it came to education. "You could see he was much less prepared than most of the kids," d'Almeida said. "That was probably the biggest problem he had. He didn't have the foundation. He needed extra schooling and from meeting his grandmothers I could tell that, while they were loving, caring people, they weren't sophisticated enough to understand what he needed as far as academics. They just didn't know the requirements. I felt this kid, with the right education, had a chance to go anywhere that he wanted. That's why I wanted him out of the city, wanted to get him into an environment where he could learn. So I sent him to Oak Hill."

Lloyd claims there was also another, more sinister, reason d'Almeida was willing to spend over $5,000 on his education: d'Almeida knew Lloyd had little loyalty and, therefore, might lose him to another club. "Want to know the real reason I went down there?" Lloyd said. "Lou was tryin' to keep me away from Riverside Church. They said they was goin' to send me to school on a bus and Lou said, 'No, I ain't goin' to send you on a bus. I'm goin' to send you on a plane.' "

So, as Lloyd said, "I took that deal. You know, 'Bigger and Better.' Comin' from where I come from, you have to get what you can."

That was how Lloyd became a student at Oak Hill, though maybe "student" is the wrong word. As Smith said, "We've never had a student like that before. We've never had anybody here who was like Lloyd."

For almost one hundred years, Oak Hill Academy deviated little from its original mandate. Founded in 1878 by the New River Baptist Association, it was built as a school for locals, one which, through the teachings of the church, tried to steer its troubled teenagers away from outside distractions and toward a more humble, more respectable, more academic life. That it went coed in the 1950s was more out of necessity than desire, its enrollment was on the wane, its till growing less and less full.

By the early 1970s, its demise was imminent. Enrollment was down to eighty-five students. The operating budget used to support its withering faculty, its thirteen worn and wearied buildings and its two varsity sports—a baseball team which almost never played games; and, a basketball team that played games against the likes of the Virginia Baptist Children's Home—was a mere $200,000. It seemed that Oak Hill was in dire straits.

Until, that is, athletic director Chuck Isner got an idea. What if, taking a page from the major-college and big-time high school programs, Isner asked his father, Robert, then the school's president, Oak Hill invested a few dollars in its miserable basketball team and used it to promote the school? Four scholarships would be all Chuck Isner needed. His father, though his head told him the school could not afford to do it, agreed. In New York City, Chuck Isner found three players and a team was born.

That was 1976. By the 1980s, the enrollment at Oak Hill had grown to nearly 200 and the budget to almost $2 million. As one writer wrote, Oak Hill used basketball to "spread the word of the Mouth."

Hearing what the school could do for troubled kids, Lou d'Almeida also paid to send Rod Strickland to Oak Hill Academy in the fall of 1984. Like Lloyd, Strickland hardly appreciated the idea. He had just established himself as a consensus all-American, having led Harry S Truman High School in the Bronx to city and state titles as a junior. But, with an offer from DePaul University hanging in the balance, Strickland could ill afford to gamble with his 1.94 grade-point average when he needed a 2.0 to be eligible. "It was do or die," Strickland said. And so, though he didn't like it, he went.

Oak Hill offered the perfect environment for athletes like Rod Strickland and Lloyd. "The same like Rod, I went there because I needed my grades," Lloyd said. "But I was, like, shocked when I got there. I was in a town with nobody and nothin'." There was nothing that would hinder a man's chances of attaining success. Nothing that would hinder him from getting his life back on track. Nothing, Strickland noted, except "blackboards and backboards."

Nothing, except a chance for education and maturation with a little bit of big-time high school basketball thrown in on the side.

Oak Hill offered a chance to learn what it meant to be responsible, and to become successful despite past failure. It taught that lesson through structure. Breakfast was at seven. Class was from 8 a.m. to 3:25 p.m., with tutorial from three-thirty to four-fifteen. After dinner, which was at five, there was study hall at six, practice from seven-thirty to nine-fifteen and lights and televisions out at ten. No exceptions.

For some of these kids, it would be the first time in their lives that they'd have positive role models. They would see kids who went to school, kids who wanted to learn. More important, for the first time in their lives they would have no excuse not to attend class. If you slept late, Davis and Smith came and woke you in the morning. Here, you were force-fed knowledge.

"The kids there go to class because they have to," said Tom Konchalski, the East Coast basketball recruiting expert who was very familiar with the school. "The dorm is across the street from the buildings where you go to class and, if you don't go, they come and drag you out of bed. They don't give you a chance to goof off. It's not like the city. They make you work."

"People have a misconception that, if you go to Oak Hill, you automatically get your grades," Davis said. "But nobody's going to give you a grade. It forces you to do things. If you don't do your homework, you don't get a zero like public school. You have to keep coming after school until you do it. The kid decides he'd rather do it the first time than keep coming after school."

Lloyd could not read more than a few words when he arrived at Oak Hill. He understood neither phonetics nor the basics of grammar. Teammates recalled how he would take a book and pretend to read it and how they laughed because he was holding it upside down. Or how he tried to read a magazine—in Spanish. Unlike most students, who needed minor refinements because of deficiencies in their educational backgrounds, Lloyd needed to restart the entire process from scratch.

"I hate to label him," said Smith, sounding familiar. "But I wouldn't even want to speculate on how low his reading and writing skills might be."

In an effort to improve those skills, Lloyd was assigned a private tutor, Lisa Smith, the coach's wife. She said that while Lloyd wanted to learn, there was "no real desire" to do the work. Partly, it was because of his dyslexia which, possibly due to a lack of specially trained counselors, had still gone undiagnosed. Partly, it was because he just didn't like school. School, after all, meant work. And, Lloyd didn't like work. "It just wasn't in him," she said. "I tried to tell him that every spare moment he had to read and write. Of course, he wouldn't. For him, he was doing a lot." But not enough.

"I didn't expect it to be that deep," Lloyd said. "Like, you just went to class then back to your room. I thought at least you go down there, go to a little party. Like a college thing. But it wasn't that type of thing. It was like, check your books, then go back to the dormitory. That wasn't Lloyd Daniels' style. I was like, 'I got to get up at seven, got to eat breakfast, and then I got to stay up from like seven to three-thirty?' I was like, 'Excuse me, sir.' You know, that wasn't me every day like that, man. I wasn't into my books that hard. I felt like I was thrown into, what you call it, formation—no, reform school. It seemed like that's what they threw me in. Oak Hill was a good school. But you couldn't take a kid like me, from the ghetto, out to that type of country. I couldn't deal with no mountains. I couldn't deal with Oak Hill."

Few could. Strickland fought the idea, threatening to quit after he'd gone home for Christmas. "I'm not coming back," he told the coaches. "I'm just going to forget it and go to a junior college." To which they said, "You've got a full scholarship to DePaul. You're going to throw it all away?"

Convinced that wasn't in his best interests, Strickland came back. But he was promptly placed on academic probation for two weeks—meaning he couldn't play ball. "I was walking around with a chip on my shoulder," he said. "I didn't want to be there. But it helped me realize that I had to get down and do my homework." Academics were screwing up his career.

But homework wasn't what concerned Lloyd. He had other concerns. After all, at Oak Hill male students were not allowed to be in a room with a girl if the door was closed. That meant no kissing. And no sex. Violation of those rules caused another city player to be expelled after he had taken the girl out of town, to a motel, for a weekend. "You can't be expectin' a guy like me, who is just start learnin' about girls, sayin' I can't kiss a girl," Lloyd said. "I mean, I got to get restricted? I couldn't take it, man. I couldn't take it. You couldn't get caught tryin' to get your rocks off. How was I supposed to deal with that? What was I supposed to have did?"

Unable to understand the need to exercise restraint or be mature enough to obey the rules, even if he disagreed with them, what Lloyd did instead was turn to drugs. If he couldn't get action, satisfaction, at least he could get high. Smith always suspected Lloyd had a drug problem at Oak Hill. "I knew he had some drug-related problems when he was here," he said. "There weren't that many drugs down here and that was his problem. The only thing you can find down here might be some marijuana. A new kid would come onto campus and he would be the first one to say hello to him. It was always, 'Hey, you got anything? Can you get me some?' "

If you were a basketball player, you could make connections. Lloyd had juice. "White guys that go home on the weekend, we used to pay them to get us a twenty-five dollar bag of marijuana," he said. "And they'd bring it in."

After all, the kids who weren't athletes, who were there not because of their club coaches, but because they'd been sent by parents who wanted to teach them responsibility, often liked the idea that they could associate with the players. It gave them power, gave them prestige—just like kids on the streets. It gave them a chance to mingle with the stars and allowed them to live out their fantasies, all while making a little money on the side.

It was a difference in maturity, a difference in priorities. While Rod Strickland decided to buckle down, decided to go to class and then go back to his room to work on his homework, Lloyd was going to class and going back to his room to get high with a few of his new-found friends.

Until, that is, one afternoon in October, when he was caught by a school dean in a room where a few students were smoking marijuana. "I swear to God, I wasn't doin' no drugs," Lloyd said of the incident. "You ask me, 'Were you puffin'?' and I would say, 'No, I didn't do no puffin'.' But I was in there, so who's goin' to believe me? I mean, I ain't sayin' I wasn't gettin' ready to take a toke. But I wasn't smokin' yet. Still, I was there. What could I do?"

"He was not caught red-handed," Smith recalled. "But there were drugs in the room and school officials felt this wasn't something they could condone." As punishment, school officials decided that, since he was a player and since he had not actually been caught smoking marijuana but had only been in the room when it was smoked, Lloyd would not be expelled. Instead, he was ordered to run laps at six o'clock every morning for a two-week period.

It was a minor punishment, one that required minimum effort to fulfill. But, with the chance for a successful future in one hand, and a chance to avoid a little hard work in the present in the other, Lloyd made his choice. Given a chance to redeem himself through an option offered only because he was a basketball player, Lloyd refused.

After all, he was Swee'pea. Why should he have to run? "It ain't about listenin'," Lloyd said. "It was just a lot of times Lloyd wanted to do what he wanted to do." As he said, "I told them, 'I ain't runnin', I ain't goin' to run. This ain't like the slavey days. And I ain't no slavey boy.' "

"We had suspected him for a long time," Smith said. "But he said so many times that he didn't have a problem that I think he seriously believed that he didn't have a problem. He'd say, 'No, I'm clean. I'm clean.' "

Having left school officials with no other options, Lloyd was asked to leave Oak Hill. He did so without hesitation.

Lloyd had lasted six weeks at Oak Hill. Now, he figured, after that stretch, which to him resembled a prison sentence, he would be headed back to New York—where he could sleep late, cut class, play ball, do drugs and, as he said, "Get fucked by all the pretty ladies." It would, no doubt, be paradise.

Lou d'Almeida had other plans. He had heard of another prep school with a big-time basketball team, a school which specialized in problem kids and in getting them eligible. The season before, the school had been home to one of the most-recruited players in America, Chris Washburn, who had gone on to North Carolina State. So what if in recent years the school, Laurinburg Institute, had seen its reputation wither, becoming known among basketball cognoscenti as a haven for shortcutters? Lloyd needed a school, needed a basketball team. Laurinburg figured to be his best bet.

Lloyd liked Laurinburg. And, apparently, for good reason. "I was smokin' pot every day there," Lloyd said. "I could smoke in my room. No one checked. I was the man on campus, that was my school. I was the new Chris Washburn."

It was a morbid comparison, especially since on the night of December 19, 1984, about the time Lloyd was finishing his second month at Laurinburg, Washburn, a frequent drug user, was arrested for breaking into a dorm room at North Carolina State and stealing a stereo system. In the wake of charges of second-degree burglary—he pleaded guilty to misdemeanor charges—it was revealed he had scored 470 on the SAT. You get a minimum of 400 just for signing your name correctly, which often led to jokes among coaches—some of whom told their players, "Just sign the test twice."

Washburn, it was said, had managed at Laurinburg because he was such a highly-recruited player, one who was allegedly pushed through and given grades despite being a functional illiterate. As one basketball scout who knew the school alleged, "The place is a total zoo. A trained parrot might have been able to pass class there." Lloyd agreed. In addition to smoking marijuana at Laurinburg, he said he did anything he wanted. Lloyd claims he even threatened coach Frank McDuffie, whose mother, Sammie, was the school principal, that if things didn't work out in his favor, he'd just leave.

"It was a wild zoo," Lloyd said. "It was so fucked up. But they listened to me because I was a hell of a good ballplayer, I was the man. They knew if they didn't listen to me, I would go. Everybody knew my record. I was goin' to leave if things didn't go well for me. I always kept a school under my belt. That may sound funny, but that's the truth. I knew if I left this school, somebody was goin' to take me. Those days, I knew everybody wanted me then. A lot of times I threatened them that I was goin' to leave and they said that they'd work things out. Then they'd sit me down to talk to them, take me out to dinner, somethin'. Next thing you know, I'd sit down and chill."

Lloyd averaged 25 points and 15 rebounds that season at Laurinburg, where he earned immeasurable respect as a big-time player. He also earned a 'C' average and five credits, the most credits he ever earned in a single year of high school. "You know," Lloyd said, "I stayed there for a whole year. For once in my life, I went to a place and stuck it out. I lasted a year, got my grades." As Frank McDuffie said, "If a person tries, should he get an 'F'?"

The best high school basketball player in America in the summer of 1985 was J.R. Reid. A shot-blocking, rebounding machine, Reid was built like the Incredible Hulk and every bit as intimidating. Every college in the nation wanted him. He would later attend North Carolina and would become the first-round selection of the Charlotte Hornets in the 1989 NBA Draft.

But that summer at Five-Star Camp, according to camp director Howie Garfinkel, Reid got "served"—the street term for getting his ass busted—by none other than Swee'pea. "Here was Lloyd, this skinny 6-foot-8 guy, and you figured he would get crunched," Garfinkel recalled. "But, he guarded him, defended him nicely. He outshot Reid, outhandled him and played him even on the boards. Here was Reid, considered the best senior in the nation, a man who was playing for his reputation, and Lloyd outplayed him both weeks of the camp. Clearly, they were the two best players in camp and it was never worse than even and, in most cases, Lloyd was superior."

Lloyd toyed with him, scoring at will, defending against him, taking him to the hoop. He would come down, freeze Reid with a head fake, and then blow by him for an uncontested lay-up. He would take him down on the low post, spin off him, and sink his shot. He couldn't out-muscle Reid. But he could use his finesse to get the best of him. And, he did.

"He was a real good player," said Reid, who even got his shot rejected once by Lloyd. "They called him the next Magic Johnson. And he was pretty good. I played against him a couple of times. He checked me for a while. He was a really smooth player. He had the skill, I sure remember that."

Ron Brown, an assistant coach at West Virginia, said there was no doubt that Reid remembered even more about Lloyd from that camp—game notes that he wanted to forget. "Everyone going in was talking about the great J.R. Reid," said Brown, a Bronx native who had watched Lloyd throughout high school. "But, coming out all they talked about was Lloyd Daniels. Lloyd took him to the free throw line a couple of times, head faked him, then took him to the hoop, smooth as can be. He did a little passing, he ran the break. He scored a few on fingertips to the basket.

"He made the great J.R. Reid, the man who was supposed to be the best on the court, lose his reputation. Lloyd was phenomenal. A few coaches were walking around going, 'They could put him in the pros right now.' When people say that Lloyd can play five positions, it was because of that camp. He showed he could play. He was just a little slicker, just a little sweeter, just a little better than anyone else there. He was playing basketball at his own level. When camp was over if you asked, 'Who's the best player in the country?' people would have told you, 'Lloyd Daniels, without question.' "

Garfinkel remembered something else, too, about that camp. Something that also had to do with the battles Lloyd had with J.R. Reid. It was about Larry Brown, then the basketball coach at the University of Kansas. "Larry was there," Garfinkel said. "His mouth was open for two days. He wanted to take the kid home with him. He wanted to adopt him. He kept telling me, 'I'll find a place for him. I'll find a family for him to live with.' He said he could get something worked out. Believe me, this kid was the real thing."

Larry Brown, who just a few years before ensured the recruitment of high school all-American Danny Manning when he hired his father, Ed, then a truck driver, to be his assistant at Kansas, never tried to adopt Lloyd that summer. And, with Ronnie and Hersh arguing against Lloyd going back to Laurinburg because they felt he needed a "more structured environment," Lou d'Almeida again made contact with school officials at Oak Hill.

Rod Strickland had stuck it out, graduated and gone on to DePaul. Chris Brooks, a senior from Samuel Gompers High School in the Bronx, was being sent to Oak Hill by d'Almeida. So, d'Almeida asked Smith, who had become the head coach after the previous season, if he and the school would consider taking another chance on Lloyd. It was a risky decision. But Smith, as well as the members of the school administration, decided to be practical. The school needed whatever students it could attract. Even ones like Lloyd.

"He was a paying student," Smith said, "and we felt, 'Hey, let's give him another chance.' He was a good basketball player. The school would get some publicity. Now, that wasn't the only reason. We were genuinely concerned. Besides, he really didn't have a whole lot of places he could go."

So, Lloyd headed back to Mouth of Wilson. But, once again, it wasn't long before he ran into problems. He was a god on the court, where, it seemed, every coach in America had seen him and become enamored with his skill—including a University of Nevada-Las Vegas assistant named Mark Warkentien, who, that October, had flown from Las Vegas to Chicago to Pittsburgh to Tri-Cities Airport in Bristol, Tennessee, and then driven two hours in a rental car just to see him practice. Still, Lloyd was again a hellion off court.

"I ain't seen nobody who can play like him," Smith said. "I'm only thirty, but I've never seen a high school player who has the talent he has. It's like he's not human. Like he's a freak show out there on the court. He can dribble. He can shoot. He can rebound. He can block shots. He sees the court. And, he does all these things at 6-foot-8. It's not like he's a regular high school player. He could have played any of the five positions here. He could have been my point guard, my shooting guard, my small forward, my power forward or my center and we don't have such a bad team. Just to watch him play, you'd never know he has any problems. Until he steps off the court."

The problems, at first, were minor. Lloyd began to doubt he could ever do his schoolwork and so he refused to even make the attempt. He slept late. He created disturbances in class—talking during lessons, telling jokes, cutting up. He disrupted team unity, went against orders. He became rebellious. He refused to play with certain players, who he felt weren't good enough to be on the court with him. And, even though he might have been correct in his assessment, his teammates were hardly appreciative of his candor.

"Oak Hill was no joy ride," said Brooks, who had played on the Gauchos with Lloyd and who would win a president's award for academic progress and good citizenship at Oak Hill, though he later failed to achieve the minimum SAT score and was ruled ineligible as a freshman at West Virginia. "But you had to think of the future. I tried to appreciate what they were doing for me there. But Lloyd acted as if school was something he was allergic to. If you said, 'Lloyd, do this' he would do it. But if you said, 'Lloyd, don't do this' then it was almost like he had to try to do it. He just got out of hand. It was like he had made a decision, like, 'I don't really belong here. Why try? I'll only do bad.' So it seemed like he tried to be out of control, almost as if he figured, 'They'll send me home.' It was like that was what he expected. I figured it was what he wanted. To be sent home."

"The things he would do, you would say to him, 'Why'd you do that?' " Smith said. "It just compounded itself daily. You kept on saying, 'You're blowing your only chance to make it.' He didn't seem to understand."

The problems multiplied. Teammates were missing possessions from their rooms. They began to blame Lloyd. There was dissension on the team. People began to blame Lloyd. "A lot of things started to go wrong on the perimeter," Smith said. As Brooks said, "People started to say, 'Lloyd's a bad apple.' "

Lloyd denied the allegations. But he did nothing to ingratiate himself to his coach or his teammates. "People on the team started saying, 'Lloyd is a shady character,' " Smith said. "I thought it was tearing our team apart. It wasn't just one player. It was ten against one. And if they suspect you, and they had good reason to, it will eventually show up on the floor, in the classroom and in everything they do. It just got to the point where I didn't want to have to fool with his everyday headaches."

So one day, Smith just asked Lloyd to leave. This time, he had lasted eleven weeks. Lloyd never played a basketball game for Oak Hill.

"It just shows you that Lloyd Daniels is his own worst enemy," said one local high school basketball scout. "He didn't want to stay the first time, and when he did leave, he wanted to come back because in his heart he knew Oak Hill was the best situation for him. And then, when he does go back, he creates a situation which means he cannot stay."

"It is difficult to understand," d'Almeida said. "But it's like people on a life raft out in the ocean. Why do some die and why do some survive? Maybe what it all comes down to in the end is willpower."

As Smith said, "He relies on basketball so much that he thinks it is going to get him out of everything. Up until now, it has. But it has reached the point where it can't keep going that way. In fact, it's a possibility, a distinct possibility, that he could be that person who never makes it. And, with all that talent, that would be a shame. But, at the rate he is going, he is a prime target to be one of the biggest athletes, one of the biggest names, never to make it. There are some people who still want to protect him. They don't want him to get a bad rap. But I think that time is long over. When people hear the name 'Lloyd,' they think of trouble. The funny thing is that I still like him. I care about him. When he pulled out of here, I watched him go down the road and felt sorry for him. I wondered if this was his last chance. If Oak Hill was his last chance. I wondered if I could have saved him."

Like all who Lloyd disappointed, he wondered if anyone could.

5 · Andrew Jackson

Alvis Brown was in class when he heard the news. There was a new kid in school. Word was, he was good, too. People said, in fact, that with him in uniform, Andrew Jackson High School might be a sure bet to defend its city title in the Public Schools Athletic League. Some said the kid might even be the best ever to wear a Jackson uniform, which made Brown wonder just a bit. His cousin, Boo Harvey, had graduated after the previous season. He had been a two-time all-city player at Jackson and was considered one of the best ever at the school—listed in the school hall of fame, in fact, next to Bob Cousy, the Boston Celtics guard who was in the NBA Hall of Fame.

"Who's the new kid?" Brown asked a classmate. "Don't know," the kid said. "His name's 'Swee'pea.' That's all I know, he's called 'Swee'pea.' "

Brown thought a moment. Back when he was younger, about six, seven years old, he and his cousin used to play ball with this kid at St. Pascal's in Hollis. Brown couldn't remember the kid's name, but he remembered folks used to call him "Sweets." He had been real good. "I was sayin' to myself, 'Couldn't be the same kid, could it?' It couldn't be 'Sweets.' "

Right after class, Brown headed for the gymnasium, anxious. It would be time for practice. And, the kid would be there.

When Brown walked into the gym, he was on the floor with a basketball—standing alone, shooting. "Sweets," Brown said to himself. "This is Lloyd Daniels," Brown remembered Jackson coach Chuck Granby told the team. "He's going to be on our team." His teammates were in the stands, watching. Whispering. "We're goin' to win the title," Brown recalled a few of his teammates said, then. "We got us another city championship."

"Here was Lloyd, out on the court, by hisself, dribbling, shooting the ball where the three-point line would be if we had a three-point line—which, at that time, we didn't 'cause the rule wasn't put in until two seasons later," Brown said. "He hit all the way around from the left side to the right, shooting righthanded all the way, and then, when he got done, he went back around the other way, hitting every shot lefthanded. Again, he didn't miss."

Brown put his thumb to the forefinger and middle finger of his right hand as he said this, kissing them and holding them aloft while placing his left hand on his chest. "I swear to God," he said. "He didn't miss not one." The new kid was good, all right.

If that little shooting exhibition in the gym had hinted to team members the skill their new teammate possessed, then the first game of the season against Moses Scurry and his team, Brooklyn's Eli Whitney High School, offered irrefutable evidence of what Lloyd could do with a basketball. It was a situation that seemed to define the essence of his game.

After all, another man, with his first big game on the line, might have panicked and rid himself of the ball too soon, the result being one of disaster—or, at least, one not of benefit to himself or to his team.

But Lloyd, who was now a junior, was no such man. And so, as the time wound down and with his team down two, he glanced at the clock and calculated in his head, it seemed to all in attendance that night at Jackson, just how far he could go before the ball would have to be released.

He had been deep in his own backcourt, having taken the inbound pass from a teammate. He dribbled to within a few steps of the midcourt line when he looked at the clock. There were just three seconds left in regulation. Jackson trailed Whitney, 62-60. Lloyd had been in this situation hundreds of times, it seemed—in his imagination, during those lonely nights back in the park in East New York. He had done fine then. He would do fine now. After all, he was Swee'pea. This was his game. And so, undaunted, Lloyd dribbled once. Then again. And then, once again. Having used all the time he had allotted for movement toward his goal, he pulled up and, to the amazement of all, squared his body to the basket. He was at halfcourt. The buzzer was about to sound. He fired. No sooner had he done so then the buzzer sounded its alarm—the ball in mid-air, mouths hushed among the patrons.

The shot could easily have missed its mark and, despite the toughness of the crowd, all would have been forgiven. In his day, the legendary Cousy had at times failed in his quest for heroics in this gymnasium. And here even Harvey, who as a senior at St. John's would hit four buzzer-beating shots to either tie or win games, had been known to come up short. Besides, Lloyd had already netted 37 points, a more-than-fair performance, even for a player of his stature, in this season-opener for both teams. What more could people expect? But Lloyd always seemed to have something in reserve, a little bit of extra magic with which to control a pressure situation.

"We was going to lose our reputation," Brown, then a sophomore, recalled of the moment. "It was all on Lloyd's shoulders with that one shot. We all felt we would lose the game. All of us had our heads down. But Lloyd was telling everybody, 'Y'all move out the way. I got the game under control. I got the game under control. Just leave it to me.' Then he took it and let fly."

It was the stuff of miracles, the stuff of legends. Because as the crowd and his teammates looked on, stunned, the ball hit dead center in the box painted on the backboard and, an instant later, fell through the opening in the hoop. Lloyd had tied the game. The gym echoed with delirious applause.

Still, he was not finished. With Jackson down, 63-62, in overtime, Lloyd put the game's last points on the board, two free throws, to win the contest, 64-63. He had gone 16-for-20 from the field and nine-for-nine from the line, scoring 41 points with 12 rebounds. He had outmaneuvered Scurry, who had twenty-eight but could only shake his head at what he had seen.

"You know," Tom Konchalski said, "the most impressive part was that, when he hit that half-court shot against Whitney, he released the ball at the precise moment of best advantage. He wasn't going to release it a dribble too soon. He timed it in his head, got as close as he could, then shot. It was pure Lloyd Daniels. It told you right then just what kind of player he was."

Coaches throughout the five boroughs already knew what kind of player Lloyd was and they accepted that he was a star who possessed talent unparalleled. But, at the same time, they also knew what kind of student he was—and questioned whether or not he should, in fact, be allowed to remain eligible based on his academic track record.

Several coaches even suggested that the league investigate the situation. Two, Paul Dallara of Far Rockaway High School and Howie Warhaftig of Beach Channel High School, filed protests after their games against Jackson.

"The kid is jumping around from school to school to play basketball, not get an education," Dallara said. "Someone has to be held accountable for the procedure which allowed him to get into school and then be eligible to play basketball. When I think of it, I feel cheated. I feel bad for my kids. I feel bad for my whole division. I feel bad for the whole system. I don't mind losing. But I like to lose fairly. This is a travesty for everybody. I have to question a system that allows this to happen."

The controversy began long before that first game against Whitney and long before Jackson would split its season series with Far Rock, a team that featured future Seton Hall University guard Oliver Taylor, Jr., who would lead the city in scoring during the 1986-87 high school season at 35.2 points per game. It went back to the first week of November, when Lloyd had first returned to New York after his dismissal from Oak Hill. Back then, Lloyd had called Ronnie's house and left a message. "Tell Ron I'm comin' to Cardozo," he told Ronnie's mother, Gloria Naclerio. "Tell him I'll be there tomorrow."

After a brief conversation with Lloyd, Lou d'Almeida had decided Cardozo would be a good school for him to attend. It was noted for its academic reputation. It had a tutorial program that could assist Lloyd in his studies. And Ronnie, who, at that time, had known Lloyd for more than three years and who knew how to handle him perhaps better than anyone who had ever dealt with him, was its coach. There was a problem: Cardozo was located in Bayside, Queens. And Lloyd did not live within the school zone.

According to officials at the New York City Board of Education, several methods allow students to attend school out of zone—areas defined by a complex geographic grid system that delineates enrollment districts. A student can request to major in a specific subject offered only in a school out of zone, such as a vocational school or one with a specialized academic program—educational options programs, or ed-op programs, as they are known. A student can also request a safety transfer, usually to protect him or her from some sort of harassment. Or a student can request a guidance transfer. Lloyd's case didn't fall into any of those areas.

Still, Ronnie was not about to argue when d'Almeida arrived with Lloyd that morning. They all expected to find some route by which Lloyd, who had developed into high school basketball's prodigal son, could be enrolled in Cardozo. Like others, Ronnie believed he could help Lloyd get his life in order. Like others, he had some selfish reasons. As Ronnie said later, "I knew if I had him I would either have an ulcer or a city championship. Or, probably, I would have had both." That made it worth an attempt.

Lloyd was given the guided tour at Cardozo. Baseball coach Ed Tatarian, who served as Coordinator of Student Affairs, talked with him about coming out for the team—something which interested Lloyd, since he had shown hints of some major league potential as an outfielder with the local youth league teams, before he quit to concentrate his efforts on basketball. Ronnie introduced Lloyd to his two starting guards, Greg (Skate) Scott and Kevin Story, whose game was all flash and glitter and right out of a playground circus, which was why they were known as the Psycho Twins. Then, Ronnie and Lloyd ran into Duane Causwell, a 6-foot-11 senior center who would become a first-round selection of the Sacramento Kings in the 1990 NBA Draft.

"Duane was in an office, studying, when I walked in with Lloyd," Ronnie recalled. "I go to Duane, 'Duane, this is Lloyd Daniels. There's a good chance he might come to our school.' Duane looks at me and goes, 'Yeah.' I go, 'Duane, he's a pretty good player.' Duane goes, 'Yeah.' It was obvious he didn't know who Lloyd was, so I go, 'Duane, he has a nickname.' And Duane goes, 'Yeah. What is it?' I go, 'Swee'pea. This is Swee'pea.' Immediately, his eyes lit up. He goes, 'This is Swee'pea?' You could see he understood what it meant."

Others at Cardozo knew what it meant, too. It meant trouble, said Cardozo assistant principal George Rosenberg, who decided to let the officials at High School Placement make the final decision on where Lloyd would attend high school. "If he gets clearance from High School Placement to come here, that's fine," Rosenberg said. "It's not unprecedented for kids out of district to come here because we are one of the best schools in the city and have a very good tutoring program. But he is not going to come here just to play basketball."

As Ronnie later said, "Maybe I should have told Lloyd to tell them he wanted to come to Cardozo because he wanted to study Russian."

Of course, Ronnie never did tell that to Lloyd, who already read English as if it were Russian. High School Placement followed the book when it ruled that Lloyd should attend Jackson, not Cardozo.

They also ruled Lloyd eligible at Jackson, because the rules governing the Public Schools Athletic League, the organization that oversees interscholastic sports among public schools in New York City, mandated that to be eligible a student-athlete had to attain a passing average the previous semester—and Lloyd had, even though some argued that his marks were questionable, passed classes at Laurinburg. Another rule states that an intra-city transfer be enrolled in school no later than fifteen days after the start of a term. Though Lloyd had not been enrolled then, he remained unaffected by the rule, because he was considered an out-of-state transfer.

His situation, some coaches said, was indicative of just how bad, how widespread, the problem of illegal recruitment and illegal transfer had become in New York. Here was Lloyd, a gun-for-hire who had little more than one-quarter of the credits needed for graduation, shopping around—at the request of his summer-league coach, Lou d'Almeida—for what would be his fourth high school in three states in two years. Shopping around for a school that could offer him good basketball and an education, though, if his past was indicative of the future, not necessarily with an equal emphasis.

"My initial reaction is one of anger," said Ken Gershon, the coach of Hillcrest High School in Jamaica, Queens, one of the schools Lloyd said he had considered enrollment in. "Since when did we go into the recruiting game? There has to be something wrong with a kid being in four schools in two years. How can he be a student? Here is a kid who, every time he fouls up in a school, leaves that school and still he has been allowed to play ball.

"He has not been penalized because of his academic problems. He just went where he could play basketball. In this case, it brought to the forefront problems with the system because of the type of player he is. The fact that he was allowed to play said something about our whole athletic system. We, the basketball society, continue to use these kids as much as we can. We stress that they belong in an academic background, when they don't, because we only want them to play basketball."

It was an all-too-common problem. Within the two-year period in which Lloyd attended those four schools—and had considered transfers to Westinghouse, the high school where Hersh worked in Brooklyn, as well as to Brooklyn's Wingate and John F. Kennedy in the Bronx—a handful of other players also jumped ship several times. Kenny Eato, a guard from Queens, went from Forest Hills High School to Oak Hill, where he was dismissed, and to Long Island City High School. Forward Adrian Carter went from Christ the King, a Catholic school in Queens, to St. Agnes, a Catholic school in Rockville Centre, Long Island, to Jackson and then Long Island City. Guard Darin Worsley left Hillcrest for Richmond Hill High School. Forward Royal Miller left Richmond Hill for Jackson. And Causwell left Jackson for Cardozo.

Some of those moves were made for personal reasons. One, the transfer of Miller, was made for what was termed "racial harassment," even though Eric Greenberg, the basketball coach at Richmond Hill, and Theresa Oropallo, the Assistant Principal in Charge of Guidance, both said that neither the school nor the local police had records of racial incidents against Miller—a 6-foot-5, 220-pound forward, who left perhaps the worst basketball team in the city to join a Jackson team that went on to win the city title in 1985.

And, those were only a handful of the documentable transfers during that period, according to Joe Varone, who served as Chairman of the Eligibility Committee for the PSAL. No doubt, Varone said, that there were many others that were never brought up for review.

"This happens all the time," Varone said. "The Board of Ed rules and regulations allow this to happen, because of the way those laws are written. People take advantage of it and, even though we know what goes on, there is really not anything we can do about it."

The reason for what happens is simple: Coaches want to win basketball games, because winning games can lead them out of the high school ranks and into college coaching; because having a great player can sometimes mean a college will offer that player's high school coach a chance to come along for the ride—hiring him as an assistant, part of a package deal; because winning can get a team into national tournaments, can get a coach sneaker deals.

As a result, the best players in the city often are given inducements in the form of sneakers, sweats, cash and an easy path through school, or, at very least, are pampered and coddled by coaches who understand that without those players, their teams wouldn't win. It has led to a battle between the local clubs, which bid for the services of players to ensure their participation in national tournaments. It has led to a battle between the local high schools, all of which compete for players who sometimes even use false addresses in an effort to enroll in a school out of their assigned zone.

Rod Strickland did it when he attended Truman, which was not his zoned high school. "I used another guy's address," he said. "I don't remember who." Pearl Washington, already a playground legend in Brownsville, did it, first attending Norman Thomas High School in Manhattan because a friend of his knew the coach at Thomas, an open enrollment school. But, after scoring 37 points in his high school debut, Washington was convinced to leave Thomas, which had a weak program, to attend perennial power Boys & Girls.

As Bernie Gober, an assistant principal at J.H.S. 8, the elementary school where Ronnie worked and one long-known for producing talented players, said, "Throughout the city of New York, if a kid is known to be a ballplayer, he is going to be approached and asked, 'Why don't you come to my school?' "

Many times, with their values corrupted by club teams that give them money, by a school system that often demands little more than attendance, by the atmosphere in their very neighborhoods and, sometimes, in their very households, the kids do. They leave one school, go to another.

"What you do is give a kid a false sense of values," Gershon said.

"A kid like Lloyd Daniels says, 'Hey, if I'm not happy at Jackson, I'll go to a school in Wisconsin or Ohio or somewhere' because he has no allegiance to anyone. See, these are high school kids. They're impressionable. From the time a kid like Lloyd—any of these kids—was a grade-schooler, he was exploited because of his basketball ability. People saw something in him. Coaches took care of him, gave him money, bought him things, found him a place to go to school. When do these kids realize that is not the way life is? When do they learn to deal with life on their own level?"

Stan Dinner was sitting at a table in The Sports Page, the cafe he owned and operated on the Lower East Side of Manhattan and a place frequented by Ronnie and Hersh, as well as college coaches and even members of the Knicks, among them Mark Jackson and Charles Oakley.

Once, Dinner had been a high school basketball coach, one known as perhaps New York City's most able recruiter. No one was better at finding kids and getting them eligible than Stan Dinner. No one was more flagrant in his "creative manipulation" of the high school recruiting rules.

His claim to fame was that he once assembled perhaps the most fucked up team in America, a band of truants and rowdies that transformed Benjamin Franklin High School in Harlem into the nation's top-ranked high school team back in the fall of 1979. "I recruited all the maniacs, the knuckleheads," Dinner said with a bit of a laugh. "But those guys, they could sure play."

There was Gary Springer, a two-time high school all-American who made two trips to the NCAA Tournament with Iona College before his career gave way to bad knees. There was Richie Adams, who later became the two-time player of the year in the Pacific Coast Athletic Association at Nevada-Las Vegas before he found himself in the big time—prison, that is. And, there was Kenny Hutchinson, a pure shooting guard who made it all the way to the University of Arkansas before substance abuse problems robbed him of his game.

Truth was that Walter Berry, who won the Wooden Award as the NCAA Division I Player of the Year at St. John's in 1986, and who played three years in the NBA with the Portland Trail Blazers, San Antonio Spurs, New Jersey Nets and Houston Rockets, couldn't even make that Franklin team. Just a sophomore who had transferred in from DeWitt Clinton High School in the Bronx, he sat out the season. An assortment of others did make the roster, though: Respected high school and playground players by the names of Wayne Alexander, Lonnie Green, Darrell

Davis and Watkins (Boo) Singletary, who later became a starter at the University of Utah.

Dinner recruited them through a network of assistants, summer-league coaches and friends, his kids often using "aquired" addresses as their heads filled with visions of the NBA. Dinner now admits that those kids probably developed a false sense of values, believing that they were somehow above the law, not subject to rules—which, being a bunch of street kids, they often never followed anyway. Then again, Dinner said, even though some saw him as a minor-league Larry Brown or Jerry Tarkanian, what they didn't understand was that everyone recruited high school players in New York City. Not just him.

"I was just the only coach who was willing to admit it," he said. "In New York, so many fucking guys get a piece of the kids that it isn't funny. But everyone else was sneaking around."

An affable, good-natured New York sort of guy—he is a bit rumpled, likes his beer and Buffalo wings, and likes sitting in his cafe talking sports—he always speaks his mind and never skirts the issue. Rules, maybe. Never the issue. "I remember Dinner coming up to our star player at a game once, saying, 'Why are you wasting your time at Stuyvesant? You could be on my team,' " one player recalled. "At least with Dinner, he was open about it."

Sure, Dinner said, maybe he sent some wrong messages to kids, sometimes allowing them play when they weren't eligible. His 1980-81 team, after all, had to forfeit all its victories for using an ineligible player—ironically, not Berry or Hutchinson, but one who was using his real address and was found to live across the street from the school zone boundaries. Still, he sincerely made an effort to teach his kids how to be responsible.

He didn't give them money for nothing. If they needed it, he made them sweep floors and wash dishes at his cafe or at a deli he owned to earn it. He loaned them his car, but only provided they first asked his permission.

He couldn't be their parents, couldn't be their guardians. He couldn't make them become good citizens, though several later did. He was just a coach. All he could do, he said, was give them a chance to get off the streets and be on his team; give them an enticement to at least get them in school. Give them more exposure than they could get in another school, and, therefore, at least give them a fighting chance to get to college and achieve some success.

Sometimes, it worked. At last word, Springer was a counselor for the Job Corps and Green worked for the Transit Authority. Still, it seems that more often than not the kids who came to Dinner found trouble on a more consistent basis than they found the classroom. Adams, Berry and Singletary never did graduate from high school; each earned an equivalency diploma. The problem, he said, was most of his players, like most of the students at Franklin, were beyond help by the time he got them. "We were a turnback school," he said. "Other schools would send us kids they didn't want."

His kids were lawless. They had, because of their environment, grown up without discipline in their lives. They were addicted to the streets.

His 1979-80 team, for instance, should have easily won city and state titles and was regarded as the leading candidate to finish the season as the national high school champion—a sort of mythical title based on polls in a host of basketball publications. Gary Reedy, the coach of Lake Braddock High School in Burke, Virginia, remembered playing that team and being in awe. "They were amazing in the warmups," Reedy said. "After watching the first few dunks, we were like, 'Let's get on the bus and go home right now.'"

Instead, considered best in the nation, Franklin later lost in overtime in the semifinals of the city tournament to an Adlai Stevenson team led by Ed Pinckney. Then again, Dinner said he expected to lose the game. After all, he said several of his players arrived for the contest under the influence.

"When they came in you could tell they were high," Dinner said. "I said, 'What are you guys doing? This game is for [a berth in] the city championship.' They said, 'Don't worry. We beat them once.' It turned out the night before was Richie's birthday party. The players got to the game straight from the party, about an hour before tip-off. At halftime, I'm pouring coffee down their throats and giving them cold showers to keep them awake." Franklin lost after a turnover by Hutchinson in overtime allowed Stevenson to score the winning basket. Twelve times, Adams was called for goaltending.

Adams was sort of typical of the players recruited by Dinner. He was an incredible talent, nicknamed "The Animal" for his shot-blocking, as well as his ferocious play around the basket. Orlando Magic forward Sidney Green, himself a notable New York playground and park player who played against Adams in high school and with him at Nevada-Las Vegas, said, "It was a thrill to watch him. He could snatch shots out of the air."

But Adams also was a terrible student. Not a dumb one, because when he went to class, he did well. He just never went. In fact, he transferred to Franklin from Alfred E. Smith High School, where he had been enrolled for two years, but had never attended class. "It took me two years not only to get him to come to Franklin, but just to convince him to go to school," Dinner said. When Adams entered Franklin, he did as a second-semester sophomore, one who had no high school credits. Still, Dinner knew he needed him to win. So he got him eligible, arranging his schedule, bending the rules.

"I'm probably guilty, as a coach, because I'd bend the rules for the good players to make sure there were no problems," he said. "Maybe that gave them the wrong idea, the wrong perception. Maybe, every time a kid failed a class, I failed a little, too. But, at the time, it seemed like something that was helping them; helping them stay eligible, helping them get to college."

The alternatives were either to slide an unprepared kid into college and hope he could learn something—even if just from being in that atmosphere—or, let him stay on the streets, where his future was already bleak. As Tom Konchalski, the high school basketball scout, said, "I think people like Stanley try to help these kids. I don't think he did anything malicious or with bad intent. He might not have done everything right, by the books. But I don't think he tried to harm anyone. He meant well."

But the example Dinner set never did much to help his players change the image of themselves as a bunch of renegades, kids out of control. Kids being kids. Kids who saw their coach bending the rules and decided to follow suit.

Just look at Adams. He might not have liked school, but he liked cars. And there was one time during the season that Adams, Springer and Hutchinson "borrowed" Dinner's. It was hours before a game when Dinner, sitting in his office with a recruiter from UCLA, got the call from the local police. Could the coach come around when he had a moment and identify half his team—all of whom had been found in his car, which had been reported stolen?

"I got the call," Dinner said, "and the sergeant asked, 'Do you know a Richie Adams?' I said, 'Yeah.' He said, 'Do you know a Gary Springer?' I said, 'Yeah.' He said, 'Do you know a Kenny Hutchinson?' I said, 'Yeah.' He said, 'Do you know a Darrell Davis?' I said, 'Yeah.' He said, 'Do you know a Wayne Alexander?' I said, 'Yeah, yeah already. Why do you want to know? What the hell did they do now?' He said, 'Please come down here and identify them. They stole your car.' "

"We were on our way to pick up someone else and all of a sudden a policeman is sticking a gun in my face," Springer recalled of the incident. "When the police saw we were Ben Franklin basketball players, though,

they didn't really handcuff us. But they put us in a holding cell for a
while. We were all like, 'Richie, didn't you tell Dinner you were taking
the car?' He said he forgot. The police called Dinner to come and get us
from the station, and he's got a coach from UCLA in his office who'd
been there to recruit me. We figured it would make a great episode for
'The White Shadow.'"

The difference, of course, was that the White Shadow—the coach on
that TV program about a fictional high school in L.A.—would have suspended his players for pulling such "pranks." Dinner was dealing with
the real world. He felt nothing he did would make a difference in the
end.

After all, there was a time when his team was leading a game by nine
with perhaps a minute left and he elected to go into a stall. "I'm sitting
on the bench and the team manager goes to me, 'Coach, what are you
doing?' I go, 'It's a stall, why? What's the matter? We're up nine.' He goes,
'But the spread is ten-and-a-half. And I got money on this game.'

"I mean, what can you do?" Dinner said, finishing an order of wings.
"Most of these kids are living in a different world, one that has its own
rules. You have to play by them if you want to survive. I was coach of the
top-ranked team in America. I had all-Americans. Norm Sloan and Larry
Brown and Jerry Tarkanian were coming to talk to me. I got wined and
dined by the recruiters. I admit it, I was impressed. Maybe, you just lose
sight of what's important. You lose sight of your job as a coach. Maybe,
you take a look at these kids and realize you're helpless to change them
and so you just decide you have to be practical."

Even when you know it's wrong.

Jack Curran had no need to be practical. He had been around too
long, had built too good a program at Archbishop Molloy, to have to
bend a few rules. His school, after all, was an exclusive one, an all-boys'
school and one of the more respected academic institutions in New York
City. It attracted only the best students, only the best athletes—a sort of
Harvard of high schools.

In a time of growing moral corruption, in a time when most public
schools in the city more resembled Benjamin Franklin than Benjamin
Cardozo, Molloy, the private school, remained well-ordered, refined. Its
students still obeyed a dress code, which demanded of them blue blazers,
button-down shirts and ties. Even the halls were immaculate. Should a

stray piece of litter dare to appear, it was not beneath a student—or, Jack Curran—to pick it up.

Curran was a respectable gentleman with an old Irish face and a brush of fading red hair. He didn't curse, was a regular church-goer and yet his voice, his mere presence, held in it a command, a power.

He had been at Molloy forever, it seemed. He had come to the school in 1958, the year it had changed its name from St. Ann's, and had replaced the former basketball coach, a guy named Lou Carnesecca, who had moved a few exits down the Grand Central Parkway to become an assistant coach at St. John's. A former minor league pitcher, Curran had once been a baseball and basketball player at St. John's, where he'd been recruited by Frank McGuire and played on a team with Mario Cuomo, later the governor of New York. But at Molloy, Curran was part of a basic two-man athletic staff with a partner named Frank Rienzo, now the athletic director at Georgetown University.

It wasn't long before Curran built a reputation, though. His baseball team was always among the best in the nation, once winning sixty-eight straight games during the 1960s. His basketball teams, too, were renowned. By the fall of 1985, Curran had coached six all-Americans, among them Kevin Joyce, Brian Winters, Billy Lawrence and Kenny Smith. Even Lew Alcindor had once sought enrollment at Molloy. But, he lived in Manhattan and told Curran he thought it might be too far to travel on a daily basis. Curran said that was a shame and wished him well. "I told him, 'Lewie, I think you're right,'" Curran recalled. Alcindor enrolled in Power Memorial and the rest is history. "It cost us three championships," Curran said. "If we had to do it all over again, we might not tell him it was too far." But, really, that wasn't his style.

Curran was not going to bend the rules for anyone, even if, like most private schools, his now received most of its players from the local club teams, which often paid their tuition to attend. He told Kenny Anderson that when the freshman guard arrived at Molloy in September, 1985. Freshmen, he said, even freshmen as good as Anderson, didn't start at Molloy. Often, in fact, they didn't even get a chance to play on the varsity. If the kid didn't like that, well, he was free not to come. Period. End of discussion.

Though just about 5-foot-10 and 150 pounds, a wisp of a kid, Anderson decided he had come too far and worked too hard not to give it a shot. With Vincent Smith and an ever-expanding group of advisors prodding him on, Anderson not only tried out; he made the varsity. By the winter of 1985, while Lloyd was tearing up the PSAL, the reputation of Kenny Anderson was beginning to grow. In the parks, they called him "Chibbs."

He was getting himself a household name.

There are four major daily newspapers in New York City—*The New York Times, The Daily News, The New York Post* and *New York Newsday*—and three of them, the tabloids, fight each other for space on the newsstands. New York, after all, is a competitive town. There are two major league baseball teams, two pro football teams, three hockey teams and two basketball teams all within a twenty-mile radius. And, with the papers fighting for coverage, the trickle-down effect even dictates how they cover high schools.

Now, high school sports are not quite so important in New York, at least not as important as they are in many of the smaller towns across America. But high school basketball is, to some extent, still taken seriously. After all, basketball is the city game. So, when a player of Lloyd's ability and stature, one with his history, goes through the kind of situation he was going through at Jackson—well, understand that the New York tabloids know a good story when they see one. Be assured, Lloyd was a good story.

"A High School Star out of his League," was the headline of one column in *The News*. "Daniels 'used' Jackson, PSAL," cried a headline in *The Post*. "The Strange Case of Lloyd Daniels," said the headline over a story in *Newsday*, which outlined Lloyd's movement from school-to-school, from state-to-state. Even the normally aloof *New York Times* was involved. "Schoolboy Star: Fit to Play, but Where?" politely asked *The Times*.

It was a sure bet Lloyd couldn't read those headlines, or the stories. But his friends could—and did. That caused embarrassment for Lloyd, whose travels and travails were now on public display. Friends, as well as classmates and the general public, now knew not just that Lloyd had jumped from school to school, but also that he couldn't read. Though Lloyd tried to remain polite to people who were polite to him, he did refuse to speak with reporters on the record. And, in some cases, off the record, as well.

One reporter who especially got to Lloyd was one from *The Post* named Steve Barenfeld. He had ripped Lloyd in a column, had written about how he couldn't read, about how he had used the PSAL for basketball. Now, all of that was true. But Lloyd felt Barenfeld had taken some pot shots at him and, one afternoon, in the Jackson locker room, he confronted him. There was no violence, nothing physical. In fact, Lloyd just wanted to put him down. Poke fun at him. The problem was, in the process, he "dis'ed" himself.

"Is this the guy who wrote I can't read?" Lloyd asked teammate Anthony Johnson, as he pointed to Barenfeld.

"I guess so," Johnson said.

"Yeah," Lloyd said. "You're that guy from *The Post*. Steve Barenfeld. You're the guy who wrote I can't read. Well, if I can't read, how'd I know you wrote I couldn't read if I couldn't read it?"

Barenfeld looked at Lloyd in disbelief. "Someone read it to you?" he said. Of course, Lloyd's teammates, knowing that was the truth, began to laugh. You could almost see Lloyd wince. It was a terrible moment, especially since, no matter what anyone thought of him, Lloyd was still just a kid.

"The kid's been going through a tough time," Granby, the Jackson coach, said, trying to explain why Lloyd refused to talk to reporters. "People keep calling asking for interviews and he's not ready for that now. So far we've had no problem with him, on the court or in the classroom. I've told him he has to do certain things, because if things don't go right here, everybody is really going to come down on him. He seems to understand."

Certainly though, Lloyd continued to play well, something later confirmed by his postseason selection as a *Parade Magazine* All-American—an honor which, strangely enough, was partially due to all the coverage he received in the press, extolling his virtues as a player, if not as a student. There was a 27-point, 12-rebound, and 15-assist performance in an easy 83-67 win over August Martin, a team that, led by guards Sean Green and Brent McCollin, would reach the 1986 PSAL Semifinal Game. "He intimidated us," said Green, who would later play at Oak Hill and then at North Carolina State and Iona College. "Just the name Lloyd Daniels is intimidating."

There was the halfcourt shot he made—it hit nothing but net—at the third-quarter buzzer later that season against Beach Channel. And, there was a tournament in Trenton, New Jersey, when Lloyd went out and made a mockery of the opposition. "We had won the first game," recalled Alvis Brown, who shared a hotel room with Lloyd on the trip, "but the crowd was getting on him because he didn't show them nothin'. That night, in the room, Lloyd and I was talking. He had like five-hundred dollars on him and I had forty-five. He said he'd bet me his whole five-hundred against my forty-five that he wouldn't miss a shot the whole first quarter of the championship game, against Trenton Central." Brown had no idea where Lloyd got all that money: A club team, a drug deal, a recruiter. Still, he told him, " 'It's a bet.'

"Well, he didn't miss a shot the whole first quarter, the whole second quarter," Brown said. "He didn't miss 'til the third quarter. In fact, he was going to the guy guarding him, 'Where you want me to shoot it from? Right about here? Here?' He was pointing to marks on the floor, going, 'Here? Here?' then shooting and hitting all net." Lloyd scored fifty-six.

"I lost all my money," Brown said.

Perhaps the most important game all season, though, was in the Martin Luther King Classic at the Nassau Coliseum. And, it wasn't because Lloyd dominated the opposing team, Wyandanch. Rather, it was because it was at that game, Arnie Hershkowitz later alleged, that he informed Nevada-Las Vegas assistant coach Mark Warkentien of plans for Lloyd to visit the school on a recruiting trip that would lead to his enrollment there.

Despite Chuck Granby's statement about Lloyd meeting his scholastic obligations at Jackson, apparently that was not happening. According to Lloyd, he rarely attended class at Jackson though he still remained eligible to compete. Some mornings, Lloyd said, he would make an effort to attend school. Other mornings, he would simply pretend he was getting ready to go and, once his grandmother went off to work, he would go back upstairs and go to sleep—just like he had back at I.S. 218.

"At Jackson, I couldn't undertstand why he was sleeping when he was supposed to be in school," said Lloyd's grandmother, Lulia Hendley, who also said Lloyd was constantly smoking marijuana—sometimes before games. "Granby would call and say, 'If he's not at practice, I won't let him play.' But he would let him play anyway. See, that's the thing with Junior. If he had respect for you and didn't lose it, he would respect you to the highest.

"I think Granby knew Junior was smoking, but he let him play anyway because he wanted to win games. And Junior would say, 'He's goin' to let me play anyway, 'cause he needs me. I don't need Granby.' He would get up, like one o'clock, take a shower, smoke his stuff and he would still play."

"When I first got into Jackson, I was goin' to classes," Lloyd said. "Even he couldn't believe it, 'cause Chuckie knew my background. The first half, I was goin'. But when I saw Chuckie was soft, that he didn't care 'bout me, I said, 'Fuck you, Chuckie. I'm stayin' home today.' See, the days I did go to class, I went to class. But there was days I went to school and I just hung out in the lunch room all day. And Chuckie knows it. If you ask me, I should have been ineligible. I should've flunked out of Jackson."

While Granby refuses comment on Lloyd—"All I can say is that he was never mine," Granby said when pressed on the matter. "I'm not going to say anything else"—Brown said that, despite the fact that, in the end, Lloyd rarely went to class, Granby tried in vain to help him.

"The reason Lloyd doesn't like Chuck is because Chuck was always staying on him, calling his house in the morning, trying to help him," Brown said. "He would call his grandma. He was going out into the neighborhood looking for him. He was looking out for him. But soon he just realized there was no helping the boy. See, it just got to the point that, no matter what you did, Lloyd just wouldn't show up. Most of his classes were remedial classes and he was embarrassed that people might find out his reading level. He'd see his picture in the newspapers and, because he knew what his name looked like, he knew it was about him. He'd say, 'Yo, read the article.' If you call someone a dummy over and over and over, they're going to tend to withdraw. People said that about him and he went into his little shell."

As one Jackson teammate said, "He turned to drugs. It was the only thing he had left in his life." Drugs. And, basketball.

Lulia Hendley said Lloyd was "high when he left the house" the afternoon Jackson met Cardozo in the first round of the PSAL Playoffs at Hillcrest High School on February 20, 1986. Lloyd protests that wasn't the case, claims he was sick, instead. "That was like one of the times, one of like the only times, I wasn't high," he said. "I just didn't feel good. I had a little cold."

Lloyd had missed two previous games, one of them, he said, for a good reason. "I was gettin' laid by a cheerleader," he said.

But now he was back. And, despite his "cold," was virtually unstoppable. He'd drive down the floor, dribbling past defenders like Cardozo guards Greg Scott and Kevin Story, both of whom were all-borough selections, to swoop in alone on center Duane Causwell. Now, Causwell wasn't much of an offensive player. In fact, he scored just two points in the game. But he was almost seven-foot tall and was a big-time shot blocker and defender. And yet, Lloyd rattled him that afternoon, put every park move he could on him, getting him in early foul trouble and getting him out of the game. One time, he'd score on a finger tip roll. The next, he'd pull-up against Story or Scott and bank one home from twenty. Or, he'd back in against Causwell—referred to by Ronnie as "Abdul Lollipop" because, despite his size, he could sometimes still be licked by the competition—spin off him, and force him to foul.

But it wasn't enough. Though Lloyd went 9-for-11 from the field and 11-for-14 from the line, one of his missed field goal attempts coming on a fierce rejection by Causwell, Cardozo upset Jackson, 69-63. Despite scoring a game-high 29 points with 9 rebounds, 2 blocks, 2 steals and 2 assists, on a team where three of his teammates were marginal, at best, he could only do so much. After the game, Granby refused to shake hands with Ronnie, the two continuing a feud that stemmed from the situation with Lloyd.

But Lloyd walked over and congratulated Ronnie and his players, including Story and Scott, who had combined for 36 points against the Hickories. Later, Lloyd said, Granby yelled at him.

"He thought I threw the game," Lloyd said. "Can you believe that? He figured since I wasn't all broke up after the game, that I must've gotten paid by Ronnie to throw the game. The team beat us, straight up. I did everythin' I could have did against them. So I went over and shook their hands. Chuckie didn't like that. But what was I supposed to do, get on my knees and cry? Chuckie's daughter came over to me after the game and said, 'How much did the coach pay you?' I had a cold. So, I just coughed on her."

After the game, Lloyd, for the first time all season, decided to talk to reporters. "Definitely," he said, "I'm comin' back next year." No more jumping around. The next day, true to form, he dropped out of high school.

Kenny Anderson moved through the traffic that congested the floor of the Rose Hill Gymnasium at Fordham University. It was the Catholic High School Athletic Association City Championship Game and Molloy trailed Tolentine High School, 66-65, with little more than a minute to go in overtime. Already the lithe, lefthanded freshman had dominated the game, scoring five straight points near the end of regulation to take the Stanners from a 60-59 deficit to a 64-62 lead with seventeen seconds remaining, before Tolentine, led by Malik Sealy came back to tie the game and force overtime. Now, as Anderson weaved through a host of defenders, almost 4,000 fans, raucous, stood and screamed.

He dribbled into the lane, backed up his man, spun off him and raised from the floor. When his leap reached its apex, Anderson, his arm already cocked, shot the ball in his most peculiar fashion—fired almost like by a shot-putter. Still, it went in, smooth, the basket proving to be the deciding points in what would become a 69-66 championship win for Molloy. "It wasn't an incredible shot or anything," Anderson said, smiling, when it was over. And, he was right. But, he had shown poise enough to take it, to take control of such a huge game at such a crucial moment, and that said a lot about him, about his game and how far he had come since his days at Lost Battalion Hall.

"He did some incredible things," said Tolentine coach John Sarrandrea, who would later become an assistant coach at the University of Pittsburgh. "I know, without him, we would have won the championship. Hands down."

That, of course, was why, when it was over, his teammates gathered under the basket and carried Anderson aloft to cut the first strand from the net. Just fifteen years old, he had just become the first freshman ever selected the most valuable player of the CHSAA Tournament, something never done by Lew Alcindor, Dean (The Dream) Meminger or Chris Mullin.

"He's the greatest," Jack Curran said, later, outside the championship locker room. And then, in reference to the movie with Robert Redford, Curran said, "He's 'The Natural.' " Anderson smiled. "Not bad, right?"

Not bad at all. Because, not only had he been named tournament MVP. But, Kenny Anderson also hit the game-winning shot in his next game, converting a three-point play with four seconds left in overtime, as Molloy beat St. Anthony's High School, 89-88, to win the CHSAA state championship—Anderson grabbing a rebound, firing it and drawing a foul against Tom Greis, a 7-foot-1 senior center who would attend Villanova University.

When the season ended, he had averaged 16.7 points, 4 rebounds and 7.8 assists. True to his word, Curran had never started Anderson, who he referred to always as "Kenneth," never even allowed him to appear in the first quarter of any game. Lloyd averaged 31.2 points, 12.3 rebounds and 10 assists to be named a *Parade Magazine* All-American. But Steve Barenfeld, who didn't like Lloyd, took a moral stand and wrote that, since Lloyd had dropped out of school, he would not be named to his all-city team. Anderson, meanwhile, would be selected all-city by *New York Newsday* and *The Post*. It was the first of four straight years he would be named to the all-city team. He remains the only player in history ever to do so.

●　●　●

Lloyd sat in a booth at McDonald's eating a cheeseburger and some french fries. It was an April afternoon and he was asked if he had been to school in the previous six weeks or so, since the end of basketball season. "Of course, I stopped goin' to school," Lloyd said, acting as if the question had been a ridiculous one. "I'm here now, ain't I?"

He put down the burger, pushed back into the seat, stiffened himself and sat straight. It was a defensive position. He licked his lips. He motioned with his hands and spread his fingers, which were greasy, to expose his palms in a gesture that almost seemed designed to halt questions stemming from his explanation. "I ain't allergic to no school," he said, straight-faced. "I just don't want to go." He said he had more important things on his mind.

Within a month, despite his high school class not being scheduled to graduate until June, 1987, and despite his inability to read, Lloyd would make what resembled a pro move: He would elect to pass up his final year of high school—sort of declare himself eligible for college—and sign a letter-of-intent to attend Nevada-Las Vegas.

The entire notion was absurd. According to Rick Evrard, the director of legislative services for the NCAA, there was almost no chance Lloyd could ever become eligible to play for the Runnin' Rebels. Evrard believed that even if he did gain his General Equivalency Diploma, the earliest Lloyd could become eligible was the 1988-89 season. Still, Lloyd said that afternoon at Mickey D's, he was going to give it a shot. After all, he said he had been "shocked" when he found out he could even get into college—quite understandable, considering he had earned little more than one-quarter of the credits needed for graduation and was borderline illiterate.

"But, you got to handle it," he said, between interruptions from a host of well-wishers, among them freshman guard Dave Edwards, who would later play one season at Georgetown before he transferred to Texas A&M. "If you can get in, you get in. You got to take an opportunity like that. Nobody can turn it down. They givin' it to you, you take it. I'd be a fool not to, right? You'd take it, wouldn't you? That's why I'm goin'. That's why it ain't worth goin' to no high school now. I can't worry about it. I got goin' to college to worry about."

"Does Lloyd have the wrong perception of how the world works?" Tom Konchalski said. "No. His perception of the system has been correct. It is the system that is not correct. But he is a product of the American athletic system. It spoils kids. It leads athletes to think that they can break the rules that they feel don't affect them. A kid like Lloyd has come to realize that, if he screws up, someone will cover for him and find an escape hatch.

"Because of that, he has not had to come to an understanding of what he has to do," Konchalski said. "Some say he is a con man, that he will say, 'Yes,' and then go out and do whatever it is he wants to do. But I think it is more of a case where the spirit is willing, but the flesh is weak. He doesn't have self-discipline right now because he hasn't felt the need to bring discipline into his life. People have always taken care of him. The question now is, 'How long will it be before he runs out of solutions to his problems?'" The answer, Konchalski said, was: "'How long before he can no longer play ball?'

"See, so far his athletic talent has kept him from being just another kid hanging out on a street corner going nowhere with his life. But that talent will only keep him from that so long. With the gifts that God gives out, he gives responsibilities. Lloyd Daniels has such great talent that, to not use it would be a sin. It would be a tragedy for him, but it would also be an oblique tragedy for the others he deprived of having the joy of watching him play. He could become the greatest player who never made it. Up until now, the greatest player who never made it was Joe Hammond. That would be a sad honor to have. But, it's up to him. He has to do the right thing."

"We've told him nothing about life," Gershon, the Hillcrest coach, said. "All we've told him is that he is a great ballplayer. And the minute that Lloyd Daniels cannot bounce that basketball, that is the moment these guys give back their piece of the rock. Nobody ever told Lloyd Daniels, 'You'd better go to class, you'd better do your homework or you can't play in the ballgame.' Instead, his talent has forced us to give him false ideals. We never forced him to develop his intellectual, social or emotional skills. We never forced him to mature. Instead, we let him do what he wanted and, sooner or later, because of that, he'll probably wind up in the parks, talking about his glory days, trying to pick up a few bucks here and there.

"See," Gershon said, "you have to try to steer these kids. You can't steer them all. You lose some of them. But you have to at least try. With Lloyd, a lot of people often just tried to take what they could get. He has abused [the system] because he has been allowed to abuse it. But he has also abused it because people used him to abuse it. He has been taught to use people the way people used him. It's a terrible thing, a sad case."

It figured to get sadder still.

6 · Swee' pea
and 'The Strip'

Nevada-Las Vegas was one of perhaps a hundred schools pursuing Lloyd. That it landed him was only because it was the survivor of the hard-fought recruiting war—a war of attrition, which counted among its casualties the likes of Kansas and Kentucky, St. John's, Syracuse and Seton Hall, as well as a host of others, including Providence College and its coach, Rick Pitino.

The process had begun as it usually does for potential major-college recruits. As far back, that is, as eighth or ninth grade, when Lloyd first surfaced among those in the know as a player with legitimate big-time skills. Once identified, he became the subject of incredible letter-writing campaigns—letters, his first arrived from Syracuse, which he could not read—as well as the subject of recruitment visits, which began in the 10th grade at Oak Hill and Laurinburg and continued to the end of his career at Jackson.

While no one actually sent him $1,000 stuffed into an Emery air mail package, the way, it was alleged, Kentucky later did in an effort to entice recruit Chris Mills of Los Angeles, that didn't mean his recruitment did not get out of hand. Coaches and street-level sources alike called Lloyd dozens of times a night just to say hello and to mention that their schools remained, as always, interested in his services. Often, coaches and assistant coaches even flew in from around the nation just to see him practice, as Mark Warkentien had done back when Lloyd was a junior at Oak Hill.

University of Michigan assistant coach Mike Boyd wrote Lloyd, saying, "I sincerely enjoyed the opportunity to watch you work out this past week. Without a doubt, you have great talent and we have a very strong interest in you." Coach Wimp Sanderson wrote, "The University of Alabama is always searching for the type of young men that will represent our University well on the court and in the classroom. We have been told that you are the type of person and player that we need to continue to be successful."

Louisville coach Denny Crum thanked Lloyd for his "interest" in the university. Coach Norm Stewart wrote, "Your ability as an outstanding basketball player and your interest in the University of Missouri has been brought to my attention. Our goal is to learn more about you and to help you discover why Missouri is one of the finest schools in the country"—as if he believed that education would be of prime consideration to Lloyd. And Pitino wrote in one of several letters he sent Lloyd, "My NBA experience will prove invaluable, as I can now help develop future pro draft choices."

"All the schools," Ronnie said, "tried to get in on him. But, because of his background, most never thought they had a shot so they backed off. A lot of coaches came around and just watched and waited, looking for some way to get him, but not wanting to tell him he had a weakness, tell him 'Hey, you're not that bright. But we got a not-too-bright program, you know, a remedial program, we can get you in.' They figured that would offend him and then they'd have no chance. So they just waited to see what happened."

One coach who tried in vain to land Lloyd was Larry Brown, who had wanted Lloyd since he first saw him back at Five-Star Camp. He wrote to Lloyd, saying, "I thought you might enjoy this article about our recent midnight scrimmage. It was a huge success + is getting a lot of nat'l. attention. I hope practices are going well for you. I hope you have a great year. Good luck! Sincerely, Larry Brown."

And, one night when Kansas was in New York City for the National Invitation Tournament, Hersh said he took Lloyd to the Essex House—a posh hotel that overlooks Central Park—to meet with Brown. It was late when Hersh said he called Brown from the lobby of the hotel. "Hey," he said, "I got Lloyd Daniels down here. Do you want to talk with him or what? If you do, you got to get down here."

"Sure," Hersh said Brown told him. "I'll be right down."

Minutes later, Hersh said, Brown, the man who brought designer suits to the world of college coaching, arrived in the lobby in pajamas with a robe hastily thrown over them. "He knew who Lloyd was," Hersh said, "and he wasn't about to keep him waiting while he changed into his clothes."

In the end, though, Lloyd barely considered Kansas. He said he didn't want to live in the middle of nowhere. And, he also barely considered Syracuse, despite what some said were the best efforts of alleged street-level recruiter Rob Johnson, who, it has also been alleged, was responsible for delivering several New York recruits to the Orangemen—among them Eugene Waldron, Tony Bruin and Pearl Washington. Syracuse officials deny Johnson has ties to the school. Johnson, too, denies he has ties to the school.

But Hersh alleges that Johnson offered Lloyd "sneakers and sweats" just to attend Syracuse practices. "I think I did give Lloyd some sneakers," Johnson admits. "But it was Rob Johnson doing it. Not Syracuse."

As Ronnie put it, "Lloyd always had money and a fresh pair of kicks on. After a while it was difficult to tell where any of it came from."

For a while, St. John's seemed to have the best chance at Lloyd. Ronnie, after all, was a graduate and knew Redmen coach Lou Carnesecca. Lloyd liked St. John's, liked the idea of staying close to home. And Ronnie and Lou d'Almeida had seen how St. John's had taken interest in players who gained General Equivalency Diplomas, among them Walter Berry. Berry earned his equivalency diploma in a program affiliated with St. John's and then had transferred to the school after a stint at San Jacinto College in Pasadena, Texas, where he had been selected player of the year after he led the team to the 1984 National Junior College Athletic Association Championship.

"It was at their Hall of Fame dinner," Ronnie said, recalling how he first informed Carnesecca of Lloyd's interest in St. John's. "Lou was having a cocktail with some big-timers when I came up and told him I had a player for him. He asked, 'Who?' When I said 'Lloyd Daniels,' he excused himself immediately—and I mean, immediately—and took me into his office."

The two agreed that Lloyd would stop by the basketball office to meet the staff at St. John's. Soon, Lloyd began receiving tickets to St. John's games at Alumni Hall, where he often sat in the third row—behind the team bench.

Carnesecca and his staff allegedly began making arrangements that would enable Lloyd to earn his equivalency diploma, enroll in junior college and gain admittance to St. John's. But then, d'Almeida said, St. John's assistant coach Ron Rutledge bummed the works. He told Lloyd to talk to Ernie Lorch at Riverside Church, which had assisted Berry. The Gauchos and Riverside were bitter rivals, and Lloyd did not like Lorch, who ran Riverside.

"He took Lloyd aside and told him to disregard all of us and work through Ernie," d'Almeida said of Rutledge. "That didn't cut it. It was wrong."

"I would never tell anyone not to listen to someone he's comfortable with," Rutledge said. "I just told Lloyd about how Walter Berry got his G.E.D. through us and that Ernie would be the one to talk to about it. I don't think there was ever any big deal about Lloyd and St. John's, anyway."

What else could he say? Because, due to his lack of political sense, he had blown a sure thing. As d'Almeida said, "Lloyd came to me and said, 'Lou, you got to know this.' When I called Lou [Carnesecca], he made Rutledge get on the phone and apologize." But, by then it was too late. After all, recruiting is a sensitive business. In the interim, Lloyd had reached his decision.

He was headed to Las Vegas.

Nevada-Las Vegas coach Jerry Tarkanian has made a career of re-cruiting and coaching misfits and vagabonds. He and his assistants often scour the nation—its inner-cities, cracks and crevices—in search of the unwanted and the unwilling, the scorned and the scornful, the maligned and the malignant. They look for the players other coaches will not take. They look for the players other coaches, because of guidelines established by their schools, cannot take. Year-after-year, it seems, they covet those castoffs, take them in and, acting much like a shelter for wayward men, care for them and nurture them. In the process, they mold the unmold-able into something cohesive. They take renegades and from them make what is perceived to be a renegade basketball team. Turn them into "Your Runnin' Rebels!"

Tarkanian does this, he says, because he himself had once been like them. He had been a hell-raiser, a kid who was an underachiever, the kid in his class voted least likely to become a brain surgeon. One whose entire life revolved around basketball—and still does. As he admits, "My wife got me to some plays and ballets, trying to get me into culture. I went to the ballet and everybody's standing up clapping. I wondered who scored."

He spent most of his teenage life at parties, rarely thinking about school, which in his case turned out to be Pasadena City College in Pas-adena, California. "It took me six semesters to get through junior college," said Tarkanian, who, after three years at the two-year school, then went on to a four-year school, Fresno State. "It took five more [semesters] to get through Fresno State. I went to every party I could find. I didn't care about school."

Then he met his wife, Lois. She was a good student. She prodded him to go to class. He did. He got all A's and one B and even went on to get his master's at the University of Redlands. It taught him something about people.

"That convinced me that with a lot of these kids, it's not that they can't do the work, it's that their priorities aren't in the right order," Tarkanian said. "Sometimes, you just have to be more patient with certain people. I wasn't perfect in college, and I know that they're not, either, and I don't expect them to be. I do what I think is right. I'm not a hypocrite. I'm not on an ego trip. How many players have been the same way, have had their priorities changed and become good students, too? But if someone doesn't give them a break, where would they be right now?"

Tarkanian points to Ricky Sobers as a prime example of this. He recruited Sobers, who attended DeWitt Clinton but who quit the team there saying he was "too good" to waste his time, out of junior college back in 1973 for his first team at Nevada-Las Vegas. Sobers achieved huge success with the Runnin' Rebels and went on to a long career in the NBA. "Ricky Sobers was a non-high school graduate from DeWitt Clinton High School," Tarkanian said. "He went to junior college in Twin Falls, Idaho, and he got his degree. He came to UNLV and played for two years. He made all-American. He played twelve years in the NBA. The last couple of years, he did the broadcasts of our games. He's the most articulate, well-mannered, well-adjusted human being you'll ever meet. He's a credit to our institution, he's a credit to himself and his family. He is just great. And, here's a kid if somebody didn't take a chance on him, what would he have done?

"The way I look at it," Tarkanian once said, "if you bring a kid in that can't read or write—somebody nobody else would touch—and you keep him here four, five years, teach him to follow the rules, make him responsible for what he does, and, at the end, if he can read and write a little, you've done him a favor. Even if he doesn't have the piece of paper [the diploma], you gave him a chance to straighten out. I don't see anything wrong with that."

However, the National Collegiate Athletic Association does. At the urging of Warren S. Brown, then assistant executive director of the NCAA, Tarkanian was first investigated at Long Beach State back in 1972. He had taken over a losing program there and, in five years, amassed a 122-20 record—never losing a home game. The NCAA suggested that Tarkanian had worked his miracle at Long Beach State because he had bent a few rules, namely that players had been provided fake test scores, among other things.

Four days after he left to become the coach at Nevada-Las Vegas, the NCAA announced it had begun an "official inquiry" into the situation at Long Beach State. Nine months later, the basketball program was charged with 74 NCAA violations and placed on two years' probation.

In 1977, the NCAA had done the same thing at Nevada-Las Vegas, placing the school on probation and urging that Tarkanian be suspended for two years. Tarkanian fought the suspension, received an injunction, and, seven years later, embarrassed the NCAA in court—a district court judge ruling that the NCAA had violated his constitutional rights by denying him due process. It would, in fact, take the NCAA four more years before that ruling was overturned and it earned the right to enforce its original action against Tarkanian. That happened in December, 1988, when in a 5-4 vote the U.S. Supreme Court ruled the NCAA is a "private actor" and therefore not bound by the Constitution to give due process to college coaches.

The long-running feud had begun when Tarkanian wrote a column for the *Long Beach Press-Telegram* back in 1972 chiding NCAA officials for their investigation of Western Kentucky University, while failing to take action against schools like Kentucky. "The University of Kentucky basketball program breaks more rules in a day than Western Kentucky does in a year," Tarkanian wrote. "The NCAA just doesn't want to take on the big boys." The feud cooled in January, 1990, when attorneys for Tarkanian agreed, in the wake of the Supreme Court ruling, that the coach would assume $340,000 in legal fees incurred during the legal battle, as well as reimburse the NCAA for $21,000 in court costs it incurred while trying to enforce its sanctions.

In the summer of 1990 the NCAA imposed a one-year probation on Nevada-Las Vegas—banning the Runnin' Rebels from the 1991 NCAA Tournament.

But in 1986 the outcome of the NCAA case still hung in the balance. "The trouble with Tarkanian," Al McGuire, the broadcaster and former coach of Marquette, said back then, "is that he's Armenian and he's got those damn eyes, dark rings under them. And, he works in Las Vegas. You hear Vegas and you think of gambling and the Mafia and cement shoes. Mother Teresa couldn't coach there without looking tainted."

"Every time I say something like, 'You can help a kid without graduating him,' it gets me in trouble," Tarkanian once told *Sports Illustrated*. "That's the biggest problem you got with education today, the hypocrisy. You say what you think, you get murdered. You talk like that guy [football coach and athletic director] Vince Dooley at Georgia, they [the NCAA] leave you alone, at least until some newspaper or magazine investigates the program and makes them come in. You ever heard Vince Dooley speak? About building character, preparing kids for life, teaching them honesty and values? He says, 'My kids are the kind of kids you'd want to go out with your daughters.' I never had a kid yet I'd want going out with my daughters."

It was understandable, because, among his players at Nevada-Las Vegas, Tarkanian had once taken on Richie Adams. Tarkanian and his assistants had seen Adams at Massachusetts Bay Community College, where, after failing to graduate Ben Franklin, he averaged 25 points, 18 rebounds and 15 blocked shots per game as a freshman. Such ridiculous numbers had even brought Tarkanian and an assistant to the South Bronx in the summer of 1981. "That was frightening," Tarkanian recalled. "I remember the elevator didn't work and we had to run up eighteen flights of stairs. I wasn't in very good shape, but I ran as fast as I could to keep up—just so I wouldn't be alone. We were yelling, 'We're Richie's coaches. We're Richie's coaches.' We didn't want the kids in the halls to think we were detectives. That's the first thing they thought when they saw two white guys with ties on, smiling at everybody."

Perhaps that was why, when Adams encountered problems at Nevada-Las Vegas—drug problems that would rob him of his career, and his freedom—and Tarkanian's son, Danny, volunteered to room with his teammate, Tark told him, "Hell no, you're not living with Richie." Then, without the slightest trace of hypocrisy, he assigned a graduate assistant to do so.

Judging by the talent in the Class of '86, grad assistants would again have to worry such fate and, no doubt, Jodie Tarkanian would thankfully again go without a date among the players. Tark and his staff not only recruited Lloyd in 1986. They had also recruited Clifford Allen, who, after failing to gain admittance to Nevada-Las Vegas, would later attend three junior colleges and be convicted of second-degree murder in the stabbing death of a 64-year-old guidance counselor in Milton, Florida. Allen, who committed the crime while in Florida for a tryout with the CBA Pensacola Tornados, told police that he killed the man during a fight after the two had sexual relations. In May, 1990, he was sentenced to 45 years in prison.

In 1986, Tarkanian had called Allen "my first valedictorian" —something based, no doubt, on his ability as a student in El Paso de Robles, a detention center in Paso Robles, California. Allen was 6-foot-10, 235 pounds and was not even eligible for parole from the center at the time Nevada-Las Vegas recruited him. Like Swee'pea, there were indications he had a substantial substance abuse problem. Only, in the case of Allen, that problem had led to petty crimes and stints in halfway houses. He once stole a car that belonged to his foster father, had robbed a man and been convicted of armed robbery. Allen signed his letter of intent from behind bars at El Paso de Robles.

Still, in effect, the recruitment of Lloyd was no less difficult. Since he was a high school junior, under NCAA rules Lloyd was not allowed to take an official visit—one paid for by the school—to Nevada-Las Vegas. So if Lloyd was to get to Las Vegas he needed to find a "rabbi." And quick.

Arnie Hershkowitz had just the man. As he, Ronnie and Mark Warkentien sat in Nassau Coliseum watching Andrew Jackson go against Wyandanch that afternoon in January, 1986, Hersh outlined the plan. His friend was Sam Perry, whom Hersh described as a "commodities broker" he knew from the local racetracks. Perry, Hersh told Warkentien, was a basketball fanatic who even helped him run a summer-league team that counted Ronnie among its players. Perry lived in Staten Island during the summer, but spent winters in Las Vegas. He knew Lloyd. He had money, lots of it. Hersh said Perry would not only be willing to pay for Lloyd to fly out to Vegas, he also would be willing to make living and transportation arrangements.

There was just one problem. There was a strong chance that the plan was a violation of NCAA rules, which forbid a booster or a representative of the school—or someone merely perceived to be acting in such a capacity—to assist in the recruitment of a player. That meant that, once Hersh and Perry made it known that they were willing to provide these arrangements, they could possibly be construed as being representatives of the school's athletic interests and could then have nothing further to do with Lloyd.

Still, this was the recruitment of Lloyd Daniels. Swee'pea. And so, despite knowing nothing about Perry, something that Tarkanian and his assistants, as well as Ronnie, would all soon come to regret, the plan was implemented. Which was why if viewers watching the national telecast of a game between Memphis State and Nevada-Las Vegas that winter had known who to look for, they would have seen Lloyd and Perry sitting behind the team bench. It was also the reason Lloyd signed a letter of intent to attend Las Vegas.

"He contacted the school," Hersh said of Perry. "He was working hand-in-hand with Warkentien at that time. The next thing we knew, they [UNLV] said [to Lloyd], 'If you want to come out here for good, then you can come back [for summer school]' . . . Sam contacted Warkentien. I told him to. He was the middle man. He [Perry] figured that would be a good way to get in with Tarkanian. Why? He likes basketball. We didn't bring a baseball player out there . . . He liked UNLV, I guess."

As Ronnie said, "Las Vegas fell into it." And how.

• • •

Considered on build alone, Sam Perry did not cut an imposing figure. He was tall, around 6-foot-2. But he was lean. One good look at his face, though, indicated he meant business. He was straightforward. His voice, eyes, made commands. He had Mediterranean looks, a deep complexion. An acquaintance once said of him, "He looks like an Arab terrorist." Now, that was not quite a fair comparison. But it made a valid point. This was a serious man, serious meaning that he was a man who got what he wanted, when he wanted it.

Sam Perry had once been known by another name. Since his graduation from Erasmus Hall High School in Brooklyn back in 1963, Richard Perry had come to acquire quite a reputation as a gambler. He had also acquired a criminal record and a nickname. They called him "Richie the Fixer." He had twice been convicted on federal charges of sports bribery.

In 1974, Perry was convicted in connection with a major New York betting scandal involving fixed harness races at raceways in both Roosevelt and Yonkers. In 1984, he pleaded guilty to conspiring to commit sports bribery as part of the notorious point-shaving scheme at Boston College. Henry Hill, the organized crime figure who became a government informant during the Boston College point-shaving trial, called Perry a gambling "genius" in the book *Wise Guy,* which chronicled Hill's life in the mob.

Long before anyone had considered it, Perry had made dozens of contacts around the nation—folks who watched the college sports scene for him, Hill said. He knew the condition of the field, knew the condition of the players. He even knew "whether the quarterback had been drunk" the night before a big game. He knew things that gave a handicapper an edge. Things he found out from sources as basic as college newspapers. Perry knew about injuries—minor ones and ones that had been kept quiet—and often got information from sources right until game time, Hill said.

Hill called Perry "the brain who figured out how to increase the odds on superfecta bets at the trotters." As he said, "For a while we were doing so well that, rather than alert the track that we were winning all the time, we had to hire ten-percenters just to cash our winning tickets." Perry, a wise guy's wise guy, apparently worked out the scheme with the understanding that by getting as few as two or three of the drivers to get their horses boxed in, a betting man could eliminate almost half the horses from the race—and, make a killing by betting the remaining combinations.

According to Edward McDonald, former head of the Eastern District Organized Crime Strike Force, Perry became involved in the Boston College point-shaving scheme when Hill, putting together the scheme in 1978, went to clear it through the late Paul Vario. McDonald said that it was Vario, the one-time head of the Thomas Luchese crime family, who suggested Perry be involved because he had an expertise in "fixing things." Perry, who had been convicted for his role in the superfecta scheme and sentenced to a $10,000 fine and two-and-a-half years at the Allenwood federal prison camp in Montgomery, Pennsylvania, served as an "advisor," McDonald said.

After spending twenty-one days in federal prison, including Leavenworth, following his arrest in April 1984, Perry pleaded guilty to sports bribery charges that September in U.S. District Court in Uniondale, New York. He was sentenced to time served and probation.

A year later Perry met Lloyd. Hersh introduced the two one night at his favorite hangout, The Entourage Cafe in Manhattan. Within hours, Hersh said, Perry had even handed Lloyd "a few bucks."

As Hersh explains it, "You want to show you have an affection for great players. Why do you love your parents? Because they take care of you. If they didn't, you would find someone else. That is what the world is about. So, he gave him some money. He likes basketball. What do you think he's doing, getting involved with these kids for betting [on] games? That was years ago. It is nothing of that sort now. He doesn't even bet on sports any more."

Even if that were true, there still seemed something sinister about a convicted gambler being associated with an athlete—especially, considering the history of basketball and gambling in New York City.

The potential for disaster from such associations first became evident back in 1945, when a scheduled game between Brooklyn College and Akron had to be canceled after word leaked out that five members of the Brooklyn team had each accepted a $1,000 bribe to guarantee their team would lose. Four years later, Junius Kellogg, the first black player at Manhattan College, told school officials that he had been approached by a former player and offered $1,000 to guarantee at least a 10-point loss against DePaul. Kellogg also told officials the player and a teammate had thrown three games the previous season, each earning $5,000. The allegations began an investigation by New York District Attorney Frank Hogan. The results would shock the nation.

Eighty-six games in twenty-three cities, Hogan said, had been fixed by thirty-two players from seven colleges between 1947 and 1950. Among the schools involved were Long Island University, New York University and Manhattan—at the time, all national powers—as well as the University of Toledo, the University of Kentucky and Bradley University. Perhaps, though, the biggest shock was that players from City College of New York were also involved. After all, just the season before, City College had defeated Bradley twice—once to win the National Invitation Tournament and once to win the NCAA Tournament, the only team in history to win both titles the same season.

The fixes, Hogan said, had been arranged when players were offered cash during summer-league games in the Catskill Mountains, where many players worked in the local resorts to earn money for school. By the time the full extent of the scandal was uncovered, seven City College players, including stars Ed Roman, Ed Warner and Floyd Layne, had been accused of shaving points or fixing games. So had four starters at Bradley—all-America Gene Melchiorre, among them—and Alex Groza and Ralph Beard of Kentucky. College basketball was in ruins. In New York, it never really recovered.

That was 1951. Ten years later, while home on Christmas vacation from the University of Iowa, a teenager named Connie Hawkins took a $200 loan from a man named Jack Molinas, who turned out to be a gambler. "Maybe he was trying to set me up," Hawkins said later. "But I was out of money and he was the only one who came to my aid."

Whatever the case, Hawkins, the best known playground player of his era—and, most all eras, for that matter—was banned from the NBA for eight years, until he won a $1 million lawsuit allowing him to play. A $200 handshake almost cost him his career.

Still, Perry did, in fact, have a genuine interest in basketball. According to McDonald, he had even coached a camp team in Allenwood. He also coached Albie's Trimmings, the summer-league team run by Hersh, as well as a team sponsored by The Entourage. In all fairness, Perry, who refuses comment on the situation, even attempted to teach the players on his team a lesson about prison. Every summer, he, Hersh and Ronnie took a few players to Comstock Correctional Facility for a game against the prisoners, though, as Ronnie said, "Lloyd always managed to finagle his way out of it."

One time, the three brought their best team to Comstock: Mark Jackson and Marcus Broadnax of St. John's; Cardozo center Duane Caus-well, who was headed to Temple; Brent McCollin, who played for August Martin and, later, Long Island University; and, among others, Malloy Nesmith, who went on to Jacksonville College, a junior college in Texas. "We didn't tell them where we were going 'til we were in the van," Ronnie said. "We were like, 'Okay Mark, you got the axe murderer.' Duane, you got 'Son of Sam.' And Marcus, 'You got the rapist.' They were like, 'Who're we playing?' We showed up and they saw it was a prison and they were like, 'You got to be kiddin'.'

"But it was good for them," Ronnie said. "It was like out of that movie, 'Scared Straight.' The inmates talked to them, told them to do the right thing. Of course, we walked in and Sam Cutchins and Mark Jackson, who both come from the same park, are walking and some guy, one of the inmates, yells, 'Yo, Sam. Mark. What's up?' They knew two guys there—a murderer and someone who got nailed for dealing drugs—so they walked over and started bullshittin' with them."

Another time, they brought a team with Wilfred Kirkaldy, a hulk of a center who would play at Oak Hill, and Lawrence (Future) Pollard, a guard who played at Boys & Girls and who, later, would attend West Virginia. "In one of the games, Future got hit so hard he got nineteen stitches," Ronnie said. "With no foul called." When the team was leaving, someone took the visitor's pass belonging to Kirkaldy so, when he tried to leave, the guard told him he couldn't, saying he would have to "stay overnight" until the situation could be resolved and he could prove he wasn't a prisoner. "He was going, 'Ron, Sam, Hersh. Tell them who I am,' " Ronnie recalled. "We were like, 'We never seen you before.' The kid was crying. It taught him a lesson."

Still, some remained skeptical of Perry's interests, though Lloyd said he never asked him anything in return for his handouts and Hersh swore that Perry only played legal blackjack and poker since his last encounter with the law. Although no allegations would ever be made that his involvement with Lloyd was illegal, McDonald was among those who said the situation should at least have raised some eyebrows. After all, here was a convicted gambler who was palling around with some of the most highly-recruited basketball players in America. "Sure, the guy could have a conversion," McDonald said. "He could say, 'Hey, look, I want to be a decent guy now.' The guy really loves basketball. He could be a straight arrow. But you have to have doubts about that, given the guy's background. How many people in this country have been convicted of fixing two different sporting events? I mean, the number of prosecutions brought under the federal sports bribery statutes, you could probably count them on one hand."

When Lloyd arrived in Las Vegas that spring he had a friend with him, a friend from 203rd Street named Steve Cropper—a friend who, among others, would later allege in a prize-winning investigative series by *New York Newsday* that the basketball staff at Nevada-Las Vegas had committed several possible NCAA violations during the recruitment of Lloyd.

Cropper was twenty-two years old and had briefly attended Hofstra University in Hempstead, New York, where he served as manager of the school basketball team. He was working for the U.S. Postal Service when Lloyd asked him to go to Vegas. Cropper saw it as his big chance, a chance to get in good with Lloyd and maybe get taken care of somewhere down the line. He saw it as a sort of "management position." So he went.

"Well, to me, college basketball as a whole was going to use Lloyd," Cropper said. "They needed Lloyd just like Lloyd needed them. They didn't want to face up to that, but I let them know that. I let Tarkanian know that he needed Lloyd there and don't think that, you know, he did him a favor by letting him come there even though he didn't have the grades, because he needed him there. He was going to bring money to Las Vegas."

And, in exchange for that service, Cropper said, he told Tarkanian that he and Lloyd would need assistance. Helping them find a place to live would be nice. Helping them find a job would be fine. Cropper alleged that, on the basis of those requests, he received a job interview—allegations both Tarkanian and Warkentien have denied—and was lent a hand finding an apartment, though he and Lloyd paid the rent.

"The first time I saw Tark, it made me laugh," Cropper said. "He looked like Yoda from 'Star Wars.' I was just trying not to laugh and he said, 'What's so funny?' I said, 'Nothing I can talk about right now.'

"But he said to me, 'Now everything has changed because you've come out here with [Lloyd],'" Cropper said. "He was like, 'So, what has to be done?' I was like, 'Could you just tell people that I'm out here with a recruit of yours and that, um, I'm a good worker and that I could prove myself.'"

Cropper said he found himself at an interview with Mike Sloan, the general counsel for Circus Circus, a well-known hotel and casino on "The Strip." Sloan, Cropper said, took him to see Tony Alamo, the hotel's vice president and general manager. As Cropper found out, it paid to know people. Soon he had a job as a money runner at the casino and, later, after he quit, he and Lloyd were allegedly set up with interviews at an ad agency. They got the job. Warkentien had also helped them find a place to live at the St. Tropez Villa Apartments. Another assistant coach, Tim

Grgurich, allegedly provided the two with a used color television and kitchen utensils.

All of those situations could be construed as NCAA infractions and, if the NCAA had anything to say about it, blatant ones. But it didn't end there.

Cropper also claimed that both he and Lloyd received small "loans" from Warkentien—allegations that were denied by the assistant coach, but were supported by a former player, Ricky Collier, who had been a reserve guard for the Rebels. "He never told me how much," Collier said. "He was always like, 'Bald-head blood likes me, Ricky. Bald-head blood loves me.' I'd laugh when he'd say that."

So would Lloyd and Steve Cropper. All the way to the bank.

As he stood in the terminal at McCarran International, it hit Ronnie that he had committed a cardinal sin, one he never thought he would make. He had trusted Lloyd. Now he realized it had been a dumb thing to do.

Earlier in the week, when he had last talked with Lloyd, this had seemed like a good idea. After all, it was late August. Ronnie needed a vacation and he also wanted to see how Lloyd was doing in his new environment. He figured he would catch a weekend flight to Las Vegas. Lloyd told Ronnie that he would meet him at the airport. It was simple.

Except for one thing. Ronnie had now been standing in the terminal for over an hour and Lloyd had still not arrived. That alone would not have been so bad, except that Ronnie also realized that he couldn't contact him. His phone had been disconnected because Lloyd hadn't paid the bill. Worse, Ronnie also realized that he had forgotten to ask Lloyd for his address.

Annoyed with himself, Ronnie called the athletic department at Nevada-Las Vegas. He figured if he could at least explain his predicament, someone there could give him an address for Lloyd. Then, at least, he could catch a cab. The problem was, it was Sunday. And, no one was at school.

Ronnie thought about checking into a hotel. He could always find Lloyd on Monday. Exasperated, he decided to explore one last option. He dialed information. Maybe, at least, he could reach Jerry Tarkanian.

"So I get the telephone operator and I go, 'Could I have the number for Jerry Tarkanian?'" Ronnie said. "I figured, at least if I could get Tark, then I could find out where Lloyd lived. But instead of giving me the number, the operator goes, 'Why do you want it?' I'm thinking, you know this operator isn't asking 'cause he figures I'm a friend of Frank Sinatra. I mean, you could tell I was calling from a phone booth in the airport. So, I figure, maybe he thinks I want to make a crank call or something and won't give it to me. I explain the situation. I go, 'Look, I just flew in from New York. I used to coach this guy named Lloyd Daniels. I'm trying to reach him.'

"I figure, no way the operator buys my story. But instead, he goes, 'Oh, I know Lloyd. He lives in the apartment downstairs from me.' I'm in shock. Next thing I know, the guy tells me he'll call his apartment and get his friend to run downstairs and tell Lloyd to come and get me. So he does."

It was about a half-hour later, then, that Ronnie, standing outside the terminal, heard this horrible noise and turned to see an old rust-bucket of a car speeding along the access road, Lloyd's head poked out the side window. "Ronnie Boy," Lloyd screamed, as he drove past. "Hey, Ronnie Boy."

"You had to see this," Ronnie said. "This car was a wreck. Junk. I mean, even if the school gave this car to him for nothing, it wasn't a violation, that's how bad it was. But here he is, winging it down the wrong side of the street doing about fifty miles-an-hour. He's got his head out the window, looking like E.T., not looking where he's going, but looking at me and yelling, 'Yo, Ronnie Boy. Hey, Ronnie Boy.' After he goes by me, he makes a U-turn, forgets to give this truck the right of way and nearly has an accident. He pulls up and goes, 'Ronnie Boy. Yo, Ronnie Boy. I finally got my license.'

"I yelled back, 'Lloyd, give me your address.' He goes, 'Why you want my address, Ron?' I said, 'Because. I'm taking a cab.' "

It seemed everyone in Las Vegas knew Lloyd. Not just the telephone operator and not just the attendants at the local gym or the workers at the school. But everyone. It was one of the first things that Ronnie noticed when Lloyd met him at the airport. Lloyd had contacts. Lloyd had power. "When I was in the airport," Ronnie said, "I saw Jesse Jackson get off a plane and two, maybe three people knew who he was. When Lloyd met me, everyone knew him. People were going, 'Hey, it's Lloyd. Hey, it's Lloyd Daniels.'

"It was like that everywhere we went," Ronnie said. "Everyone knew who Lloyd was and, if they didn't, once his name was mentioned they knew what it meant. In the casinos, in the restaurants. He was a celebrity."

When Lloyd first arrived in Vegas, Ricky Collier had taken him on a guided tour of town. He had shown him the places to hang out, the places to avoid. He had shown him the places where a basketball player—or, more specifically, a member of the Runnin' Rebels—could put the touch on folks because of his situation. The community loved the Runnin' Rebels, a team that seemed to reflect the very soul of Las Vegas. They loved their run-and-gun style. They loved their outlaw image. And, of course, they loved that they won. Better still, they loved the players, because in Vegas, like in Hollywood, everybody loves a star. The team even has a section known as "Gucci Row," where season tickets sell for around $1,500.

"The thing is," Tarkanian once said, explaining the relationship, "Las Vegas doesn't have anything else of its own. You know, they got things coming in all the time, the greatest entertainers in the world. But everything else leaves after the show. UNLV is part of the town. None of the boosters' kids go here. They go to Southern Cal or Stanford. The boosters never went here. The *alums* didn't even go here. But they love us."

In true Las Vegas fashion, Collier showed Lloyd how to capitalize on that stardom. He took him out on The Strip. He estimated that he took him to at least ten hotels for meals, always, he said, making sure to introduce him to the right people. "I'd say, 'This is Lloyd Daniels' and they'd flip, because Tark talked about him so much," Collier said. "They were like, 'Come any time. If you need anything, call me.' " And, Lloyd always did.

After all, like other players, Lloyd was not about to let his status go to waste. Free meals, free drinks, free time at the Las Vegas Sports Club, where members paid an initiation fee plus monthly dues, but where players were allowed to use the facilities—which included a regulation basketball court—at no charge, according to a club executive. This was heaven for Lloyd, who had the soul of a con man and who, it seemed, was always trying to get something for nothing. It was the way he had been taught in school, where, if he performed on the court, he was often allowed to slide in the classroom. It was the way he saw some in his old neighborhood spend their entire existence. Las Vegas offered him a perfect forum to perform his routine to the fullest. Minimum effort. Maximum gain. Lloyd knew the score.

They didn't call it fame and fortune for nothing.

"He had a tremendous amount of juice," Ronnie said. "It was incredible. We went to one or two casinos where we got a steak and all he had to do was sign for it. He went to jewelers, looking to get the best deal he could on gold. In fact, Lloyd was always trying to make a deal with the local jewelers, going for his con. He wanted to find out jewelers where he could get a ridiculous deal. With everything, he was always looking for a guy who knew a guy. You know, anyone in that position is going to take advantage of the situation, try to work his con. But with Lloyd, he does it to the nth degree."

Still, there was a reason Lloyd had so much juice in Vegas. It was because Tark had been quoted in the local papers saying what people had said about him for years, that Lloyd was the second coming of James Naismith. You know, every time he touched the ball, he reinvented the game. "When they write the final chapter on guards," Tark once said, "they'll start with Jerry West, Oscar Robertson, Magic Johnson and Lloyd Daniels. He's the best I've ever been around." Folks took that to heart on The Strip.

Ronnie recalled how, when Lloyd walked into The Sports Club, where he practiced daily on the immaculate indoor court, people would give him the once-over. "By the time he had laced up his sneakers," Ronnie said, "a crowd would be filing around." Jarvis Basnight, then a junior forward, would tease Lloyd. "You better get eligible," Basnight said. "You better do the right thing, because you're putting me in the NBA with those alley-oop passes."

One bystander even told Ronnie, "What's he doing in college?"

"I figured," Ronnie said, "the guy's going to tell me, 'He's not smart enough. He's not a student.' Instead, he goes, 'This guy should be in the NBA.' "

Consider the game when Lloyd and Sam Perry teamed to face future U.S. Olympic Team members Stacey Augmon and Barry Young, both recruits who would later sign with Nevada-Las Vegas. Lloyd and Perry won. Consider the game when Lloyd busted Sidney Green, the former Rebels star who came out of New York City and was then with the New York Knicks. As Green struggled to defend him, Lloyd toyed with him—banking home jumpers, talking trash about how good he was, how it wasn't nothing for him to hit a few "J's." "This kid always shoot like this?" Green asked Perry, in disbelief.

And, consider the game when Lloyd, Ronnie, two guys who had been working out in the gym and future Arizona recruit Matt Othick went against Armon Gilliam, Freddie Banks, Gerald Paddio, Mark Wade and Eldridge Hudson—a team that would go on to become ranked first in the nation. "We won," Ronnie said. "That's when I knew Lloyd could be ungodly, that everyone else next to him was a joke. He was making these guys look like high school kids. This kid was the best."

Maybe that was also why, when Lloyd and Ronnie ran into George-town coach John Thompson in the Barbary Coast Hotel, Thompson told him, "Stay out of trouble and I think you've got a good chance to be the two-guard on the Olympic Team." As Ronnie said, "To this day, I still tease Lloyd that he cost the U.S. Team the 1988 Olympic Gold Medal."

Lloyd signed his national letter of intent April 11, 1986. And, despite not having graduated from high school, by the time Ronnie left Vegas, Lloyd had earned fourteen college credits. Though he would leave Ne-vada—Las Vegas that fall and not return until the spring semester, before Lloyd finally left Las Vagas for good in 1987, he had even acquired a tutor.

"'He had trouble reading and we felt that, if we could get him with a reading specialist, we could monitor his work academically," Tarkanian said. "We thought we had a chance. We knew it was small. We knew it was a small chance. But I felt we had a chance."

According to Mark Warkentien, Lloyd was "in absolute wonderment over the dictionary." And, Warkentien said, Lloyd was even "amazed at punctuation marks, at what they could do." But some suggested that the inference that Lloyd was learning was, at best, misleading.

Ronnie recalled how Lloyd would have one book open to his left, another open to his right—each on different subjects. He would attempt to answer one question out of the first book, then attempt to answer a second question out of the other book. Often, his efforts were in vain.

And, it wasn't long before he "fired" at least one tutor. The reason? The tutor who once said Lloyd had a "primitive style", told Lloyd he had a learning disability.

"He, of course, has done nothing as far as his education is concerned," the tutor told Ronnie. "He refused to work with me anymore because I said he had a learning disability. He was appalled at the fact that I would say anything like that about him. He fired me as his tutor. We laughed our brains out about that one. It is the joke around here—Lloyd Daniels fired his tutor. It never ceases to amaze me what he'll do next."

Still, at least Lloyd was going to school on a regular basis during the summer of 1986. "What was he taking?" Ronnie said. "He was taking pre-med, what do you think? At least he looked good going to class. I mean, he sat in the apartment and tried to do his homework. He carried his books. It was like he was trying to be normal. Imagine that."

7 · Guardian Angel

If Larry Brown had suggested, not so tongue-in-cheek, to Howie Garfinkel back at Five-Star Camp that he had a family Lloyd could live with in Kansas, then Mark Warkentien, the assistant basketball coach and "recruiting coordinator" for Nevada-Las Vegas, took the idea one step further. On August 26, 1986, Warkentien filed a petition in the Eighth Judicial District Court of Clark County, Nevada. And, in that petition, Warkentien stated his desire to become the court-appointed legal guardian of Lloyd Daniels.

It was a strange request, considering his position and considering that Lloyd already had two legal guardians—his grandmothers, Lulia Hendley and Annie Sargeant—and that, though he had signed a letter of intent with Nevada-Las Vegas, according to the NCAA he still was viewed as a "potential recruit" until his actual enrollment at the school on a full-time basis.

Some said the proposed arrangement would violate NCAA rules, if not in fact, then at least in theory, and provide Nevada-Las Vegas with an unfair advantage in his recruitment. Common sense implied that it would, since in his petition Warkentien asked for the power to borrow money and obtain loans for Lloyd, as well as assist him in his financial affairs—all potential NCAA violations. Others simply found the request to be in both bad taste and poor judgment.

Pacific Coast Athletic Association commissioner Lew Cryer said he had some "concerns" over the situation and, later, initiated an exchange of correspondence between Nevada-Las Vegas and the NCAA. The NCAA later notified athletic department officials at Nevada-Las Vegas that the matter would be investigated by its Legislation and Interpretations Committee.

Still, Warkentien—or, as Lloyd called him, "Stein"—elected to move forward with the legal process. "The proposed ward has the potential to be a successful human being, student and athlete," Warkentien stated in his petition to the court. "He has shown great promise in athletics, and, given the right direction and encouragement, has the potential to be a successful professional athlete. However, the proposed ward, despite being eighteen years old, barely reads at a third-grade level. Without the

94

guidance, support, encouragement and counseling of a special guardian, the potential for exploitation of the proposed ward is great."

The petition painted a sad, tragic picture of a kid who had been born into poverty, been raised in a home situation where he seemed to amount to little more than an afterthought, been passed through an educational system that showed little concern for whether or not he actually was educated, and who had been a pawn in a societal system where concern for his well-being seemed to begin and end with his ability to play basketball.

What the petition did not mention was that Mark Warkentien was an assistant basketball coach at Nevada-Las Vegas.

Warkentien said he could not understand how outsiders could view the situation as unethical or exploitative. But Warkentien and his wife, Maureen, did not choose to become guardians of other students at the school. Just Lloyd. In fairness, Warkentien, like others who have known him, did seem to have a genuine affinity for Lloyd. "I loved him," Warkentien said. "He has the key to my house. He baby-sat my daughter. Around my house, I consider him family. In the human existence, you do what you can for people."

Still, Tarkanian admitted, Warkentien made the move so Nevada-Las Vegas could exercise greater control over Lloyd, monitor him more closely and, therefore, have a better chance to get him to do the things he needed to do to become eligible to play basketball there. Lloyd went along with the guardianship proceedings because, while he did want to "be part of a real family," as Warkentien put it, he also realized the situation could provide him with access to money, access to a car, access to material things he did not have, including a shot at the pros via a career at Nevada-Las Vegas.

Though Lloyd, as usual with what he viewed as "that negative stuff," said he would not discuss the situation, team members at Nevada-Las Vegas, among them reserve guard Ricky Collier, alleged that one of the things Lloyd seemed to like most about the relationship was that Warkentien would, on occasion, give him money—usually, in the form of an allowance.

He said Lloyd sometimes stopped by the athletic offices for closed-door meetings with Warkentien. When Lloyd needed cash, Collier said, he would say: "I'll get some money from Stein." And, Collier said, after those meetings, Lloyd would say: "Yeah, I got some money now." The "guardian angel" might also be construed as the "goose who laid the golden egg."

• • •

There was no need for Kenny Anderson to have another legal guardian. He had his mother, Joan, who worked hard to keep him in line. Still, it was certain that Kenny needed more support, needed someone to keep him in check, keep him from letting success go to his head. That job fell to an organization Tom Konchalski, the scout, called "Team Anderson."

"Team Anderson" was a network of advisors, headed by Vincent Smith and a friend of his, a lawyer named Pierre Turner. What they did, and what the other members of the team did, was keep track of Kenny at all times. If he was in the park, they knew it. If he was talking to the wrong people, they knew it. "Vincent became his security blanket," Jack Curran said of Smith, who had also become an assistant coach at Molloy—just to keep better track of Anderson. "He had everything covered."

The network was so extensive it even included Kenny's barber. "We even know when he gets his hair cut," Curran said.

If the guardianship situation with Lloyd and Las Vegas smacked of exploitation, the network established by Smith and Turner seemed to be a welcome alternative. Because, despite rumors on the street that the two had some ulterior motives in the deal, such as ensuring themselves of a cut if and when Kenny was ever able to turn pro, the two were the main reason he had been able to find as much success as he had. And he *had* found success.

Kenny Anderson was perhaps the best player in the city by the fall of 1986, an intriguing notion, considering he was still just sixteen years old, a first-semester sophomore—one who had yet to even start a high school game. Already, calls had come in from coaches around the country and, in his office closet, Curran had a box full of recruiting letters from places like Kansas and Kentucky, Syracuse and Stanford. The goal now was to ensure all that "pub" didn't get to Anderson, didn't give him what teammate Ralph James, a Harvard-bound senior swingman, called "an ego overflow."

The cure was simple. First, Curran met with Anderson on a regular basis, the two talking about the recruitment process, as well as about the career development of the star guard. Second, Curran relied on the members of "Team Anderson" to make sure things didn't get blown out of proportion with recruiters and with the local club teams—though Kenny did eventually play for three: Madison Square Boys Club, Riverside and the Gauchos.

"It could become a problem," Curran said of the chances of Anderson being spoiled by success, getting sidetracked. "But I don't think it will happen. We talked about it and I told him the situation could be good for him, as long as it doesn't affect the way he behaves. He's not a wise guy and doesn't act like this is a big deal, though he could have. But, what I told him is you have to be suspicious of people. A lot of people want to be connected with Kenneth, because they realize that he is going to be something. It's up to Kenneth not to associate with those people—you know the old story, 'Show me your friends and I'll show you who you are.' The problem is, at his age, he thinks he can just say 'Hello' to them and not be affected. But you can't."

"What I've done is take everybody's advice, use the information I thought I could use and sort it out," said Anderson, who, despite remaining traces of street in his voice and in his actions, was a likable kid with a quick wit and sharp sense of humor. "It's always good to listen to people and hear what they have to say. The people around me help keep me level-headed. I don't think I'm great because I'm a good basketball player, because there are people who can do things I can't do. Some people here can't play basketball like me, but they have academic skills I don't."

Of course, primarily due to the efforts of "Team Anderson," Kenny had been able to achieve a B-minus average as a freshman. And, because of that support, throughout his time in high school Anderson would never stray far from the straight and narrow. "People here had a fear he might slack off, but I think he really grew up and realized the world doesn't revolve around basketball," Ralph James said. "Besides, if he would ever start to stray, people would pull him aside and make sure he did things right."

"His salvation," Tom Konchalski said, "is that he has enough people around him who will keep his hat size the same." As Curran said, "I think he really understands the dangers of being this good, this young."

"Maybe some people think I'll get a swollen head," Anderson said. "But I'm not like that. I just want to be myself. People can say you're great all they want. But you have to remember that every time you step on the court you can prove them wrong." But not all kids get such good advice or learn those lessons as well as Kenny Anderson.

In order for Mark Warkentien to obtain legal guardianship of Lloyd, who at one point was identified by the court as "an adult minor," it had to be proven that Lloyd was not able to make "all of the decisions necessary to his own care." In other words, that Lloyd could not survive on his own. That without the aid of yet another in a seemingly endless string of benefactors, one who would vow to act "out of concern" for him and in his "best interests," Lloyd would become just another lost soul on the streets.

To obtain evidence needed to support those contentions, Lloyd underwent examination by a family and marriage counselor, Dr. Joan Elaine Owen, the director of the Center for Diagnosis and Development in Las Vegas. In a five-page affidavit, dated August 7, 1986, and attached to the petition filed by Warkentien, Dr. Owen outlined the findings of her exam.

She testified that Lloyd had been presented with "a full battery of diagnostic tests" and that he was "quite easily discouraged during the test taking." The results of several tests administered—among them, the Bloom Sentence Completion Survey, the Wechsler Adult Intelligence Scale-Revised, the Leiter International Performance Scale, the Bender-Gestalt Test, the Wide Range Achievment Test and the Peabody Individual Achievement Test, which were all designed to test intelligence levels, as well as verbal and non-verbal communication skills—indicated that Lloyd was a dyslexic who needed to be tutored as would "a blind or deaf student."

"He has made numerous school moves which have interfered with continuity in his life," Dr. Owen stated. "He admitted that he had substantial absenteeism and had felt humiliation and embarrassment with the limited academic growth. Thus, he avoided school rather than face the continued failure." As Dr. Owen wrote, "He admits that he is angered by the media for embarrassing him due to his poor academic success. He stated that what bothered him more than anything else was not being able to read. He stated further that if he only had a mother and a father, 'These school things would have been different.' " According to the sworn statement, Lloyd also told Dr. Owen, "I feel that this is my last opportunity to get an education before I am too old. I know that I will not be able to play basketball for all of my life and I must prepare for another career as well."

How someone like Lloyd would be able to attain a college education prior to being provided years of tutorial assistance was beyond all comprehension. Especially, since Dr. Owen said that, while Lloyd possessed an understanding of "addition, subtraction, multiplication, division and simple fractions," his math skills were that of a student in the sixth grade. His reading comprehension tested out at a grade level of 2.8.

Still, though the entire situation seemed to make a mockery of the college athletic system, based on the testimony presented by Dr. Owen, Warkentien and Lloyd, District Court Judge Thomas A. Foley appointed Warkentien legal guardian on October 24, 1986. By that time, though, Lloyd was already living in Walnut, California. He had become a "student" at Mount San Antonio College.

8 • Mount Sac

Even though it was three days after his nineteenth birthday, Lloyd still could not read when he arrived at Mount San Antonio College in September, 1986. Although basketball coach Eugene Victor said he knew Lloyd was dyslexic and described him as being "educationally disabled," neither he nor members of the school administration felt compelled to let such mere formalities interfere with his quest for a formal college education.

Lloyd was going to be a "normal" student. He was going to attend classes on a regular basis. He was going to pass courses. And, if all went according to the elaborate plan laid out by Jerry Tarkanian, Mark Warkentien and Victor, Lloyd would graduate with a junior college degree from Mount Sac, as it was known, and become eligible to compete at Nevada-Las Vegas.

The plan was masterful and, by its design, would neatly circumvent the eligibility guidelines established by the NCAA. Those rules, Rick Evrard, the director of legislative services for the NCAA, had said, required an athlete be a high school graduate or hold a General Equivalency Diploma to receive an athletic scholarship at a school in Division I. Lloyd had neither.

Because of that, Evrard said back when Lloyd was at Andrew Jackson, the earliest he could receive his equivalency diploma would be one year after the graduation of his high school class—or, at best, in time to become eligible for the 1988-89 season at Nevada-Las Vegas. If then. If ever.

But the plan conceived by Tarkanian, Warkentien and Victor took into account one obscure and all-but-overlooked fact: California law mandated admission to state-run institutions for any adult "who can profit from the instruction offered." A student need not be a high school graduate. A student need not prove competence in scholastic areas. A student need not even be a resident of the state. The only requirement is that a student be breathing, and be at least eighteen years of age. Lloyd qualified on both counts.

Although admission policies suggested a prospective student take a minimum three years of college prep courses in mathematics and four years in English, and even though he had never even spent one full year in any high school or come close to learning how to read on the high school level—or, for that matter, had made little or no progress toward receiving his high school degree—Lloyd was eligible to become a full-time junior college student in California. With a junior college degree, he would then be eligible to transfer to Nevada-Las Vegas—on a full athletic scholarship.

It seemed ludicrous. But with additional credits received in intersession classes, Lloyd might even be able to graduate ahead of schedule and be eligible to appear for the Runnin' Rebels in 1987-88. It was brilliant. Better yet, it would work. Even tuition, which was $90 per credit for out-of-state students, would be taken care of, paid for with federal grants.

"Is this a loophole?" Warkentien said, sounding almost shocked at the suggestion, when questioned about the situation. "No. The bottom line is that Lloyd is doing what he is supposed to be doing. It is his expressed desire to become a student. At this point, he is more excited about reading than about basketball. And, if it's for the kid and it's the right thing to do, then I really don't worry what people think."

Still, the entire scenario seemed implausible. Especially since, based on his past, it was apparent Lloyd had little desire to become a student, except if it meant he could play basketball. And yet, it had happened.

"I guess we were wrong, that he will be able to play next season if he is a junior college graduate," Evrard admitted with reluctance after the plan was outlined. "It is pretty clear what they [Nevada-Las Vegas] have done and why it was done, but there is nothing within the legislation to prohibit it. It certainly seems they have found a way to bend the rules.

"The Lloyd Daniels case is obviously extraordinary because he is such a talent and because he is not a student at all. The membership is aware of what has happened and they may decide to take action to see where, why and how this can be done and if it was done to circumvent the rules. I've seen some pretty strange cases, but none as far-reaching as this one. I don't think this whole situation is over."

That was an understatement.

Still, there was little concern about threats made by the NCAA back at Mount Sac in the fall of 1986. There were more pressing concerns. The first was to get Lloyd a class schedule, one he could handle.

It proved to be a challenge, though after some effort it was worked out and Lloyd was assigned a full course load, eighteen credits. Among his classes was an ethnic studies course called "The Black American," as well as several physical education courses related to basketball: "Strength and Conditioning," "Recreation and Fundamentals of Sports" and "Fun-

damentals of Team Sports." Lloyd had four other classes. Two of them
were in physical education, one was in biology and one was remedial
English.

The reading course, titled "Reading 67" was, according to the course
catalogue at Mount San Antonio, required for students who failed a placement test for freshman composition, the basic first-year English course,
or the placement exam for the basic remedial course, "English 68." But
it soon became evident that Lloyd could handle neither the biology nor
his reading course and he was forced to withdraw from both.

"I had placed him in 'Reading 67,' " Victor said. "It was not even
remedial reading. It was just trying to read. But Lloyd couldn't do the
work."

There were no such problems in the other classes. As Victor said:
"I dropped him from all the classes he wouldn't attend. All he had left
was P.E. classes. Lloyd did all right. There was no heavy reading. Just say
they were all 'activities courses.' "

One of those activities courses was "Fundamentals of Team Sports,"
a class open only to members of the basketball team at Mount Sac and
taught by Victor and his assistant coach, Ralph Osterkamp. According to
the course catalogue at Mount San Antonio, the class offered "instruction
in the skill and technique of playing basketball, including offensive and
defensive strategy." The catalogue stressed that "students who repeat this
course will receive more advanced instruction leading to skill improvement."

Bizarre though it seemed, Lloyd Daniels, the former *Parade Magazine*
All-American and one of the most sought-after, big-time basketball recruits in the nation, was scheduled to receive two college credits for being
on his junior college basketball team. This was his "education."

Then again, Lloyd wasn't the only city kid in junior college back in
the fall of 1986. In fact, Boo Harvey and Moses Scurry were "doin' time,"
too.

Graduation day was May 10. Boo Harvey had it marked on his cal-
endar. He had been waiting for the day for almost two years, ever since
he first came to San Jacinto College in search of a second chance. He
would have traded the junior college national championship he won his
freshman season, when the team was unbeaten in thirty-seven games, just
to have back the scholarship to Syracuse—the one he forfeited when he
left Andrew Jackson in the spring of 1985 with a city title, but no grades.

In fact, he would have traded it all just to be anywhere except San Jacinto, the junior college nestled between the oil refineries in the Houston suburb of Pasadena, Texas.

"When I first got down here," Harvey said then, "I looked around and said, 'What am I doing here?' It hurt. I remember when I first came home. Everybody said, 'Where you goin' to school?' I kept on thinking, 'I shouldn't be here. I shouldn't.' But being here made me realize that basketball might not be there all the time, that I needed something to fall back on. This place helped me mature. I took a fall. But now, I'm coming back."

Coming back is what junior college is all about. For years junior colleges, like prep schools, have served as a home for wayward student-athletes. A place where the academic indigent can, if they can just learn to use their heads and show even faint dedication in the classroom, in their studies, stake a claim to a higher education as well as their rightful place in the world of college basketball. A place where they can get a second chance.

It is not a simple process, since many of the athletes who find themselves in junior college—referred to as thirteenth and fourteenth grades by the hopelessly cynical—are much like Lloyd. Few cases are as dramatic, mainly because few players involved in such situations tie all the major elements—the incredible talent, as poor a scholastic background and as high a profile, in this case due to the hands-on involvement by Nevada-Las Vegas—into one neat little package the way Lloyd did. But that doesn't mean that there aren't, and won't continue to be, hundreds in similar situations.

"We get kids for three reasons," said San Jacinto coach Ronnie Arrow, who would later become the head coach at the University of South Alabama. "First, because they aren't doing it academically; they have the big-time tools, but they didn't predict. Second, because they've had problems off the court. Third, because they're just not ready for Division I.

"Mostly, for the first reason."

San Jacinto is perhaps the most renowned junior college in the nation, even more well known than Hutchinson Community College in Hutchinson, Kansas—site of the annual junior college tournament. Just about every inner-city player in America has heard of "San Jack." And, though they all admit that it probably isn't such a bad place, they still don't want to go there. Just down the block from the bar, Gilley's, home of the original "Urban Cowboy," San Jack specializes in big-time, small-time college basketball and the education of the heretofore uneducable—the new urban cowboys.

Since it opened back in 1960, San Jack had won three national junior college championships—including the previous season when Harvey, then a freshman, helped the Ravens go 37-0. In fact, since 1966 when Ollie Taylor came from the Bronx en route to the University of Houston and the New York Nets in the old American Basketball Association, San Jack had given a second chance to eleven future professional players, among them Tom Henderson, who came out of the Bronx to attend San Jacinto before heading to the University of Hawaii, the Houston Rockets and the Washington Bullets. Even Walter Berry, who had gone on to St. John's and the NBA, found himself at San Jack after failing to graduate from Franklin. Denied enrollment at St. John's, he earned his equivalency diploma, led the Ravens to the national junior college title as a freshman in 1984, and headed back to St. John's, where he helped the Redmen to the 1985 NCAA Final Four.

"I was told by more than one Big East guy," Arrow recalled of that team, "that we could have finished fifth, maybe fourth in the Big East."

Of course, most of these kids—kids like Harvey, kids like Scurry—would have gone to major colleges in the first place. It's just their academic pasts wouldn't let them. "Some of these kids you call up keep telling you they got their grades and you know they don't," Arrow said. "But they'll go down to the last minute saying that until someone slaps them silly and says, 'Hey, you big dummy. Who you kidding? You ain't going to graduate, so what you going to do now?' The problem is, a lot of these kids live in a dream world. They've been stars all their lives. They don't need a junior college.

"These kids have always had someone to look out for them and so have always been able to land on their feet. But from the moment they get here they realize that will no longer be the case. It hits them upside the head. By the time we get done with them, they realize from now on there will be demands made in their lives. But first they have to admit to themselves that they screwed up. They have to come down a notch to rise two notches."

"Everyone thinks that these are dumb kids," said assistant coach Scott Gernander, who would later become the head coach. "But, for the most part, they're not. It's just that a lot of them didn't go to class. I bet most of them have never studied in their lives. It was just easier to hang out."

That transformation was difficult for both Harvey and Scurry, a freshman during the 1986-87 season, when Harvey was finishing his second year at San Jacinto. The first inclination of both was to resort to their old ways, to cut class. But, unlike the old days, they couldn't get away with it.

"If they miss a class—and, if they miss one, we find out—Scott gets them up at 6 a.m. and runs them," Arrow said. "If they don't turn in a paper on time, Scott runs them. The third time we have to run them, we add an eleven o'clock curfew. Now, Scott's a runner. He gets up at five-thirty every morning and he's going to run whether he has company or not. But we've had guys who run with him twice a week, and one year we had guys who could've gone out for the track team. But we tell them, 'We damn sure didn't bring you here to get you up at six every morning to run.' "

Some, like Harvey and Scurry, eventually do get the message. Maybe they don't change completely—as Harvey admitted, "I had to run once or twice"—but at least they change some. "I'm here trying to make it," Scurry said. "I never thought it would come to this, but now I realize my mistake. It's a real big change. But I found out that when you work hard, you can do it."

"A lot of these kids have never been punished," Arrow said, "and so they are one-dimensional. With them it is, 'I'm going to do what I want to do when I want to do it.' We teach them to accept structure in their lives. If they don't accept it, they may end up on the street spending their whole lives blaming their problems on someone else. But if they can accept that their reason for being here is their fault, then they can succeed. We give them a horizon to shoot for. The rest is up to them."

Despite his success back then, Harvey, whose teams combined to go 73-1 in his two seasons at San Jacinto, would later be ruled ineligible at St. John's, missing the 1988-89 season before coming back to lead the Redmen into the 1990 NCAA Tournament. And Scurry, too, would later be ruled ineligible for part of his senior season at Nevada-Las Vegas in 1989-90.

Still, at least those two got something out of junior college. They earned a chance to move on, to regain a foothold on the future that had always been theirs for the taking. Some, though, never learned enough to even make that jump. They got as far as junior college. But, they couldn't clear the streets.

The Terminator stood perched, momentarily, at the foul line, trying to analyze the situation. Three defenders, nowhere to go. The perfect situation for a man of dangerous means, a man with an outlaw heart who did what he wanted, whenever he wanted. He was a modern-day version of an Old West gunslinger; the kind of man willing to take his chances and roll the dice, but one who always made sure to have more than enough ammo to make an honest stand. He dribbled once. Then again. He wanted to score. He was going to score. He knew that. But why make it easy, he thought?

Why not instead taunt them a bit, like a cat swatting around a mouse before the final death blow is administered? One-on-three was no problem for him. Why not have a little bit of fun?

The Terminator dribbled again, then flashed a half-grin, the kind a gambler flashes when he has been called, knowing he has an ace up his sleeve, ready to drop it on the unsuspecting field, all of whom figured he was about to fold. He looked at one defender, glared at another. Glowered at the third. He said not a word. Didn't have to. With his eyes, he sent the message. *Go ahead, stop me if you can. I know you can't.*

He stutter-stepped one man, juked him, and slid past the next before there was time to react. Finally, in the boldest of moves, he took the ball right at the third—over the third, in fact—spun 360 degrees and dunked. The crowd erupted. People fell out of the stands, rolling about, as they laughed at his opposition. Jeered them, taunted them. Then, The Terminator turned and slowly trotted up the court. Mission accomplished.

Behind him, the trio—Eric Brown, a 6-foot-6 forward from the University of Miami; Eric Johnson, a future member of the Utah Jazz and the younger brother of Detroit Pistons guard Vinnie Johnson; and, Darryl Middleton, a 6-foot-9 center who teamed with Eric Johnson at Baylor University—shook their heads in wonderment. And disgust.

"Hey," The Terminator said with a certain bravado after the summer-league game in the gymnasium at the City College of New York. "Sometimes, you got to make a point out there. You got to show you're hard-nosed, that you're not going to take nothing from no one."

Ron Matthias, alias The Terminator, has always made it clear he isn't weak, that he will not be pushed around on the basketball court. He learned the importance of being strong when he was comin' up, when he had to fight to get his due in a household of eight kids, five brothers.

"They'd push me around," he said. "I was told what to do all the time. If I wanted something, I learned I had to assert myself."

To his detriment, he forcefully made clear to society outside the confines of the inner-city, the one which doesn't really understand the realities of the daily fight for survival; clear, that he would not be weak, would not be pushed around off the court, either. That reluctance to trust anyone but himself, that reluctance to back down even an inch, probably explains why, after all these years, The Terminator, can still, like so many other potential city stars who fell by the wayside, be found on playgrounds in Manhattan and the Bronx. So what if, once, he scored more than 100 points in a game?

In the end, he managed to do what no opponent ever seemed capable of: He stopped himself. And, in the process, he became a has-been before he had a chance to be an ever-was.

Before, opponents couldn't touch his game. Now, no one in basketball will. Too many problems. "I did have a 'rep,' " he admitted. "And, I still have one. Problem was I would get defiant. But now, I'm learning how much I messed up. I know now I got to keep my nose clean. Maybe, I still got a chance."

The future seemed bright back in Evander Childs High School in the Bronx. Sure, Matthias rarely attended class. But he averaged 24 points a game, leading Evander to the city title for small public schools. Even though he failed to graduate, he did manage to earn his equivalency diploma and a spot on the team at Palm Beach Junior College.

But, wherever he went, his unbridled rage forced people to shy away from him.

He was leading the National Junior College Athletic Association in scoring during the 1985-86 season, averaging 41.4 points, when he was dismissed from Palm Beach. It seems the school administration frowned upon his taking textbooks he received for free and trying to sell them to the bookstore; frowned upon his making sexual advances toward a female professor; frowned upon his showing up at halftime for one game.

Matthias admits his parts in the incidents. He claims he was merely being an entrepreneur, that he needed the money from the books to pay his tuition, and that the professor had it in for him because of the book situation and because he was an athlete. As for missing part of a game, well, he said he had a good reason. "I was a victim of circumstance," he said. "I had to visit my probation officer in New York." What's a guy supposed to do?

A 6-foot-3, 195-pound guard who ripples with muscles, biceps bulging, thighs taut, calves ready to spring him skyward in an instant, Matthias launches awkward, one-handed running shots from every conceivable angle and yet, somehow, makes them fall. He seems out of control, but has the knack for making the right play at the right time. He appears bored at times on the court, then on a moment's notice, explodes with the fury of someone who needs to prove a point to both himself and the world.

As a freshman at Palm Beach, he once scored 63 points in a game against Miami-Dade North, which had a front line that averaged 6-foot-8. He once scored eighty-one in a Rucker League game against a team that had Walter Berry. And once, back in 1985, he scored 107 points in a game in the Upward Fund Tournament in Manhattan. "Hey," he said, smiling his half-grin smile, "sometimes you get hot."

"The kid can't shoot a lick," said former Palm Beach coach Howard Reynolds, who was a graduate assistant to the University of Kentucky's legendary Adolph Rupp in the 1960s. "He just takes it to the hole. But I tell you, I seen a whole lot of good basketball players when I was at Kentucky. This kid was good enough to start for any Top Twenty team. Miami-Dade had a 6-foot-9 kid and a 6-foot-8 kid and that night he dared those two kids to step out in front of him. He has no fear of anyone."

Maybe that explains why Matthias received five years' probation on assault charges after he "punched out a drug dealer" in front of his Bronx apartment in 1985. He refuses to say whether he did so because he despised drugs or because he despised drug dealers who gave him a bad count.

Whatever the case, at Palm Beach, Reynolds said, that attitude fast made The Terminator a student out of control. "You would sit and talk with him and really feel like you were getting through to the kid. But once he got away from the office, on campus, and things went against the grain with him, he just lashed out." No one was spared. Not professors, not coaches. "Not even the president of the college," Reynolds said. "It was like he just went out of his way to paint himself into a corner and, after a while, you just couldn't get him out. Finally, he just had to be dismissed from school."

"They said it was in the best interests of both of us," Matthias recalled.

Until his dismissal, Matthias had been recruited by a host of major college teams. But seeing all the problems he got himself into at Palm Beach, those schools stopped calling. Saying he had learned a lesson and pledging to make a new start, he turned up in the fall of 1986 at South Junior College in Savannah, Georgia. Quickly, he made his presence felt—both on and off the court. He averaged 34 points a game, again, best in the nation. But the unruliness continued. "He passed class," said Brien Crowder, then coach of the team. "That is, as long as he went to class. And, on the court, you couldn't stop him. One-on-one, two-on-one, three-on-one; he can score on anybody, anytime, anywhere. His problem is that you have to follow rules. And Ron doesn't always like to do that."

The problems started small. Matthias had his girlfriend in his dorm room, which was forbidden under school rules. "You would tell him not to have a girl in the room and then he goes and does it," Crowder said. "You tell him not to do it again and so he does it again. And again. And again. Finally, he was kicked out of the dorms." Then, Crowder alleged,

Matthias became a "suspect" in several dorm break-ins, though he was never charged in any of the incidents. Finally, Crowder said, he was asked to leave.

Matthias was supposed to attend St. Mary's College, a school in Orchard Lake, Michigan, that belonged to the National Association of Intercollegiate Athletics. He never showed up. Later, he said he would attend St. Thomas Aquinas, an NAIA school in Sparkill, New York. Again, he never arrived.

These days, you can find Ron Matthias hanging out in the parks, still trying to make it. Chances are he never will. See, there is a lesson to be learned here, one about buckling down, making the most of a bad situation. The Terminator never learned that.

"I'm trying my best to keep things under control," he said. "I still have a temper, but now I try to catch myself. You've got to grab a hold, concentrate. A lot of people might not want to take a chance on me because of my past. But that's up to them. Either they're right, you're right or no one's right. That's just the way it is."

Based on the results of his first collegiate game, and considering the course requirements, Lloyd probably deserved those two credits at Mount Sac. The game was at Santa Monica College on November 19. And, though Mount Sac lost, 84-77, in overtime, it had little to do with Lloyd. He dominated the contest, scoring 30 points and grabbing a game-high 16 rebounds.

"He played every spot on the floor," said Santa Monica assistant coach Bill Smith. "Center. Forward. Even point guard. He brought the ball down, shot 25-footers like lay-ups. He had about ten turnovers and I'd say nine of them were because his guys weren't ready for his passes."

After that, Lloyd appeared in just one more game for Mount Sac, against Orange Coast College in Costa Mesa. It seemed, Victor said, that due to "a conflict" with his tutorial sessions, Lloyd had missed too much practice time. So, when he scored just 5 points with 8 rebounds against Orange Coast, Victor, who had welcomed Swee'pea because of a long-time friendship with Tarkanian, decided Lloyd would not be able to remain on the team.

"I decided that was enough," said Victor, who implied Lloyd had also created disturbances on the team, much like he had back at Oak Hill. "He had to make a commitment and his commitment was to get into UNLV, which I don't blame him for. When I saw the handwriting on the wall, I just backed off. When I found out he couldn't sincerely go to practice like the other players—I've got a lot of nice kids here—I could not deal with it. So I made that decision. And Lloyd agreed. He badly wanted to play at UNLV."

Though Lloyd said he would not comment on his situation at Mount Sac—"I ain't talkin' 'bout none of that"—by their own admission, Tarkanian and Warkentien also wanted Lloyd at Nevada-Las Vegas. As Tark said, "Our plan was to put him in junior college, watch him in junior college and get him eligible." And even Victor had said, "Hey, if Jerry sent him here, I'll make sure he gets him back." According to allegations leveled by two players at Mount Sac and revealed in an investigation by *New York Newsday*, Lloyd clearly understood to what lengths Tark and Stein were willing to go to do that—and he was willing to milk it for all it was worth.

When Lloyd arrived at Mount San Antonio, he was driving, according to records supplied by the Nevada Department of Motor Vehicles, a 1983 Dodge Aries K leased to an advertising firm owned by a member of the booster club at Nevada-Las Vegas. The firm was R&R Advertising. The owner was Sig Rogich, who had hired Lloyd and Steve Cropper as "runners"—or errand boys—for his firm the previous summer.

Rogich was a man of power. "Ronald Reagan used to call him all the time," Cropper recalled. "Marvin Hagler, Bill Cosby. Everyone who was anyone knew Sig. He had juice. He had an awful lot of juice."

He had, according to several published reports, been "instrumental" in bringing Tarkanian to Nevada-Las Vegas in 1973 and was a man who later would become a Regent at Nevada-Las Vegas. He had helped a lot of folks secure gambling licenses in Nevada, among them Frank Sinatra. He also had been one of the three directors on the "Tuesday Team," which in 1984 had conducted the $20 million advertising campaign that secured Reagan's landslide election. Later, he would serve as the "quiet partner" in a team with Roger Ailes, supervising the television commercials for the 1988 Presidential Campaign of George Bush. Most notable among their endeavors were the negative commercials about the pollution in Boston Harbor and the tale of ex-convict Willie Horton, who had committed a rape after his parole by Massachusetts Governor Michael S. Dukakis. Rogich, in fact, would come to be among the "inner-circle" of White House advisors to President Bush. He would come to hold a position in the Bush administration. His title: Assistant to the President for Public Events and Initiatives.

Strange, how people are connected. In the fall of 1986, Lloyd Daniels—an uneducated basketball player from New Jersey Avenue in the crime-ridden, poverty-stricken section of East New York; a player who had been brought to Las Vegas via arrangements made through a convicted gambler who had served time in federal penitentiaries—was driving a car that just happened to be leased by a major national advertising agency owned by a future presidential assistant and one of the most powerful men in America.

As one school official said of Lloyd, "What power. I have never in my life seen anything like this kid. If he runs for mayor, he'll win."

Lloyd said Rogich sometimes even let him live at his house. "He saw the good side of Lloyd Daniels, when Lloyd Daniels was straight," Lloyd said. "You know how people see the good side? He saw the good side some days. He saw a lot of fucked up days, days I would call in, say, 'I'm sick.' And how can you be sick in a hundred degrees? But he saw the good side. When have you ever known a man like him, who works with the President, let you stay in his condominium with all big, fancy stuff? He even let me drive his cars."

According to records, R&R Advertising had leased one of those cars, the Aries K, through a firm called Master Lease Plan, which was owned by Norm Jenkins, also listed as a booster club member at Nevada-Las Vegas. Rogich said he had leased the car in June, 1986, when he hired Lloyd. Rogich told *New York Newsday* he had let Lloyd keep the car at night, but allowed other runners the same privilege, thereby distancing the school from possible NCAA infractions. He also said that the only reason Lloyd still had the car at Mount Sac, long after he had terminated his employment at R&R, was because of a "slip-up" in paperwork. "We notified the lease company that we wanted out of [the lease]," Rogich said, "and they said they would. They said someone else was going to take it, and that's the way we left it."

Still, on September 14, six days after classes began at Mount Sac, Lloyd was involved in an accident and ticketed for failure to decrease speed at an intersection in Las Vegas, according to municipal court records. He had been involved in a two-car crash in which his car passed another car, side-swiped it and left fifty-two feet of skid marks. The accident report described the car as a blue 1983 Dodge. The license number, according to records at the Motor Vehicle Department, showed the car was leased to R&R.

Little more than two weeks after the accident, Lloyd brought a car into a Chevron service station in Pomona, California. The engine needed to be rebuilt, according to the mechanic, Jose Flores. Later, a rental car company sent a truck to take the car, Flores said. On the work order, Lloyd had listed the car as an "84 DOD ERZ." It was his description of a Dodge Aries.

According to Collier, team members at Nevada-Las Vegas had always referred to it as a "cereal box car" or a "detective car" because it resembled the kind used by undercover police. Lloyd always responded by telling them that soon he would get a new Nissan Maxima. "He was bugging them about that Maxima, too," Collier said. "I know he was, because I was there when he said, 'Stein, when am I getting my Maxima? Rick doesn't believe I'm getting it.' He kept saying it. And Stein would say, 'Lloyd, just wait. Just wait.' Lloyd said, 'Watch, Rick. I'm going to have a Maxima. You guys rap me in my blue car. Wait 'til I get my Maxima.' "

Though Warkentien denied he ever promised Lloyd a Maxima, records on file in Pomona Municipal Court showed he was driving a vehicle registered to Warkentien when he ran a stop sign in Walnut on November 12. The vehicle, according to records supplied by the Nevada Department of Motor Vehicles, was purchased by Warkentien for $1,792 on November 5. The dream car turned out to be a motor scooter.

In the wake of claims that Lloyd had been provided with a car, two Mount Sac players—James Jones and Cletus Jarmon—said that, at the request of Gene Victor, they had allowed Lloyd to live rent-free in their three-bedroom apartment in Pomona. Jones also said that Warkentien would visit Lloyd at the school "maybe three to four times a week."

"When Lloyd first came, he really didn't want to [attend Mount San Antonio]," Jones said. "Mark was coming down constantly. Mark and Lloyd would talk. Mark would ask, 'Are you going to class?' Lloyd would say, 'Yeah.' But if Lloyd said, 'No,' then Mark would be on his case about that. The things that Lloyd wanted Mark to do for him, if Lloyd didn't go to class, Mark wouldn't do them." Jones said that Warkentien would give Lloyd clothes and small amounts of cash as rewards for attending class. Warkentien said as incentive he also told Lloyd, "If, in a year, your reading is better, your mode of transportation [may be] better."

Needless to say, the NCAA took an interest in the situation, which its investigators construed as a possible violation of recruiting rules—rules which, if broken, would give Nevada-Las Vegas an obvious advantage in the recruitment of Lloyd, whose letter of intent became void when he enrolled in junior college. After all, NCAA rules limit the number of times a coach can contact a prospective recruit to three visits at the prospect's school and three away from it. Those rules also bar a coach or booster from supplying financial aid or other benefits to a recruit, his family or friends.

For their part, athletic department officials at Nevada-Las Vegas protest the school and its staff did nothing to violate those rules.

"'I'll guarantee we didn't do one thing," Tarkanian said. "We were not involved in one thing. Believe me, we would not have stuck our neck out on anything on him. I mean, you've got to be a damn fool to think that anything with him wasn't going to be checked out, wherever he played. I don't care what school he went to. And particularly being us, there was no way we would stick our neck out in any way."

Warkentien, meanwhile, defended his actions because, as he said, he had only acted in his role as legal guardian. "It was all perfectly legal," he said. From a legal standpoint, it was just that: Legal.

Still, NCAA officials offered another opinion. On January 22, 1987, those officials informed Nevada-Las Vegas athletic director Brad Rothermel that the guardianship arrangement was not allowable, based on a decision by its Legislation and Interpretations Committee. That committee had ruled that coaches cannot become legal guardians of recruits, unless the guardianship was based on factors unrelated to recruiting—and that the relationship predated the recruiting process. In other words, Warkentien would have had to be Lloyd's guardian before he ever recruited him—"recruited his skinny ass," as Warkentien put it—back at Oak Hill. "The [guardianship] question has come up a number of times in the past, and the interpretation from this department has always been that a coach could not be involved," said Evrard, the official from the NCAA of the rule is now known as the Lloyd Daniels Rule. "It wasn't like this was the first time this was ever interpreted or reviewed."

Two months later, in March, the school administration announced it would conduct an internal investigation of the entire situation.

None of this, however, seemed to concern Lloyd. Neither did the final exams at Mount Sac, which were scheduled for January 21-28. He knew how badly people wanted him to play basketball. So, even though he left campus right after finals and moved back to Las Vegas to enroll for the spring semester at Las Vegas, when grades were posted on the glass-enclosed bulletin board in the administration building at Mount Sac, Lloyd was listed with the other students who had passed their courses.

And, Lloyd didn't only pass. But there, alongside the names of students who had aced courses in analytical trigonometry, bacteriology, microbiology, physics, foreign languages and literature, was the name: Daniels, Lloyd.

Swee'pea made the Dean's List.

Back at Vegas, Lloyd continued his new-found quest for knowledge. Now a full-time student at Nevada-Las Vegas, one who had acquired twenty-six college credits despite being illiterate, he was assigned classes in Elementary Composition, Appreciation of Theatre, Internship in Sports Management and Juvenile Delinquency in the Juvenile Justice System. With a bit of luck, it would not be long before he might reach his goal and become eligible.

Lloyd would also be provided with another chance, one that would allow him to acquire invaluable knowledge about the legal system and its inner workings. More interesting, the knowledge would all be firsthand.

9•Gone Bust

"Lloyd," the cameraman asked, as Swee'pea was escorted from the house to a waiting van by an officer from the Las Vegas Metropolitan Police. "Do you realize what you may have done to your career?"

Lloyd looked at him for a moment as it all sank in. Here he was, a burgeoning star, his hands now cuffed behind his back like a common criminal, an undercover officer holding him. He had just been arrested and charged with attempting to possess a controlled substance, rock cocaine. He appeared to be under the influence of drugs. His world was coming apart at the seams. Worse, he was on television, a cameraman from WVBC-TV Channel 3 filming his arrest for all the world to see.

Swee'pea lowered his head. This was real. There was no doubt about it. This was bad. From inside the van, where a handful of other suspects were seated, also handcuffed, came the voice of a man. "Fucked up," the man said, almost in assessment of the scene, as he watched it unfold.

"They're goin' to put me on the news," Lloyd said to the other detainees as he reached the side of the van. "They like that."

The officer guided him into the open side door and, as Lloyd ducked his head under the roof line, leaned in and stepped toward the crowded rear, he twitched and twisted his hands. As he did, his left hand slipped out of the cuffs, which were formed from a simple notched plastic band wrapped tight and fastened to bind the wrists.

"He's out of his cuffs," someone said. But Lloyd continued to make his way toward one of the remaining seats as if nothing had happened.

"Lloyd," the officer said. "Daniels. Come on back out here." And, as Lloyd backed out of the van and stepped to the ground, the officer grabbed his hands and called to another undercover officer. "You got some regular cuffs?" he said. "We need some regular cuffs."

For a few minutes, Lloyd was held outside the van. And, as others looked on, he presented a curious study of a man trapped between his mortality and immortality. What of his career, he thought. His future. What would happen now? He licked his lips. His mouth was parched. The cool, night desert air seemed to swallow and consume him as he stood there and waited for the next move. Was he finished? Was this how it ended?

115

"Oh, shit!" he said out loud to himself. He shook his head in self-contempt and cursed himself for being so stupid as to let this happen.

As the officers recuffed his hands, this time his wrists bound too tight for them to move, Lloyd watched the cameraman again focus in on him. "Hey. Yo, man," Lloyd said, as the light illuminated his face against the dark winter night. "Want to move that camera? You goin' to end my career."

"That's the idea," the man from inside the van said, adding a dose of his own wisdom. "It sells newspapers."

Lloyd was still a moment. "That's life, man," he said to the man. He shrugged his shoulders as if to indicate he didn't care. After all, he was here now. What could he do about it?

"Like I said, we'll get you," a female undercover officer told Lloyd as he was once again placed in the van. "Every time."

Of course, Lloyd was not the first basketball star ever to run into trouble because of problems related to drugs, drug use or the streets. Countless pro players had—from Denver Nuggets all-star guard David Thompson, whose cocaine addiction led to problems with the Internal Revenue Service, to Micheal Ray Richardson, the former all-star guard for the New York Knicks and New Jersey Nets whose addiction earned him the distinction of being the first player "banned for life" from the NBA. And playground legends like Earl Manigault, Joe Hammond, Fly Williams and Pee Wee Kirkland had often been arrested in connection with an assortment of crimes—from petty thefts to bank robberies—stemming from their drug involvement.

The streets have power. And no one is spared. Not David Thompson, not Micheal Ray Richardson. Not Lloyd, not Joe Hammond, not Fly Williams, not Pee Wee Kirkland. Not even a two-time high school all-American from Astoria, Queens, named Red Bruin—a man whose life was once described by a friend as "a picture from a storybook." A man whose fall said a lot about how a man's weakness can ruin his life.

Handcuffs and chains shackled the woman's wrists and bound her hands fast to her waist as she stood before the judge on what was a hot and unpleasant mid-summer morning in Onondaga County Court in Syracuse, New York. She had been charged in a homicide and, what with her attorney in the midst of making pretrial motions and without much place to go considering her state, she stood and watched, bored almost, as nearly indecipherable legalese was exchanged between barrister and bench.

The courtroom was crowded, near full, and considering the number of sinners present and the choice of box-like seating, formed to resemble pews, it could have passed as church during penance.

A legion of the hardcore sat, then, five together, off to one side of the court, bound by a length of linked steel and their common disregard for the law. Their times had come and gone and the decisions rendered had been largely unfavorable. Now they awaited their return home—to the steel bars, to the hardened beds, to the unclean sinks that smelled of urine and the toilets with their brackish water and no real seats.

Here, amid the world of the incorrigible, sat Tony Bruin. He looked out of place, more than just a bit, as he awaited his turn before the bench.

"Are you Abraham Bruin?" Judge William J. Burke asked, when Bruin was brought before him on that morning, August 4, 1987.

"Yes," Bruin answered, in a quiet, almost hushed tone.

"Do you understand," the judge asked, "that there are allegations that you were in violation of your probation?"

"Yes," Bruin said, again.

The judge looked down from his bench. He had piles of papers, which outlined the details of the case, but had little need to look at them, knowing quite a few of the details from personal experience. Still, he looked to see that Bruin, who had tested positive for drug use while on probation on drug charges, had just completed forty days of inpatient care and rehabilitation for a substance-abuse problem. He read the recommendations from a multitude of municipal agencies which suggested the man now before him had a chance, this time, to succeed in his full rehabilitation. Satisfied, the judge once again turned his attentions to the man who stood before him.

"You're a troublesome person to deal with," Burke said to Bruin in a stern voice, having announced that he had restored him to full probation, thereby causing him to avoid jail time. "You're a high-visibility person, looked up to by the members of the community. You have to make an effort to live up to that. I trust you will. I don't expect to see you back here again."

"Believe me," Bruin said, once he had made his way outside the courtroom and into the corridor. "I don't want to see him again, either."

How Abraham Anthony Bruin III came to be in court that morning was a tribute to the abilities of each new generation not to learn from the mistakes of ones previous. Because like Lloyd, like many who had become fallen stars, the streets once had offered him an easier, smoother road.

He had been the all-American boy-next-door and that was not rumor left open to interpretation, but fact twice proven if you believed the reports in all the magazines, which—despite the fact that one of his teammates was Vern Fleming, who went on to the University of Georgia and the Indiana Pacers, and another was Dwayne Johnson, who attended Marquette—named him among the best in the nation two consecutive seasons at Mater Christi High School in Astoria. He was the man with the untouchable game then, the man who seemed destined to soar to new heights.

"The elastic man," his coach, Jim Gatto, called him. He was 6-foot-4 with a forty-two-inch vertical leap. He could dunk at will, do just about whatever he wanted. "He could just go up and up and up and stay up," Gatto said. Scout Howie Garfinkel called him "the Benny Goodman of swingmen."

But, while all the attention he received for possessing such abilities was very nice, it put quite a strain on Tony Bruin. Subjected to the unrealistic expectations of others—as Jim Boeheim, who coached him at Syracuse, said: "There had been such incredibly high hopes"—Bruin, like most legends, turned out instead to be an ordinary kid who one day found himself up on a pedestal, only to find out he didn't know how to get down.

"I feel like I'm coming back from a war," Bruin said, as he sat in the office of his attorney, Donald J. Martin, after his court date. He seemed tired, used. "I don't know how to react, what people are thinking about me. I feel bad for the embarrassment I caused. I feel like I'm still on eggshells."

Court had reminded him how fast his life had spun out of control, how far he had fallen. He had once been Red Bruin, the man who had it all. He was the one who had been named to the Big East all-tournament team as a sophomore, the one who scored twenty-five points on national television against DePaul, the one who finished his collegiate career with 1,294 points—then fourteenth best in school history.

But what that all counted for now, no one knew. He had turned his back on the good will wrought by those accomplishments long before pro scouts realized he was a forward trapped in the body of a guard—Philadelphia made him the 162nd overall pick in the 1983 NBA Draft, effectively ending his basketball career before it ever began—and long before he ever pleaded guilty in May, 1986, to having sold $420 worth of cocaine to an undercover detective in Syracuse on two separate occasions in April, 1984.

Since he first began college and maybe, some said, since even earlier than that, he had wagered high stakes on his ability to withstand the seductive force of cocaine and, in a game of Russian roulette, committed career suicide. He had forsaken most of his options in basketball and forfeited a $20,000-a-year job as a youth counselor at the Spofford Juvenile Center in New York City after he was named in an indictment on October 28, 1985. He also paid the price in the loss of his self-esteem.

Under a plea-bargain agreement, he was given a probated sentence. Five years. Less than seven months later he was stabbed in what police termed a drug-related incident. On March 21, 1987, he again tested positive for drug and alcohol usage—in violation of his probation—and underwent rehabilitation at the Benjamin Rush Center in Syracuse. What he had when he emerged was nothing. He was twenty-five years old and in debt, the unmarried, unemployed father of a three-year-old son.

"How this happens is hard to figure out," said his father, Abraham Bruin, Jr., who worked as a laborer on Rikers Island.

Because of where he worked, the elder Bruin had been more aware than most parents about the dangers of the streets. While Lloyd and others had no parents to teach them right from wrong, the elder Bruin would tell his son to be careful. He would see those of bad influence, of bad faith, and warn his son about the dangers of association. He assumed that the message had gotten through. He assumed wrong.

"You know," he said, "every day on the streets of New York there are hundreds of kids selling drugs. Near our apartment, on 36th Avenue, there are five, six kids every morning. The same on 35th Avenue. The same on 34th. And, this is Astoria. A good neighborhood. I used to see those kids and wonder how come nobody stopped them. Then I realized they have parents, too, and they couldn't stop them. After all, I didn't see it coming."

"It is a real scary thing," said Robert Czaplicki, commissioner of probation for Onondaga County and one of those officials who recommended Bruin be restored to full probation. "Tony is the kind of guy who, if you ever met him, you'd say, 'This is not a bad guy.' Now, I'm not a believer that someone else is at the root of your problems. But, I think it is real easy to see how this could happen to him or someone in his situation.

"We put athletes on a pedestal they may not deserve. They're subjected to a dream world. Everyone told Tony he would be the next Dr. J. Then, when it didn't pan out, what did he have left?"

The undercover detectives at first thought their eyes had deceived them. Just a few hours earlier on February 9, 1987, the narcotics officers from Metro Police had staged a raid on the pink-and-white single-story house on Clayton Street in the downtrodden section of north Las Vegas and had seized "several" cigarettes laced with PCP, a "small quantity" of cocaine and had arrested four persons for selling drugs.

Now, having established a "sting" operation at the house, they watched as the latest of the clientele walked toward the door.

"Looks like we got trouble," one officer said.

"What do you mean?" asked another member of the surveillance team, not as quick to catch on.

The members of Nevada-Las Vegas basketball team were well known in the community, almost as famous as the stars on The Strip, if not more so it seemed at times. It was no surprise, then, the first officer had immediately recognized the man headed toward the door of the crack house. After all, at 6-foot-8, he was hardly inconspicuous. And, he wore a sweatshirt that read "UNLV Runnin' Rebels" and a hat that read "N.C. State Wolfpack."

This was the prospective big-time recruit almost everyone in this town had heard about. The one Tark had spoken of time and again.

"Lloyd Daniels," the surveillance officer mumbled under his breath, as Lloyd walked toward the front of the house and knocked on the door.

No sooner had he said the name, than an undercover officer answered and the attempted purchase commenced—recorded on a video camera in the room. "Is Neil there?" Lloyd asked, already on tape.

"No," the officer said.

"Well, I need a rock," Lloyd said. "I want a rock."

According to Lt. Jerry Keller, head of the department's street narcotics unit, Lloyd then paid the undercover officer inside the house $20 in an attempt to purchase the crack, known on the streets as rock. He was arrested on the spot, one of sixty busted during the sting operation.

"Lloyd Daniels appeared to be under the influence of a controlled substance," the police report read. "Based on [his] actions—[he was] for example, very talkative, fidgety, licking his lips and constantly sniffling—and physical signs such as dilated pupils, red and runny nose, it appeared that he was possibly under the influence of cocaine. Daniels told [the arresting officer] he was under the influence of cocaine."

Lloyd was remanded to the Clark County Detention Center. It was there he came to realize just how serious this business was.

The charge of attempting to possess a controlled substance was a felony and carried maximum penalties of three years in jail and a $5,000 fine, according to Clark County Deputy District Attorney Bill Koot. The charge of being under the influence, also a felony, carried the maximum penalties of six years in jail and a $5,000 fine, Koot said.

Despite his well-chronicled history of problems, he had never before been arrested. Now, he was searched, fingerprinted, photographed, processed and placed in a holding cell to await a bail hearing. It scared him. But, really, not because of the jail cell. Not because he felt isolated or because he felt like that scared little kid who had been left to fend for himself. And, not because of the possible jail term that awaited him, if convicted.

Rather, he said, it was because—based on his experiences back at Andrew Jackson—he knew what the newspapers might do.

"I ain't goin' to lie," Lloyd said. "Jail didn't scare me. You know what scared me, know what hit me the hardest? When I realized it would be in the papers, nationwide. I swear to God on my mother's grave, if they had just kept that quiet, I would have goed out the next day and got high. What shook me up was when I realized it was goin' to be in the papers and everybody would know, that my grandmothers, that Ronnie would know. I told the cops, I swear to God, I told the cops, 'Beat me up, man. But don't have it in the papers.' I would do six months if they would keep it out the papers. I wasn't worried 'bout jail. I knew how to get over in there."

Lloyd remained in jail for some time, because it was hours before Mark Warkentien found someone to arrange his bail. Sam Perry's signature and $1,500 managed to get him released in the early hours of Tuesday morning.

"He was petrified and very embarrassed," Warkentien said. "He knows how many people have been in his corner wanting him to do well. Then, this happens. I told him, 'You're going to carry this with you, whether you get off or not, for a very long time.' "

Though he was scheduled to be arraigned in Clark County Court on March 3, when he left the building at least the worst part of the nightmare seemed to be over for Lloyd. "Once I got out," he said, "I thought I was home free."

Tony Bruin thought he was home free, too. After all, he had cocaine, enough of it in his possession to make a deal. He had been in the car with an acquaintance. The acquaintance had brought a friend. Bruin sold the friend $110 worth of coke. Another time, he sold him an amount worth $310.

But the friend of a friend, a man named Paul Pendergast, turned out to be an undercover officer with the Syracuse Police Department. Eighteen months after the two first struck a deal, Bruin was named on two warrants charging him with third-degree sale of a controlled substance and third-degree possession of a controlled substance, felonies which carried a maximum prison sentence of twenty-five years.

Police records showed Pendergast once asked Bruin why he sold drugs. "You got to make money somehow," Bruin said.

But there was more to it than just money. Bruin had first used cocaine, he said, because it was available, because his friends did it. He used it because he felt good and wanted to feel invincible, because he felt invincible and wanted to feel immortal. Later, he said, he used it because he felt depressed and just wanted to feel normal again.

"There are plenty of bad characters who missed their boat, who are not going anywhere, who want to steal some of your shine," Bruin said. "They're like parasites and leeches. But they're taking you to parties and there is drinking and drugs and they're giving it to you for free, and you don't think about it. It smoothes right in. Pretty soon, you're overcome.

"With cocaine, no matter how bad you feel, it makes you feel good. No matter how hungry you are, it makes that hunger go away. No matter how tired you are, it makes you feel like dancing all night. If you were a businessman you'd say, 'Let's package this and sell it. We'll get rich.' You just don't realize how bad it is for you."

Bruin admitted he "occasionally did coke" while at Syracuse. He denied rumors that he used cocaine in the locker room at halftime, that he had played games with coke stuffed inside his socks, that he had served as the middleman in several drug deals for other players in the Big East—a vague implication made by former Villanova guard Gary McLain in an eighteen-page, first-person account of his own drug problems in the cover story of the March 16, 1987, issue of Sports Illustrated.

There had long been indications that he might have had a problem, even though, as Boeheim, among others, said, "Tony was one of the nicest kids we've ever had in the program. I didn't know about him using drugs. It came as quite a shock to me." But, like Lloyd, Red Bruin—the man of whom Gatto, the coach, said "everyone who knew Red knew he was a nice, down-to-earth kid. Even refs liked him"—turned out to be a drug addict.

On probation after having pleaded guilty to reduced charges in his drug case, Bruin was ordered to donate 500 hours of community service at the Southwest Community Center in Syracuse. He was to work with kids, get them to overcome the obstacles presented by the neighborhood.

Bruin liked working with kids. They liked him. "I taught them ball," he said. "But I also tried to give them a message. I'd tell them, 'Learn from other people's mistakes so you don't have to go through what I went through.' I figured if you could talk to ten, you might be able to reach one."

"I am strictly against drugs," said Carmellita Boatwright, who was the acting director of the center. "Drugs ruined my family and that was in the back of my mind when I heard about Tony and so I figured I wouldn't want to get to know him. But, as the months went on, I realized he was a thoughtful, caring person. Just a good person. He was the type of person who just took time. You take time with kids and they don't forget."

The community center is located on South Avenue in Syracuse, just down the block from Fredette's Lounge, the Tadros Market and Chicago Market, which long ago had its windows boarded to keep out the trespassers. It is not far from Rezak's Silver Star Grocery and the Pillar of Truth Church of God in Christ, Reverend Benjamin Jamison, Pastor—a parish more than needed to assist the sinners here, it seemed, seeing as how across the street was an adult movie theatre sandwiched between the Tippin' In Lounge and an enterprise known as J+J Liquors. Near the center, on Marginal Street, folks lay in the littered grass in the park, drinking at the otherwise respectable hour of three-thirty in the afternoon.

Faced with the constant assault on his senses, the constant temptation, Bruin gave in to his weaknesses. He forgot to listen to his own advice.

The trouble occurred in the wake of a car accident, when Bruin received $2,000 from his insurance company. That same day, he had a fight with his longtime girlfriend, Tracey Johnson, the mother of his son. Angered, he cashed the check and headed for a local club which, according to Czaplicki, was a known drug location. There, Bruin met a man named Phillip Stokes, and the two went back to his house—allegedly to do some coke.

Not long after midnight, two men wearing ski masks broke into the house and demanded Bruin give them all his cash. According to Stokes, Bruin told the two would-be robbers, "Hey man, I got cocaine here. You don't have to do this." Then, he said Bruin stood and said, "Hey, I'll give you some money."

But instead of turning over the cash, Stokes said, Bruin rushed the pair as he yelled, "Let's get them." Problem was, the pair turned out to be Elmer (Butch) Stokes and his brother, Leroy, who, in a move of comic proportions, had set up their own brother in a desperate effort to rob Bruin.

Leroy, holding a knife, slashed Bruin in the arm and he lost a significant amount of blood as the assailants ran off. Later, under threat that their younger brother would testify against them, Elmer and Leroy both pleaded guilty—Elmer to charges of second-degree robbery, Leroy to attempted first-degree assault. Because the situation was viewed as a one-time incident, Bruin remained as a worker at the community center, but was ordered to submit to regular drug testing.

"Think about what happened," Boatwright said. "He was arrested for a drug problem, then he comes into an area with all the poverty, drugs. I don't think it was wise to put him in that environment. It just don't seem right to have put him there. There was too much temptation."

It was a delicate situation, one Boatwright understood from firsthand experience. She had seven children. One daughter, she said, worked for a lawyer. One son, she said, was in prison on robbery charges stemming from his involvement with drugs. Her husband, she said, had been a drug addict when he died. Like Bruin, she knew the pain.

"The thing is you have to remember that all these addicted folks got a problem, that they are really just like you and me," she said. "They have the same weaknesses. Maybe, the problem was they just didn't want what society said they should have. Maybe, they just didn't know what it takes to become a success or how to handle the disappointment when they failed.

"When my husband died," she said, "I saw junkies and winos come to pay their last respects. Anytime a junkie takes time from a fix or a wino takes time from a drink to come see a man in a coffin, that person can't be all bad. Must have a bit of good in him to pass them things up.

"Like, I'll never forget this wino I always used to see in the neighborhood. Used to call me 'lady with the smile.' One day he said, 'Hey, lady with the smile, how come you ain't smilin' today?' I said, 'I ain't got no money to pay the grocer.' He said, 'Don't worry. I'll take care of it.' When I went to pay the grocer the next time, he said, 'It's taken care of.' That wino had come and took care of my bill. I haven't seen him since that day. But that shows you how there can be good and bad in every man. I always say, don't never look down on a man, unless you stoppin' to pick him up."

With that in mind, Boatwright would sit down and talk on a regular basis with Bruin. She would give him advice, lend him support.

"I had no direction," Bruin said. "And the problem was, every time I got that empty feeling, I went to look for 'those guys.' "

The relapse came in late March and early April, 1987, just after the story by McLain. Bruin tested positive for drug and alcohol use on three separate occasions and was ordered into the in-patient drug treatment program.

"Red is a very honest and moral person, but he got a little frustrated with some of the things in his life," said Hank Carter, who runs a charity basketball game in New York called the Wheelchair Classic and who had known Bruin since his days at Mater Christi. "He saw that golden piece over the rainbow and then, when he didn't get it, well, he gave in to temptation. I see that every day in my community. What you have to learn is to keep doing the right thing. If you're consistent with it, they can't get to you.

"But you have to continue asking yourself, 'Who am I hurting by doing this?' If you know the right answer, you'll stop."

It isn't always quite that simple, though. For Tony Bruin the road has been long and hard. He understands how fragile his situation remains, will remain, and uses that knowledge to make a strong commitment to himself and to his future. "I used to be happy-go-lucky and that was my problem," he said. "I trusted people. You had to do wrong by me before I would write you off. Now, I'm more cautious, more of a realist.

"I have no room for stumbling now. I have to say, 'No.' The things I did can't cause you nothing but trouble. I know that now. The thing is, when the spotlight is on you at a young age like that, you immediately think everyone is your friend. You don't see all the angles. You don't realize this guy might have a friend who's an agent, that this guy might hope you get into a college so he can go along, too, and get a coaching job, that this guy may want to deal you drugs. You lose perspective. All of a sudden, ten White Castle hamburgers don't satisfy you any more. You want lobster. The hard thing is to learn to be strong. I think I've learned that."

"You know," Boatwright said, "when you have kids, you have these dreams that the boys will grow up to be doctors, lawyers, have good jobs and that the girls will grow up and get good jobs or find a good man and get married. Nowadays, in this world, it seems like you just got to hope that the boys grow up to be boys and the girls grow up to be girls."

As Abraham Bruin said, "If Tony hadn't gotten arrested, who would have ever known this was happening? If Len Bias hadn't died, who would have ever known about his problem? He would have been in Boston, just another all-American. It makes you realize this can happen to anyone. It happens down on the stock market. Geraldine Ferraro was running for Vice President of the United States and it happened to her son. As a parent, that's scary. You start to think maybe there is nothing you can do."

There was nothing Lloyd could do. The news footage of his arrest had been shown on television that night and had been reported the following day in newspapers from coast to coast. But despite the evidence against him—as Sgt. Ed Pitchford of the street narcotics unit said, "It's not the strongest case, but it's not the weakest case, either"—and the bad publicity, Lloyd maintained that the incident was a misunderstanding.

"This is somethin' serious," he said. "But I'll be all right, 'cause this was nothin' I done. I didn't try to buy no drugs. I was just in the wrong place at the wrong time. That's all it was. People can say, 'He fucked it up.' But I didn't do nothin' wrong. I didn't buy nothin'. I just got caught in the house. How was I supposed to know it was a crack house? If you had knocked on that door like I did, you'd be under arrest, too."

Truth was, Lloyd said, he had gone to the house in search of a former summer-league coach who was to have supplied him with tickets to a basketball game. Truth was, he said, he knew the man only as "Tony."

"I went there to get some tickets," Lloyd said. "I get to the door. I'm knockin'. I walk in and a guy said, 'What you want?' I said, 'I want Tony.' He said, 'Well, Tony ain't here and you're under arrest.' I said, 'What I'm under arrest for?' He said, 'Comin' to a crack house.' There was nothin' I could do. The motherfucker cop pulled a piece and said, 'Freeze.' I just said, 'Whoa.' I ain't goin' to get shot. I didn't know what was goin' on."

The truth also was, no one, least of all the members of the Clark County District Attorney's Office, believed the scenario. Especially since Tony Milner, the man identified as the "summer-league coach" Lloyd described, was arrested for allegedly attempting to purchase crack at the house just twenty minutes after the arrest of Lloyd. Especially since, just two weeks before on January 29, a sting operation at the residence had resulted in arrests and the confiscation of thirty-four "Sherm Sticks"—joints dipped in PCP.

"Everythin' was goin' real good," Lloyd said. "But this one incident could end my career. I thought about that when I was in the slam. I said, 'Think Lloyd. Think.' Whatever I do now, it got to be correct. My feelin' is that the papers are goin' to write what they want and people are goin' to say what they want. But my life ain't goin' to change because of that.

"They got people out there doin' murders and shit. As long as I know deep down that I ain't guilty, I'm not goin' to feel like I killed four people. When my day comes, we'll see who's right."

Nevada-Las Vegas coach Jerry Tarkanian did not share that optimism. He had always worried that Lloyd might be using drugs and had confronted him several times with his suspicions. Time and again, Lloyd denied the drug usage. "Give me a test, I'll take a test," Lloyd told Tarkanian. "C'mon, I'll piss in a bottle right now, Tark. Right now, I'll piss. Right now."

"It was only later, after the arrest, that Lloyd admitted to me he was just doing that to cover himself," Tarkanian said. "He told me, 'That's the way us drug guys are, Tark. You got to be a good liar if you want to get away with it.' He must have been a good liar, because we believed him."

Part of the problem was, like Jim Boeheim, Tarkanian was not an expert on drugs, on drug use, or, on the warning signs. He was a basketball coach and, lacking expertise on drugs, was misled by a seasoned con man. And, possibly, he didn't want to look too hard because, if he had, he might have found a problem, whether he understood drugs or not. And, no doubt, that might have affected his chance to win basketball games.

Now, confronted with the arrest, Tark understood the situation was bad—and not only because it had become apparent that Lloyd had a problem. Tark had a problem, too. A big one. One that called for damage control.

His team was 24-1, ranked Number One in the nation. He was still locked in that court battle with the NCAA. As if those two factors had not focused enough attention on the Rebels, the arrest of Lloyd had sent a host of curious reporters scrambling to Las Vegas to find out how a player with such suspect academic credentials could have been admitted to college.

Then, of course, there was the most immediate problem. Three years before, in an effort to clean up its image, Nevada-Las Vegas had begun a drug-testing program which tested, at random, the members of all its athletic teams. It was a state-of-the-art program, implemented two full years ahead of the program designed by the NCAA. The university had not only used it to benefit the athletes. It had also used it as a public relations tool. Players went around to the local schools and warned students about the dangers of drug usage. Tark spoke out about the perils of drugs. Players wore T-shirts that backed the anti-drug campaign being conducted by First Lady Nancy Reagan. "Say No to Drugs," the shirts read.

On one wall in the basketball office there was even a section dedicated to newspaper clips about the drug-related deaths of athletes. The most prominent article was the one about Len Bias, the all-American from the University of Maryland, who had died from a seizure caused by "cocaine intoxication" in June, 1986, little more than a day after he had become the first round draft pick of the Boston Celtics. Above that article, the coaches had placed a sign that read: "Are You Next?"

And so, Jerry Tarkanian was forced to make a decision. He could either wait for the outcome of the arraignment hearing and subsequent court case and then, based on whether he was convicted or acquitted on the charges, decide if Lloyd was to remain on the team. Or, in an effort to save face for both his program and the school, he could view the situation as a worst-case scenario and make an immediate announcement: That Lloyd was banned from the team regardless of the outcome of the charges.

On Monday night, when news of the arrest first became known, Tarkanian went with his gut instinct and immediately tried to distance Lloyd from the basketball program. "Lloyd Daniels," he said then, "is not a member of the basketball team or on scholarship. He was a potential recruit." That was all.

On Tuesday morning Tarkanian, left with no alternative, acknowledged that Lloyd was, for better or worse, associated with the team. However, he stressed that Lloyd would be dismissed from the team "if proved guilty." On Tuesday afternoon, after he had a discussion with school officials, Tarkanian considered the athletic department policy—which called for an immediate suspension of an athlete who has been arrested, pending trial—and decided he would, indeed, take those recommendations one step further.

"We have been extremely proud of our position on drugs and of the young men on our team who have similarly taken a strong stand against drugs," Tarkanian said in a statement made at a news conference in his office in the Thomas & Mack Center. "Lloyd Daniels is an extremely gifted and, basically, good human being who unfortunately appears to be involved to some extent with drugs. If the information we have is accurate, Lloyd can never be a member of the University of Nevada-Las Vegas basketball team. Lloyd Daniels will not play for the University of Nevada-Las Vegas."

With his weathered features, forever half-closed eyes that are outlined and accentuated by thick brows above and darkened bags below, Tarkanian almost always gives the appearance of being worn, haggard. His nickname, Tark the Shark, acquired for the way his teams have devoured opponents, is reinforced by the way those eyes never seem to focus on one thing—but rather seem to cut right through a man's very soul, as if he weren't there, the way a shark does when he comes at you in search of his meal.

Something about those eyes often makes it impossible to tell what he really feels. But, after most of the reporters gathered at the news conference had left and Tark sat and talked to a few stragglers, he seemed even more worn than usual, more weathered. Those eyes said he was hurt.

"Lloyd is very hurt by what happened," Tark said. "He made a big mistake. It's really sad because the guy is so talented. This was such a great opportunity for him to do something with his life. He had made great, great progress but he went the wrong way. It's unfortunate he made the wrong turn [because] we never had a player come close to his ability. He's the best basketball player I've ever been associated with, the most-talented kid I've ever been around. If I had a Top Ten, he'd be my first nine. But we told him, if he messed around with drugs, he'd never play here. All of our kids know our position on drugs. I won't tolerate that in any way."

Tarkanian said he made the decision after a closed-door meeting during which Lloyd admitted he had gone to the house to purchase crack. "How could you be so stupid?" Tarkanian asked Lloyd.

"I don't know," Lloyd told him.

"He was in tears," Tarkanian said. "He said he had never used anything harder than grass before. He said it was his first time. But he was there, it's on television. It's not like it was a case of mistaken identity. We had checked with Metro. They told us there was no doubt he was guilty."

"Jerry runs one of the strongest anti-drug programs of any school," said Lois Tarkanian, the coach's wife, who also assisted as an academic advisor and counselor for the team members. "Jerry believes very strongly that you give everybody a chance. But after the drug arrest, he just couldn't have Lloyd on the team." As Tark said: "We're in the third year of our drug-testing program. It would be hypocritical not to kick him off. I don't want to make it look like we're giving him an out." His decision, he said, was final.

It took less than twenty-four hours for Tarkanian to again reassess the situation. Wednesday, Tark softened his stand and announced that his decision to ban Lloyd had been a "knee-jerk" reaction. "You should never use the word 'never,'" he said. "It doesn't give a guy a chance to recover."

Tark also said he "could neither confirm nor deny" that Lloyd had told him he had gone to the house to purchase crack. As Tark told at least one reporter, "You must have misunderstood me."

"The thing Jerry said, which he probably now regrets," Nevada-Las Vegas athletic director Brad Rothermel said, "is that 'never' would Lloyd be a member of the basketball team. Certainly, if the conditions change, I would hope the institution would reconsider. If the charges are dropped or are reduced to a gross misdemeanor—and that's one possible scenario—and if Jerry offered me a recommendation, I'd take it under advisement. I'd discuss it with other individuals at the university, legal counsel and other people.

"I think very few things in life are final. I would hope in any case that, if the facts are overwhelmingly against the decision that was made, we'd at least take the time to reconsider our decision. We may not render any different decision, but we must be willing to consider other possibilities. That would be the truth in any case."

The reason for the sudden about-face was two-fold. Hearing the early news that Tarkanian would ban Lloyd from the team based solely upon his arrest and not his conviction or acquittal, Larry Brown said Kansas would still be interested in trying to "assist" Lloyd on his way to the NBA.

"It all depends on his grades and transcripts and things of that nature," Kansas assistant coach Mark Freidinger, who even called Warkentien "just to inquire about Lloyd's whereabouts," said during an interview on radio station KROL, Kansas, just after the announcement by Tarkanian. "[Brown] saw the immense talent he has. He knows his future is in the NBA."

Even though it was remote, a possible scenario that ended with Lloyd in a Kansas uniform bothered folks at Nevada-Las Vegas. They had already made too much of an investment in Lloyd, taken too much heat in the form of bad public relations, to have him appear in college for someone else. Besides, it now seemed that, according to David Chesnoff, the Las Vegas attorney who represented Lloyd, the charges against him just might be reduced—giving officials at Nevada-Las Vegas good reason to soften their stand.

Chesnoff was thirty-one and from Sea Cliff, an affluent section on the North Shore of Long Island not far from New York City. He liked to play basketball. In fact, he said he first met Lloyd during a pick-up game at the Las Vegas Sports Club. Chesnoff said he had given Lloyd his card, told him if he ever had a problem to call. It just happened he specialized in criminal law. "Federal criminal law," Chesnoff said, when pressed. "Sting federal."

Word Up. Swee'pea flashes his familiar sweet smile at age 13. Who'd ever suspect he was already a drug dealer as well as a seasoned con man? Family Pho

On the Prowl. Driving past a defender from Wyandanch, Lloyd is already thinking of his next move as he brings the ball up-court at the 1986 Martin Luther King Tournament in Nassau Coliseum. © 1986 David L. Pokress, *New York Newsday*

Can't Touch This. Head-to-head, Eli Whitney star Moses Sourry, who would go on to be a member of the 1990 NCAA Champion Nevada-Las Vegas Runnin' Rebels, proved no match for Swee'pea back in November, 1985. Lloyd had 41. © 1985 Bill Davis, *New York Newsday*

Kid on the Move. Kenny Anderson, hardly an average freshman, brings the ball up-court for Georgia Tech—a team he led to the 1990 NCAA Final Four in Denver. Georgia Tech Photo

Action Jackson. Mark Jackson, perhaps the third-best guard in Queens as a high school senior, became an NBA All-Star with the New York Knicks. Here, he drives around Isiah Thomas. New York Knicks Photo

Contemplation. Lloyd ponders his next move, as he holds the ball out during a game for the CBA Topeka Sizzlers in 1988.
Brett Garland/*Topeka Capital-Journal*

Postcard from the Edge. Perhaps already flirting again with illegal substances, Lloyd posed for this photo at Mount Rushmore while a member of the Sizzlers in November, 1987. From left, Lloyd, Chip Engelland, Ron Kellogg and Brian Rahilly.
John Valenti Photo

Jam Session. John Salley, who was underrecruited out of Canarsie High School, developed into a star at Georgia Tech and won NBA Championships with the Detroit Pistons, in 1989 and 1990. His idol is Malcom X. "He turned a negative into a positive," Salley said. Detroit Pistons Photo

The Goat. Earl Manigault, once called "the greatest player his size in the history of New York City" by no less than Kareem Abdul-Jabbar, reflects on his life in Rucker Park. Manigault Family Photo

The Elastic Man. Tony (Red) Bruin, the man with the 42-inch vertical leap, seemed to live on the edge at Syracuse. Syracuse University Photo

Slidin' By. Lloyd, always ready with a smooth move to get himself out of a jam, slides under an attempted block by Pete Myers of the Rockford Lightning for an easy lay-up. Brett Garland/*Topeka Capital-Journal*

Throwin' it Down. Swee'pea soars in for a dunk in the 1988 CBA Dunk Contest. Admittedly battling his cocaine habit, he didn't win. Brett Garland/*Topeka Capital-Journal*

Chesnoff said he had faith that Lloyd would be acquitted or, at worst, because he had no previous convictions, be granted a light sentence—more than likely, a suspended sentence or probation. That took into consideration that, while Lloyd had admitted to police that he had taken cocaine, he also had refused to submit to urinalysis at the time of his arrest. Without such evidence, the assistant district attorney would probably have to drop the charge of being under the influence for lack of evidence.

"I'm not a big fan of sting operations, because they have their own inherent problems," Chesnoff said. "The people involved often don't commit the crimes, though ofttimes the police running the operation report that they do. They want people to think that someone is doing something that they might not have done. They might as well have asked him to walk over hot coals and, if his feet were burned, then found him guilty.

"Everybody is eager to condemn a young kid. But I care about this kid. He is a great kid. I'm confident in Lloyd as a young man and hopeful that this rush to judgment—after all, his arrest was on television—will not prejudice his case, that people will give him a fair chance. I told Lloyd, 'Go back to school. Keep your head held high.' I don't think he has anything to worry about. I don't think we're worried about anything."

As usual, someone figured to save Lloyd, bailing him out of a bad situation. Of course, for some others it was already too late.

10 · The Life

The locals, cigarettes in hand, lined the walls of the building in search of an ever-fleeting patch of shade and a brief respite from the searing rays of the midday sun. They sat, leaned hard against cool bricks, talking, drinking, laughing amid the smell of this place—its odor, hung in mid-air, hovering over the littered asphalt, the smell old, unfaithful. It smelled of warmed beer and of stale tobacco, of urine and of bodies and of their sweat. It smelled like life, in all its impurity. It smelled, it seemed, of death.

Only the morning before, Len Bias had been buried down in Maryland. Friends, as well as strangers, had cried at his funeral. He'd been too young to die, they'd said, over and over; just twenty-two, in fact, when his life ended. Though no one will ever know for sure, he had, in a moment of weakness and in circumstances unforeseen, taken one false step in a life filled with an array of sure-footed moves.

If Lloyd's lapses in judgment and the lapses in judgment by Red Bruin had brought arrest and shame, then the result of the lapse in judgment by Len Bias brought the harshest of revelations in the early-morning hours of June 19, 1986. Less than forty-eight hours after he had experienced the high of having been the first-round draft pick of the Boston Celtics, who had selected him second in the NBA Draft, the former star forward from the University of Maryland had felt the wrath of "cocaine intoxication"—a lethal buzz, if you will—and died a sudden, premature death.

"Lenny was vulnerable," the Reverend Jesse Jackson had said when he eulogized Bias, using his death as if to measure the tragic extent of human fallout from illegal drugs, from their usage. "But, all of us are. It takes years to climb a mountain, one slip and we face oblivion. God sometimes uses our best people to get our attention. He called him to get the attention of this generation. On a day the children mourn, I hope they learn."

Message delivered, it seemed to have fallen on innumerable deaf ears that afternoon in the neighborhood that surrounded the courtyard of I.S. 59 on Springfield Boulevard. Little more than a block north of Merrick Avenue in Springfield Gardens, Queens, this appeared to be an area far different from the destitute environs of Harlem, East New York and the South Bronx. The school stood amid a well-ordered middle-class neighborhood, home to a host of single-family and two-family houses, as well as several relatively well-kept apartment complexes just a few miles from where Lloyd's grandmother, Lulia, lived in Hollis.

The illusion created—the one of a safe, serene environment—was shattered with a ride just a few blocks west, where Guy R. Brewer Boulevard crossed the Belt Parkway and headed north from Kennedy Airport toward Jamaica. There, an incalculable amount of drugs were dealt to both motorists and the walk-up crowd alike in an almost open-market atmosphere, distributions made by teenaged sellers in front of ramshackle storefronts, their routines, replete with "def" hand-signals, body language and street jingoism, hinting at a sort of blue-collar stock exchange—their business risks weighed between the sporadic patrols of passing police cars, instead of the trading bell.

Even here, even now as some kids ran an informal five-on-five game on the basketball court that bordered the school, herbal essence wafted over from the local viewing audience and doctored the air with the thick, pungent aroma of marijuana. Underfoot, the crunching of vials once used to store rocks—pellets of crack cocaine—provided physical evidence that one death, no matter how significant, would do little to change the nature of the beast overnight.

"It might get to certain people," Marlon Crawford, a sixteen-year-old from the neighborhood, said as he took a moment between games. "But not a lot. They'll keep doin' it, because a lot of people live to get high. They'll do anything for the fifteen minutes of action. Some might say no. It may get to the athletes with a chance to make it. But for the others, well, I don't think there's nothin' you can do."

If the cocaine death of Len Bias in Maryland, the arrest of Lloyd and Red Bruin, and the rise and fall of other playground basketball legends—and, the apparent apathy of the folks whose hopes and dreams they represent—seem to be indicative of a larger problem, it's because they are.

The statistics are grim. According to the Institute for Advanced Study of Black Family Life and Culture in Oakland, California, best estimates are that 1-in-10 black males in America will die by murder, compared to 1-in-80 for white males. And, the institute found that, for black men between the ages of fifteen and twenty-four, the leading cause of death is homicide—with one out of every three black men who die between the ages twenty and twenty-four dead a homicide victim.

Some are innocent victims of street crime. Some are not. But most have that common thread, related in some way, shape or form to drugs; to what is known on the streets as "The Life."

"Not since slavery has so much calamity and ongoing catastrophe been visited on black males," said Health and Human Services Secretary Louis W. Sullivan, one of the highest-ranking black officials in the Bush administration. "I do not think it is an exaggeration to suggest that the young black American male is a species in danger."

According to a study conducted by two doctors at Harlem Hospital and published in the *New England Journal of Medicine,* drugs are a significant reason why the life expectancy of a male born and living in Harlem is likely to be shorter than that of a male born in Bangladesh, one of the Third World's poorest nations. And almost half the deaths, they found, are linked to violence and drugs, as well as to acquired immune deficiency syndrome—AIDS—which, in most inner-city environments, is often related to drug usage.

Not that danger hasn't always been inherent in such environments. But, in the past, it came in different and much less caustic forms. It came in the form of poverty, which continues to plague the residents of inner-cities, and in the form of resultant poor medical care—factors which made life hard, even in the best of times. And, it came in the form of street crime.

But the harsh realities of the streets seem to have become harsher still with the advent of mass-appeal drugs like cocaine and crack, which have caused increased stresses on a societal framework already stressed to the breaking point. Black families have seen a significant breakdown in their structure. According to the U.S. Census Bureau, almost six out of ten black families with children under age eighteen were headed by a single parent, usually a female, by the mid-to-late 1980s. Factor in other components—including the fiscal crisis of the 1970s, which caused the closing of hundreds of inner-city community centers—with the lack of a father figure, as well as with impoverishment, poor education and low-paying honest work, and the result is that many youths in the inner-cities of America have become sidetracked by drugs, either as users or as dealers or both.

Surviving by making "cash money," as it is known, has brought with it a new social class: The new jacker. The nouveau riche.

New jacker dopeboys—and girls—are new-world entrepreneurs. They can make anywhere from $200 to over $2,000 a day making crack, selling it and stashing it, as well as a variety of other illegal drugs. Better still, to do so they don't need a formal education, don't need to conform to societal rules. All that is needed is the merchandise to be dealt—and, for new businesses, this can usually be purchased for a modest investment; about $1,000 for one ounce of cocaine, enough to manufacture crack pellets to fill about a thousand $5 vials—the street workers to sell it and the enforcement arm to protect against the threat of street-level corporate takeovers.

The risks are high: Often, the result of a bad business decision is death. There are rival crews, rival posses to contend with. But, considering the possible gains and considering the alternatives, more than a few figure that such entrepreneurial activity is worth the gamble.

"We are dealing with an economy that has its own rules and order," said one assistant district attorney in Queens. "It makes sense to deal drugs."

"Take crack, for instance," said Bob McCullough, Sr., a former member of the old NBA Cincinnati Royals and the man who directed the Rucker Pro Tournament, which matched pros against street players on an outdoor court in Harlem before it gave way a few years back to something called The Entertainers Classic. "These people are dealing with survival. Their attitude is, 'If people are willing to buy crack, I'm going to sell it to them.' They are not dealing with the morality of the situation. They are dealing with putting food on the table. Now, after a while, that changes. Then it becomes a quest for a new car, new clothes, something for their woman. But it usually doesn't start that way. It starts with trying to find a way to survive."

Drugs relate to inner-city basketball because more often than not the playgrounds reflect life on the streets. The lone difference being that, sometimes, if a player is receptive enough to want to learn, basketball can teach him order, something which often is missing from his life. It can earn him an education, teach him a work ethic and teach him responsibility. It can make him mature and stabilize a life otherwise filled with instability.

For those who need it—and not all do—basketball can enable them to sidestep the street element and find success. It can open doors that seemed to be forever closed to them. Still, faced with possible success, some fail.

"The thing is, out here, you've got to be strong-willed because you can't plan twenty years into the future," said Sonny Johnson. "There are too many ways to get sidetracked. So, what you have to do is set short-range goals. And, you have to be extremely careful."

Once, Johnson was a member of Young Life, a team that featured
Earl Manigault and was unbeaten for several summers on the playgrounds
of Harlem. He had played ball with Manigault in 1964 at Laurinburg
Institute—the school Lloyd later attended—and was the first black player
to attend Gardner-Webb College in a place called Boiling Springs, North
Carolina. Years later, he became recreation director for the New York
State Division for Youth in Brooklyn. His job was to work with kids who
had been through the judicial system. "One out of every hundred kids
at the center have skills to play college ball," he said. "But they have no
goals, no expectations. On the playgrounds, the number of kids who can
go on to college ball is probably more like one out of ten. They have the
tools to get by that street element. Basketball in the city, in particular,
keeps a majority of kids out of jail.

"See, kids at the Division for Youth talk about basketball. They don't
play it. But most of the kids on the playgrounds have decided that when
the guy comes and says, 'Hey, let's go stick up the candy store,' they can
say, 'You take "let's" and I'll stay here.' They have an alternative. Their
thrill for the moment is in the park, basketball. They have a work ethic,
where the other kid ain't working for nothing. The problem is the bad
guys find a way to pick off the good guys—mainly because you've got so
many bad guys."

He walked with a comfortable gait. Not an attitude walk, the kind of
strut owned by new jack punks and assorted common street hoods, but
rather a step like that of a man who had once been a king but who had
never quite found it to be his role in life. It was humble, dignified. It was
a walk that cut the fine line between self-assurance and self-doubt.

He was wearing a pair of old black-and-white Chuck Taylor Cons.
In one hand he held an unlit cigarette and, in the other, a brown paper
bag, the business end of an aluminum can stuck through its opening, tab
popped. He seemed quite in control of his faculties, and he was. But as
he approached, a sense of alcohol seemed to overwhelm the fresh morning
air, air as fresh and upstanding as it could be at ten o'clock on a humid
mid-summer morning on the asphalt of Harlem.

"Hi," he said, eyes cast downward in sudden, sheepish fashion, yet
with a voice possessing a certain strange resonance, low and with a gravel
edge that undercut its mellifluous tones with betrayal. "I'm Earl."

The man was an intriguing contradiction. There he stood, skin dark,
rich and deeply textured, body surprisingly lean after all these years, legs

still strong. But missing were two lower front teeth that seemed to make his face, when you looked close, appear hardened and worn. Endless railroads ventured across his arms, their lines darker than that of his darkest days, their maze of scar tissue an eerie sort of avant-garde reminder of the bad habit that had nearly killed him. His weary, weathered eyes remained fast to notice interest. Almost instantly he offered up his arms, the tracks.

"Curious?" he asked. There came a nod.

"It's from 'The White Lady,' " he said with what sounded to be a hint of self-contempt. "*Her-ron*. The old days.

"You know, on the streets I still hear people say, 'There goes 'The Goat.' He used to be the baddest dude in the world. But drugs brought him down.' People tried to show me the way, but I didn't want to listen. At the time, I really enjoyed doing it. Later, I found out it wasn't shit.

"It lost me my whole career."

Twenty-five years ago, it seemed Earl Manigault soared over every park in New York City. He could entertain the crowd, picking quarters off the top of the backboard during warmups. He could spin and shake defenders almost at will. He commanded a repertoire of moves unmatched and unparalleled. Though just a thinly-built, 6-foot-2 forward, he often challenged the likes of Wilt Chamberlain, Connie Hawkins and Lew Alcindor. He would even throw it down on them. Just because of what it said.

On the uneven asphalt courts blended into the fabric of a neighborhood bordered by a world of burned-out buildings and burned-out dreams, he dominated the playground game with a flair and panache that earned him a street reputation as a player with few equals.

So moved by his ability, Alcindor, later Kareem Abdul-Jabbar, once called him "the best basketball player his size in the history of New York City." To those who could not pronounce his last name, he became known simply as The Goat. On the streets, the name alone commanded respect.

"No question, but that from fifteen feet in you weren't going to stop this man," Sonny Johnson said. "From the foul line to the basket, if he put a move on you, he had you. Period. You had to get it in your mind that you had to face the embarrassment. He might put it down backward on you. Or anything he wanted. The other nine players, two referees and everyone watching knew he was the center of attention."

"I still remember the first time I saw him," Bob McCullough, Sr., recalled. "I walked into this gym and there was this kid playing with weights on his ankles. I said, 'Why don't you take them off, so you can move?' He told me, 'Oh, it's all right.' Then, like he was runnin' up a wall, he came in and dunked something fierce. The man could defy the laws of gravity."

But for some there is also a wicked gravity to be found on the streets of New York, its lure so illicit, its power so overwhelming that only the most strong-minded can overcome it. Earl Manigault couldn't.

As a result, he never made it out of the playgrounds and into the National Basketball Association, even though he briefly played in the Eastern League. Instead, he became a heroin addict by his late teens, a convict by his early twenties and a symbol, as predecessor to the likes of Lloyd, Joe Hammond, Fly Williams, Red Bruin, Richie Adams and a host of others, of everything both good and bad about the inner-city, its playgrounds and its players.

"Sometimes," Johnson said, "no matter how good a person you are, you can't help but fall prey to the sidewalks of New York."

Some men are afraid of success, some merely too impatient to wait for it to come, and so they fail. And some, like Earl Manigault, simply wake one morning and realize the reality that, sometimes, talent isn't nearly enough; that due to no particular fate, their chance for success has passed and, with it, their hopes and dreams. "The city," Manigault said, "can take it all away. For every Michael Jordan, there's an Earl Manigault. We all can't make it. Somebody has to fail. I was the one."

On the streets of New York there is a phrase used to recall the pure days, the time when life was unadulterated, uncluttered by all those societal constraints—things like the need for education, need for a job—that hold a man down. It goes, simply: "Back in the days."

Those words evoke memories of a simple time, the time spent on the playgrounds, the time when command of a basketball alone could make a man a god. For Lloyd, it was the time he spent alone at night shooting a ball. For Joe Hammond, it was the time he tap-dunked home a teammate's miss after sailing into the lane at Rucker Park while pros like Dr. J stood helpless. For Fly, it was a time when he ruled the parks, ruled college ball; before he wound up in the old Eastern League wrestling an 8-foot-11, 1,875-pound bear named Victor in a publicity stunt that earned him $300, even though as he later said: "I thought I won. But the bear got on Johnny Carson."

For Earl Manigault, it meant a time before two heart operations made him old before his time, a time before jail and a time before nodding out on street corners robbed him of friends. A time before heroin robbed him of most of his talent and, for a while, all of his ambition.

A time before he ever dreamed he'd lose his virgin veins. A time when the world was a playground and a basketball, nothing more.

Back in the days, Earl Manigault was as close to a god as a mortal dare be. With what are now referred to on the streets as "stupid-fresh springs," in other words, supple jumping equipment, it seemed he could almost leap to the moon if he wanted. And often, he did.

In Harlem, they still recall how The Goat dunked a ball backwards thirty-six times in a row to win a $60 bet. And, they still remember how the major-college recruiters flocked to its playgrounds, as the stories of his dunks and shot-blocking ability spread like the word on the street.

Manigault already was considered one of the premier players ever to play in the city when he led Benjamin Franklin High School to the Public Schools Athletic League championship in the 1961-62 season.

"The good old days," he called them. "We was young. And everybody was looking to make some sort of reputation."

Like Lloyd, he had honed his skills during endless hours of practice in the parks, borrowing moves from the best players of his day and working them into his game, making them his own. As a kid, he would sneak out of his bed at night, jump down the fire escape of his apartment on 95th Street and West End Avenue and head up to the park on 130th Street and Seventh Avenue—site of the old Rucker Tournament—to work on his game. His goal, like the goal of every kid in Harlem back then, was to earn a spot on the roster of a league team. When he did, he often faced the best the NBA could offer, from Wilt Chamberlain to Earl Monroe, known in the parks as "Black Jesus." Often, Manigault got the best of them, as did some others.

"There were so many bad guys out there," Manigault recalled with a fondness as he sat in Rucker Memorial Park, now located at 155th Street and Frederick Douglass Boulevard across the street from the Polo Grounds Houses—site of the old Polo Grounds—and a place so revered because of folklore and the legends it gave birth to, it remains one of the few litter-free parks in the city, preserved almost as a shrine. "Wilt Chamberlain, Dick Barnett, Oscar Robertson," he said. "When you went to sleep, you'd envision ways to be like that. Sometimes, you couldn't even go to sleep. My mom used to put me in bed and as soon as she shut the door, I'd climb out the window and go to the park. I seen Jackie Jackson taking quarters off the top of the backboard and I went home and dreamed about doin' it. I seen Connie Hawkins and Elgin Baylor and I said, 'Listen, I'm gonna do that, too.' You took a little bit from each guy and put it all together into your own thing."

Manigault was the master of the in-your-face dunk. Size of an opponent was immaterial. Like the time Manigault, Alcindor, Hawkins, Johnson, Jackson and Bob Spivey, who had played at Marquette, headed to Riis Park for a day at the beach and found themselves on the basketball courts.

"We didn't go to play ball," Manigault said. "I had on my shoes." But, finding his path to the basket blocked on one possession by Jackson and Hawkins, Manigault, shoes and all, still did what he did best. "I got the ball and I came through the middle. I went right down the middle on Hawk and Jackie and I dunked it. Put it down." Right in his face. Embarrassed The Hawk, the man who once failed to show for even one game during the Rucker League—a summer-league which pitted pros and legends on the asphalt of Harlem, the legends often getting the better of the pros—and still was named the league's most valuable player.

"If you were small, like I was," Manigault said, "you had to put fear in people." After all, every street game offered up challenge. It was man against man, image, ego and reputation at stake. "So many people would always be there to watch you defend your title," he said. "They would be callin' your name when you went on the court. I was always jumpin' around, 'cause if I didn't, my knees would have been shakin', I was that nervous. But you were always thinkin', 'How can I capture the crowd?' "

Back in the days, not many men could capture a crowd like the man who seemed able to outleap the gravitational boundaries of Planet Earth. He was the man who could do the unthinkable, something he called simply, "The Double Dunk." He would take off at the foul line, jam the ball into the hoop, catch it and slam it through again before being reunited with the ground.

It was almost a metaphysical experience.

Johnson recalled one game at Laurinburg when Manigault was offered a direct challenge. "We were playing in Durham [N.C.] at Hillside High School and before the game some guy came up and said, 'Who's The Goat? You The Goat?' Then he said his name was The Goat, too. He said there was only room for one Goat on the court. Well, Earl must have scored thirty-five that night and pinned the ball on the glass two or three times on the kid. After the game, the kid came up and apologized. 'You're The Goat,' he said."

But being The Goat, the man who could soar over basketball courts at will, was hardly enough to enable Earl Manigault to reach escape velocity on the city streets, where he proved to be all too earthbound, too human.

Dismissed from Ben Franklin in his senior year after being accused of smoking marijuana in the locker room, a charge he still denies, he managed to earn his degree at Laurinburg—he graduated second-to-last in his class—then continued to struggle in the classroom at Johnson C. Smith University, a traditional black college in Charlotte, North Carolina. But after less than one year there, and after a falling out with the coach, who was tired of trying to help him, he found himself back on the streets in New York, no future in sight.

"I never realized you could make a living playing basketball," said Manigault, who, maybe because he lacked maturity, maybe because no one had ever placed real demands on him, seemed unsure of himself—seemed insecure. "I thought it was over. That's when I went right to the bottom."

"It was really a matter of two years, when his game went from the ultimate to the damn-near ridiculous," Johnson said. "It was a tough time for all of us. It was a difficult time for him and damn difficult for the people close to him." And, it was all because of drugs.

David Daye wore a T-shirt that read, "Crack Wars: Use Your Brain." As he said, "I ain't 'bout none of that. Thing is, you got to understand what all that can do to you." He was just seventeen. He was standing in Montebello Park, not far from I.S. 59 in Springfield Gardens. The place isn't really called Montebello, it's just that no one can pronounce its real name—Montpelier. The name hardly mattered, though, because as Daye said as he and a handful of friends stood around under one of the baskets, "This park is dead."

It didn't look dead. It was clean, well-ordered. Off to one side of the court, two older gentlemen played checkers on one of those permanent stone checker boards that have long vanished from vandalism in most parks. Kids were playing ball. "Wait until dark," he said. "You'll see."

Dusk settled in and, with it, came a changing of the guard. Kids moved off, in search of refuge, as an older and more threatening, less concerned element moved in to take their place. Occasionally, a kid with a basketball still stopped in. But those figures, once in abundance, are now few and far between, it seems. And, it isn't that way only at Montpelier.

It happens at Marcus Garvey Park on Mount Morris Park Avenue in Harlem. It happens at Reader's Digest in Manhattan, Ajax Park in Jamaica, and at 66 Park on Stone Avenue in Brownsville, the park where Lloyd Free first came to be known as "World." It happens because a number of kids no longer feel it is worth the risk to go to those parks—to endure the threat of physical harm merely to play ball. It happens because some of the kids who once played ball have moved to the other side.

"You see heroin, cocaine and reefer—even whores—in some parks," said Daye. "It's the drug element. At other parks, it's more subtle. See, you want to play in a park where you don't have to worry about no one trying to take your bike, your bag, your money . . . *your life*. Sometimes, you won't even play because of that. But, sometimes, if you want to play bad enough, you'll go to a park like that anyway. Just so you can shoot around.

"Now, I ain't goin' to be no dealer," Daye said. "I got a job as an apprentice butcher in a meat market. But I knew kids who used to play every day. Really good players. Some started selling drugs, and now it's 'No more ball.' See, sometimes, you see someone driving a BMW and you're walking. You say, 'I could use some easy money, so I could get one, too.' Sometimes, the environment just gets to you."

Billy Thomas learned about the environment firsthand. Where he came from, on 143rd and Third Avenue in the Bronx—the Patterson Projects, once home to Tiny Archibald—trouble was something dealt with on a daily basis. It seemed as if folks sometimes had to fight their way in and out of hallways, guns drawn. Drugs and violence were commonplace.

It had been in those projects that Thomas, known on the street as Billy Bang, first learned basketball. Having developed his game, he took it to Lehman High School, and became an all-city player in 1975. But Billy Bang also found trouble—or, trouble found him when he became the victim of a street shooting—and, though he refused to explain how that trouble came about, he did explain that it changed his entire life, consigned him to life in the projects, robbed him of a future because it kept him from basketball.

It is terrible that kids see it that way, that they see basketball as their only escape. Terrible, because sports are over-emphasized—on TV, in school, in the neighborhood—and so they put all their stock in their athletic future as a means of escape, neglecting what is really important. School, education. As Thomas said, echoing a common lament on the streets, "I had one 'bad experience' and it cost me. I turned to the streets. It was my decision. I didn't think I had nothing else. That's the thing. You do a stupid thing and it could be the end for you. It's so easy to get sidetracked."

Around his neck, Thomas wore a medallion inscribed with two revolvers and the words, "Billy Bang." On his hand he wore a three-finger diamond ring that spelled out "Billy." That was just for show, he said. Because, down through the years, Billy Bang had learned a valuable lesson: That if you fight the streets hard, sometimes you can beat them. Or, at least, not let them get you, steal your soul. Now twenty-six, he was fighting back. He said he ran a summer-league team for little kids, a team called Orange Crush. He said that he had taken a stand against drugs and urged others to do the same.

"Like, I was goin' somewhere in a cab one day and the driver up front was doin' crack, while we were drivin'," Thomas said. "I had to say, 'Can you let me out, 'cause I can see you ain't interested in gettin' me where I want to go.' But, that's the problem. Nowadays, with crack and all the other drugs, it's gettin' harder to avoid trouble. It's like, if you have some money you have to decide, 'Do I buy a loaf of bread or drugs?' If you go to the store, maybe it will be one where you can even buy them in the same place."

Such is life, such is the environment in New York, where illegal merchants—some just kids, like Lloyd was back in the days—sometimes ply their drug trade sitting on milk crates propped against store fronts, or even, as Thomas said, from inside the stores themselves. And, such is life in New York, where even the best sometimes fall prey to the environment. After all, in a backhanded way the environment even got to Herman (Helicopter) Knowings, the infamous "Helicopter Man of Harlem."

Back in the days, it was said that Helicopter could jump so high that he once went up to block a shot—and wound up sitting in the basket. It wasn't true. But this was a man who could attain serious altitude. He could leap, could soar. And, often he did against the best the streets and the pros had to offer in the Rucker League. Earl Manigault said that one time Helicopter leaped skyward to block a shot, something he did with lightning quickness and amazing regularity, and found himself having been faked by his man. With no other options, Helicopter treaded air like a swimmer treading water, and hovered until the man who was going to shoot got called for a three-second violation.

"It isn't just a story," Manigault said, with admiration. "It really happened. I seen it happen. Copter could fly."

That legendary jumping ability allowed Helicopter to soar over his competition. Folks in Harlem remember with pride the summer of 1968, when Helicopter was selected for a team called the Colonial All-Stars in the Rucker Tournament. There was a game against the Rucker Pros, a team loaded with players, among them five players from the New York Knicks—Howie Komives, Nate Bowman, Emmett Bryant, Willis Reed and Freddie Crawford, who also managed the Pros. It seemed like it would be an overwhelming match for Knowings, who was 6-foot-5. But, it wasn't.

"I'm not going to mention names, because they are my friends," Bob McCullough, Sr., once said. "But there was one play where the Pros brought the ball down, and Copter blocked a shot. *Whap*! The guy passed the ball to a teammate, who tried to shoot. *Whap*! Blocked again. The next guy passed the ball to a third Pro. *Whap*! Blocked again. Get the picture? Copter blocked three shots in a row by professionals."

But, while Helicopter could soar over the parks, like Manigault his ability did not guarantee him fame and fortune. Folks in the NBA wouldn't give him a shot, because he was a center—one who was too small for the pros, one they said couldn't shoot well enough to become a small forward or guard in their league. And so, though he briefly played in the Eastern League and with the Harlem Globetrotters, Helicopter had to get a job that made him just another mortal. And, he paid the price for not being able to escape his environment, the one that consigned him to the fate of the working man; a man who, unlike a lot of other legends, was playing by the rules.

The founder of his own taxi cab company, Helicopter was driving his car to earn a living one night in April, 1980, when another car jumped a divider on the 145th Street Bridge. It proved to be the one obstacle he couldn't rise above. The car crashed into his cab. Herman Knowings died at age thirty-seven.

You have to wonder, then: What does it take to survive?

"That's why education is so important," Ron Brown said. "I always tell kids, 'If you can play ball in New York, you can go to college in the United States. And, if you can go to college in the United States, you can get an education, make a better life and get out of the environment.' It's that simple."

Brown, the assistant basketball coach at West Virginia, came up in the Bronx River Projects on 174th Street and Bronx River Avenue. It wasn't the worst neighborhood in the world. Still, it was one where advice—stuff like, "Don't sit by the window at night with the shades up," the understanding being that it only makes you a target—was geared toward survival.

Unlike a lot of folks, Brown listened to the advice. He went to school. He got an education at Evander Childs, then at the John Jay College of

Criminal Justice. He worked for an organization called the New York City Criminal Justice Agency assisting the impoverished who had run afoul of the law. And eventually he became a basketball coach, first at Pratt, a small college in Brooklyn, and then at West Virginia University. Now, the first thing he tells a recruit—and even players whom he doesn't recruit—is this: "I went through the same doors you want to go through. I sat in the same desks you want to sit in. Listen to me: Get an education.

"You try to reach who you can," he said. "If you don't get an education, you lose. If you leave school without a degree, the only place you're going is home. Too many players came out of the playgrounds in New York City and didn't make it because they didn't realize what was important. They thought that basketball was important. But basketball is not the message. Education is the message. Basketball is the ticket to get on the train to where you want to go. But education is the train you want to get on.

"I always ask kids, 'Where do the smart kids in the classroom sit?' And, they say, 'Up front, coach.' I tell them, 'See, that just shows that you have to be where you need to be to find success.' If you want religion, you don't get it in the gas station. If you want food, you don't find it in church.

"A lot of guys from New York City didn't make it. Guys who went to jail, guys who were on drugs. You don't even have to mention names. People in the streets know who they are. The problem is, often you're around people who are just interested in getting by. You lose perspective of what is important. But if you've got an education, you got a chance to be successful. If you keep your record clean, you got a chance to be successful. If you stay away from drugs, you got a chance to be successful. But, if you strike out in any of those areas, you don't have a chance. I've seen a lot of players who were good on the courts, but who didn't have enough life components to stay out of trouble off them. It's sad. Real sad."

Bricks litter the abandoned, rubble-strewn lot on Frederick Douglass Boulevard in Harlem, a scene comparable to Dresden, Stalingrad or Hiroshima in the aftermath of World War II. Razed high-rise buildings line the lot, their remains ankle-deep. Others that still stand remain only as empty shells, long ago converted from living space to space for the walking dead; a place for shooting up, a place for crack, a place to do the bad thing. "Heroin Heaven," Manigault said, as he pointed out the window of the car, pointed to the surroundings. "This is where I shot all my *her-ron*. Right here. Every grain of it. This is where I fucked up my career."

Near 115th Street, reminders of what a lost world this is are visible just feet from the wreckage of those buildings. In war-torn, war-ravaged cities, men who had no role in the destruction walked in tatters, rags, scouring for morsels to feed aching, empty stomachs, searching for the strength to reclaim what they once had. Here, some men sit back and let it all be, trying to make the best of a bad situation they figure they can't change, opting to sometimes spend the equivalent of yearly salaries on vanity gold, fine clothes, kangol hats and the latest mode of transportation in an effort to blot out the real problem: Their environment, their lives.

"You got to understand, there's a lot of frustration here," Manigault said. "Life here is hard. That's why some of the richest guys in the world come out of this neighborhood. If you're willin' to go in for 'The Fast Life' as your means of escape, you can make five-thousand dollars a day on the street. Sometimes, people just see that as their way out. You have all your sucker friends. There is jewelry, cars, women. You don't think consequences. You go for the easy money. There is not a block in Harlem that doesn't have the bad stuff. Matter of fact, here the bad stuff is all around us.

"But, while the bad stuff is on every block in Harlem, on every other block there are at least five ballplayers, I guarantee you, badder than any cat in the NBA. They could all be there." That they're not is due to human frailty.

After all, it is here Manigault went for the life, too, realizing his lack of foresight meant he was never going to make it off the playgrounds. Realizing that, for him and so many others, the courts where they earned their reputations were all that stood between fame and a life destined to end in a potter's field. From being anonymous, forgotten men.

Soon, he had a $100-a-day habit. And soon, he was going out on the streets, down to the garment district to steal mink coats, out to the mom-and-pop groceries to take whatever he could from the register. Seeing that, soon some of the local dealers, out of compassion, simply began to give him the goods. "I was The Goat," he said. "They told me that I could have as much as I wanted. They didn't want to see me stealin' for it."

In 1969, the year the Milwaukee Bucks made Abdul-Jabbar a rookie millionaire in the NBA, Manigault was first arrested for possession and spent eighteen days in the Manhattan House of Detention, otherwise known as the Tombs. There, he kicked his drug habit and overcame his desire to commit suicide. But that did not save him from a transfer to Green Haven, a medium security prison in upstate New York, where he served sixteen months of a five-year sentence. Later, in 1977, he gave in and started using drugs again and one day, with nothing else better to do, he hopped into a car with some friends and headed off to do a robbery in the Bronx. Where Manigault ended up was in the Bronx House of Detention and, later, the maximum security correctional facility in Ossining, a prison better known as Sing Sing.

"We had a plan to steal six million dollars," Manigault said. "But we got busted. They figured I was the ringleader. I got two years."

Twenty-five years after he first made his reputation, Earl Manigault remains a legend on the streets of New York. A shy, almost apprehensive speaker, one whose speech shows great care and forethought, he displays a gentle, human quality. That alone makes it difficult to understand how he once turned to muggings and robberies to support his habit. It also fills you with compassion for a man who wants no pity, a man who never physically hurt anyone except himself, but then hurt himself so badly that it cost his most valuable possessions. His ability and, for a time, his pride.

It makes you cry for the time in 1965, when he returned to the Rucker Tournament, the place where he made his reputation, only to lose his balance, stumble twice and fall, embarrassed. It makes you wonder about the self-inflicted pain he must have endured, earning his only shot at a pro career in 1970—it was shortly after Bill Daniels, then owner of the Utah Stars in the American Basketball Association, read about him in *The City Game* by Pete Axthelm—only to discover that, at age twenty-five, he had abused his body so badly it would no longer respond to his commands.

Manigault, a man of compassion, a man without a sense of self-pity, seems to find the bright side to it all. He smiles, nods appreciatively whenever he returns to Harlem and the people stop to notice, ofttimes whispering, "The Goat. It's The Goat." "The things I done comin' up," he said, "I shouldn't be here right now. Just as far as bein' alive, I appreciate it. I thank the Lord every morning. I'm the last of the crew."

He remains especially proud of his legs, which are clean, unmarked. Unspoiled. Not at all like his arms. "When the veins in my arms were full, it was tempting to go to my legs," he said. "But I always loved my legs. No matter how bad it got, I always went to another spot in my arms. I must be a rich man. Just look at my arms. All of my money is in my veins."

Then again, come from a neighborhood like this and, perhaps, the greatest homage you can pay a man is to say he survived. Earl Manigault is a survivor, albeit a struggling one. He lives hand-to-mouth in Charleston, South Carolina, where years ago he moved in with his mother, as well as two of his seven children, Darrin and Earl Jr. He headed South trying to prevent his life from again heading in that direction, too, trying to protect the interests of his sons. Now in his forties—"Forty-bucks, plus," he calls it—he works odd jobs, painting houses and mowing lawns.

He worked for the local recreation department before his heart problems caused him to be laid off for a time and, still, wherever he goes, he makes a sincere effort to advise both adults and children on how to avoid the dangers that felled him. After all, he is living proof of what can happen to a man, no matter how good or well-intentioned he may be.

"What I try to tell them is that they have a future," he said, as he walked through the park at 97th Street and Amsterdam, the one the locals now refer to as Goat Park in his honor. "They just have to give themselves a chance. I say, 'First, see what you can do out there. The drugs will always be there.' If that's what they want to do with their lives, do drugs, then they can always come back to it. But, if they give themselves a chance, maybe then they won't get sidetracked."

"He is a guy who I have a lot of respect and admiration for," Johnson said, "even after everything he's done. I respect him for kicking the drug scene. I respect that he gave it his best shot and was able to survive the streets as well as he has. I don't think there's an individual who has had to face the adversity he faced through the years and still looks so good.

"The older I get, the more I see kids today play basketball, the more I respect him and the way he played. I wish somebody had videotape back then. Because right now his game lives only in our memories."

The pole stands better than a hundred feet tall. It rises with a certain majesty and defiance above that old, lifeless lot on Frederick Douglass Boulevard. At its apex, someone years ago placed a basketball net. Legend has it that, once, Earl Manigault jammed a ball through that basket. He never did, of course. But as he said, "I'm the only man alive who could have done it. The only man." A moment later, he turned and walked away.

It was sad. But, what with Earl Manigault still serving as an all-too-visible reminder of what can happen, and what with Len Bias dead from cocaine, Lloyd and Red Bruin having been arrested for drug violations, all while the folks out on Guy R. Brewer Boulevard are still cutting deals, you have to ask what it will take to make people finally understand.

"Maybe people who seen these things happen to someone big in basketball might say, 'Yo, money, like maybe this can happen to me,' " said Rynell Calloway, as he stood on the court that afternoon at I.S. 59 talking about the death of Len Bias—or, as the cover of the June 30, 1986, issue of *Sports Illustrated* called his tragic passing, "Death of a Dream."

Calloway was a precocious, slick and streetwise kid. He was from 138th Street and Lenox Avenue in Harlem and had come to visit a few friends in Queens. He wanted to believe that the death of Len Bias, that the death and misfortune of so many others, would make a difference. But, he knew the streets, knew the score. So, in his heart, he had doubts. He was thirteen.

"There's peer pressure all around you," he said. "So much that it's kind of tough not to get involved in the life. But you have to have a strong mental mind. Sometimes, you can look out the window and see people die. You read about it in the papers. You have to know that you can get hurt, that those things is something you shouldn't do. That's why what happened to Len Bias is a 'dis' to all of us. We all have dreams that we can be the man, be in the NBA. He had his dream come true and he let it become a nightmare. Face it, the man fucked up. And, now we know we can't fuck it up, too. Thing is, it ain't always that easy, 'cause lots of people just figure, 'Hey, a little reefer here, a little crack there helps keep the doctor away.' "

All too often it is easier said than done. "Here's a guy, everything going for him," said Craig Davis, a twenty-year-old student at LaGuardia Community College. "Money. The Celtics. He was going to make it. He did make it. And then, he goes and kills himself with drugs. You just have to shake your head and say, Look what happened to Len Bias. Look what can happen to me."

After all, viewed from a distance, there can be a certain enchantment to the life, with its lure of material wealth and good times. But, more often than not, that promise remains unfulfilled. Because once its hooks have been set, a soul is almost never delivered from evil, but rather to it. And the usual result is that a life once of promise, of potential, is sapped of its strength and of its goodness, only to be left abandoned, ruined. Or worse.

Sometimes, a few are able to escape its clutches and gain a second chance. Sometimes, a few are able to survive. Sometimes, a few are lucky enough to be granted a virtual clean slate and a chance to start over from scratch. But precious few, however, are ever that fortunate. Lloyd was.

He had not died. He had been issued a warning, rather than a penalty. He had been granted a chance to make amends before it was too late. Lloyd still had his talent. He still had his youth. He still had a chance for a normal life. All he had to do now was make an effort to save himself.

Now, if only the message could get through.

11 • Topeka, Kansas

A cold wind blew hard across the frozen ground outside Landon Arena, its teeth gnawing to the bone despite the best efforts to keep warm. It was a vicious wind, the kind that stabs at you and saps your strength; the kind that seems only-too-at-home on a late November morning in a lonely, earthen place like Topeka, Kansas. Across the lot Lloyd raced the brisk morning air, as he made his way from the rental car to the offices of the Topeka Sizzlers. It was time for practice and, already, the sound of basketballs could be heard on the court inside the arena. It was just a few days before the start of the 1987-88 season in the Continental Basketball Association. Everyone seemed a bit anxious. Lloyd, just a month out of in-patient rehabilitation for his substance abuse problem, had barely made it on time.

Barred from playing at Nevada-Las Vegas, Lloyd had signed with Topeka in September. Faced with possible jail time, Lloyd agreed to a plea bargain. Under the terms of the agreement, reached in June, Lloyd pleaded guilty in Clark County District Court to a misdemeanor charge of attempting to purchase a controlled substance. He was ordered to enter a three-month drug rehabilitation program and undergo urinalysis on a twice-weekly basis at a local hospital. He was also fined $600, as well as $200 in court costs.

A month after entering the program, Lloyd tested positive for cocaine and marijuana. Because he had violated the terms of his court agreement, Lloyd was faced with additional penalties. David Chesnoff, the Las Vegas attorney who represented Lloyd, worked out a deal. He had contacted Sizzlers owner Bernie Glannon, who knew Jerry Tarkanian, and asked if he was interested in Lloyd. Glannon flew out to Las Vegas, met with Chesnoff and Lloyd. He also spoke to Larry Brown, who, Glannon said, was "extremely high on Lloyd." A plan was worked out in which Lloyd received permission from the court to enter a rehabilitation program in Topeka.

In August, he entered the Keystone Program at Memorial Hospital. It was a twenty-eight-day program. According to hospital spokeswoman Debbie Norton, Lloyd completed it in forty-five days.

"The fact that it took him forty-five days to complete the program,"

151

Norton said, "should in no way reflect a relapse. Some people just take longer than others. Treatment is a very personal kind of thing. You have to identify the problem, then you have to find the right way to treat it. Addiction is a disease and, because it is a disease, that means that it may be different with each person. There is no thirty-day quick-fix here."

The Keystone Program uses group therapy as part of its treatment and is recognized by both Alcoholics Anonymous and Narcotics Anonymous. It also has an outpatient aftercare program that lasts fifteen months, but is not mandatory. Norton said that, in the case of someone like Lloyd, who had a cocaine addiction, use of any kind of chemical—alcohol, included—might constitute a setback in his treatment.

"It's just too bad he is such a hot item, right now, so early in his recovery," Norton said after Lloyd was released from the program on October 7. "That puts a lot of pressure on him. It's a pretty difficult position for him to be in, because, as I understand it, if he suffers a relapse, a million people the next day are going to know about it. It won't be easy."

According to Brad Marten, a member of the Sizzlers' front-office staff, Lloyd understood how hard it would be. After all, as part of his contract, he would be required to submit to random urinalysis and would be asked to maintain his attendance in the aftercare program. "He said drugs were bringing him down," Marten said. "I don't know if that is just lip service, because he's pretty good at telling people what they want to hear."

What Lloyd said was what he had always said. That this was his "last chance." That he planned to stay in Topeka for two seasons, then move on to the NBA. That he had learned his lesson. "Topeka's not so bad," he said upon his arrival there. "It's not like I have to spend my entire life here. From what I hear, the scouts aren't worried about me on the court. All I've got to do is keep my nose clean, keep myself clean off the court."

And what, he asked, would be so hard about that?

On the court inside Landon Arena, rookie guard Cedric Hunter talked to veteran swingman Ron Kellogg. The two had been teammates at Kansas. Nearby, another former teammate, second-year forward Calvin Thompson, was shooting jumpers and Chip Engelland, a second-year guard from Duke, was joking around with Brian Rahilly, a center from the University of Tulsa. Other players milled around. Lloyd quickly changed into his gear and took a seat on the sideline between JoJo White and coach John Killilea.

"Yo, what's up?" he said, pretending not to notice their concern. Both men looked at him, then began a brief conversation, going over some game strategies. It was just after 9 a.m. Practice was about to start.

For a while, the team ran drills that morning. Then came a scrimmage with Lloyd at the point, White at off guard. It was a strange combination, the kid and the old man. Lloyd was just twenty, a free spirit prone to act on a whim and without a grasp of the fragile situation that surrounded him. A situation where one mistake could jeopardize his chances of making it into the National Basketball Association.

White, meanwhile, was a man who seemed to reek of conservatism, a man who understood the game within the game and had paid his dues and achieved success. A man who had seen his career come and go and who now was back in basketball more as a teacher than a student.

Lloyd was street. He wore blue leather jackets—"The real jimson," he called it. The real thing—sneakers and sweats. White was gentrified. Top coat, imported leather gloves. The best. He had made it.

White was forty-one. He had been a first-round pick out of Kansas when Lloyd was two. Lloyd had just six years on his eldest son. White had been a seven-time all-star with the Boston Celtics and had led them to NBA Championships in 1974 and 1976. He had come to Topeka not only to see if he could still play the game—a scenario which seemed somewhat of a guise, though he was still slender and graceful and his game still had its delicious moments—but also, it seemed, as part of the reclamation project whose final goal was to save Lloyd from himself. Bernie Glannon did not hide the fact that part of White's job description was to work with Lloyd. He was hired to be a steadying influence on Lloyd, who needed to be steadied. White went along partly because he wanted to investigate coaching.

"You've got to understand he never had to work for anything," White had said in an aside just before practice that morning. "People have always told him how good he is, how talented he is, and he believed that he could get by on that alone, rather than trying to develop and refine that skill. He doesn't understand the seriousness of what he has, of where he is.

"He wants to be something, but doesn't understand the price you have to pay to get there," he said, his voice serious. "Part of the reason I'm here is to help him understand the price he has to pay."

The two seemed to work well together. Lloyd would make a sound pass. White would offer a word of encouragement. He'd slack off, get sloppy with the ball. White would bust on him, then offer a word of advice. Lloyd respected his new backcourt partner. He knew what he was, knew where he'd been. And, he knew why he was there.

"JoJo's my man," he'd said. "JoJo wants to see me make it."

But the question remained: Could White's presence be a significant factor in the battle to spark Lloyd toward success?

The results had been favorable. White would work out after practice, shooting, running drills. Eventually, Lloyd got the hint and began to stay late, too. White taught him the tricks of the trade, skills acquired during a twelve-year-long NBA career—a surgeon showing an intern how to master a bevy of intricate operating techniques. Lloyd seemed, at times, to hang on his every word. He worked harder than he had ever worked before.

But now, with the season just two days away, White appeared a bit distant. Partly, it was because he had grown unsure of himself, unsure of his ability to come back. Partly, it was because of Lloyd.

Despite his best intentions, Lloyd still tended to goof off. He was doing more than he had ever done before, but he still didn't hit the weights as often as he should. He still didn't run as often as he should. He rarely attended his aftercare program at Memorial Hospital. And, sometimes, just coming down the court during practice it was apparent he didn't push himself as hard as some of his teammates.

"The trouble with him," White said, "is he's kid-minded. He's as green as the god-damned grass in Kansas." It seemed the air held a violent storm just beyond the horizon in the Land of Oz.

Willie Glass stripped the ball, broke loose and raced down court. The swingman, who had been known as Hollywood back when he was on the 1984-85 NCAA Final Four team at St. John's, had just been cut by the Lakers—his problem an all-too-common one. He had talent. But he was 6-foot-5. And undersized swingmen who can't handle the ball and who don't shoot from downtown don't cut it in the NBA.

So Glass was here in Topeka. A place he knew, for him, was the court of last resort. "I've got to give it my best shot," he said. It was all he had left. As he ran down the left wing, Hollywood was making sure to make known his desire. There was venom in his eyes, fury in his action. He leapt at the foul line, soared skyward and when he reached the basket, arms outstretched, he sent a thunderous tomahawk dunk crashing down over the head of Jerome Batiste. This was raw hunger, the actions of a man who desperately wanted a job, but who knew only a last ditch effort in this final preseason scrimmage could save him from being released by late afternoon; from seeing his dream die a tortured death.

While Glass fought hard against the odds, in the background, Lloyd trotted down court at half speed, as if not to care one way or the other as he drew icy stares from Killilea. As the scrimmage continued on around him, the trot became a noticeable limp. Moments later, as Glass and the others living on the edge continued to sweat out the session, Lloyd stopped running altogether, walked off the court, grabbed an ice pack and sat down—as if to inform the staff that he was done for the day.

It was 10 a.m. Practice was less than an hour old.

"What's wrong now, Youngblood?" Killilea asked, his voice laced with a hint of disdain and contempt. This was an act he had seen before. He had grown tired of the kid stuff. Lloyd winced. He looked at Killer. He looked wounded by his words. No faith, coach? No trust?

"Hurt my knee yesterday liftin' weights," he explained, sounding as if he might never be able to practice again. "Can't run no more."

The con didn't work. Killer didn't bite. "Too bad, Youngblood," Killilea said flatly. "Final cuts are today." He shook his head in sympathy. Like he was paying last respects. Lloyd stared at him for a moment.

Was he serious? No sense taking a chance, he thought. After all, he really did want to make the team, no matter how he acted. His action was more a childish cry for attention—done to see if anyone cared enough to discipline him—than a real challenge to authority. Message received, Lloyd put down the ice pack, dropped a towel and ran back onto the court, his limp cured.

Killilea looked toward the heavens for an answer to this riddle. None came. Across the arena, assistant general manager Bruce Carnahan laughed. He explained that this had become an all-too-common sight at practice. "Oh, he's hurt, all right," Carnahan said in a mock-serious tone. "He slept on his knee wrong last night and his brains drained out through his ears."

The scrimmage went on. Lloyd was just being Lloyd.

It was lunchtime and most of the players had already scattered in search of food and a brief respite from practice when Lloyd, dressed in gray sweats, red-striped Avias, a red Sizzlers jacket and a CBS hat, reached the outer offices. It was the final session of double workouts and, by the time lunch was over, Killilea, who had retired to his office to contemplate the fates, would have his decision on who would go and who would remain.

Lloyd looked worried, the incident from the morning session fresh in his mind. When he saw Al Quakenbush, the beat reporter for the *Topeka Capital-Journal,* standing in the hall near the exit, he stopped cold.

"What you think?" Lloyd asked Quake, more than a trace of insecurity in his voice. "Think I'll get cut?"

Quake seemed taken aback. There was no chance, he knew. Lloyd had too much talent, showed too much promise. He was a special project. Bernie Glannon had made that clear. There had already been too much investment, in both time and money, not to go forward as planned.

"No, Lloyd," he said. "I think you're going to make it."

"How you know?" Lloyd said.

"Why, you worried, Lloyd?" He looked it, though he was trying hard to seem complacent. "I don't think you should be worried, Lloyd."

Lloyd looked at Quake. "Who you been talkin' to?" he asked.

"Go to lunch, Lloyd," Quake said. "You're safe."

Lloyd mulled it over for a moment and then, finally convinced, he walked out the door. Quake shook his head. He liked Lloyd. But, like everyone else here in the heartland of America, it was obvious that he really didn't know what to make of him.

Just down the hall in his office, Bernie Glannon leaned back in a chair behind his desk. "You know," he said, "Lloyd is the backbone of our team and I've never, for what may be selfish reasons, denied that. But here, we are making Lloyd live a life of responsibilities for the first time in his life. We don't just hand him a wad of money and be done with it."

Glannon was in his late middle-age. His hair was silvered, his face rutted, his nose bulbous. He had a gentle-but-firm quality that suggested the time when your father became a grandfather, something most probably related to having raised six children. In his baritone voice you could hear concern for Lloyd, as if he had been one of those kids. He sort of was.

Glannon allowed Lloyd to live in his house in Overland Park, Kansas, before he moved into a place of his own in Topeka. Glannon arranged for his daughter, Kristi Gillam, who served as office manager for the team, to teach Lloyd how to open his own checking account at a local bank. Glannon found an apartment for Lloyd in the complex where

Killilea lived. And, it was Glannon who, seeing Lloyd in an '80 Mercury with no floorboards, arranged for him to drive his leased 1987 Ford Taurus station wagon.

Glannon also made it clear those courtesies were not without a price. In his children he instilled values, among them respect for others.

He demanded that if Lloyd used his car he be responsible for giving other teammates a ride to and from practice. He demanded that if Lloyd lived in his home he be treated not as a guest, but as a resident. He would be responsible for keeping his quarters clean. He would be responsible for locking doors, doing dishes, turning out lights. So it figured that, when Lloyd abused that privilege and Glannon received a phone bill that included a call to New York for 101 minutes, he treated Lloyd as if he were his son. "I promptly handed him the bill," he said.

Not all of his actions were done out of love. Part was just good business sense. After all, Glannon owned a professional team and was a good businessman, one who understood the value of a sound investment. He had made a career as a travel agent and, by the time he sold his operation in 1984, had turned an investment of $25,000 into an agency that had eleven offices nationwide. He understood that despite Lloyd's fragile state, with the right tact, the right amount of effort and a little luck he might prove to be a valuable commodity—a player who could become a bona fide national star, who could draw fans with his exciting play, who could become a hero of epic proportion, who could be his best investment yet. So he kept Lloyd on a tight rein.

"But," Glannon said, "even though some of what we do is for selfish reasons, out of our interest for the ball team, I think Lloyd can see the difference in what he has here. Here, Lloyd does not receive special privileges. He is given his per diem like anyone else. Not first, not last. But when he gets on the bus. Still, there is no question that I am more concerned where he is at all times of the day than I am with other players. I do call Lloyd several times a day, just to see what he is doing.

"But at lunchtime I don't go to the restaurant where many players hang out, to see if he is with nine girls or drinking four glasses of whiskey. And, I don't go over to his apartment, walk in and check around, looking in the cabinets and under counters. That isn't my job. I just like to make sure he is not hanging around somewhere and getting into trouble."

As league commissioner Mike Storen explained: "We're not a social center. We're not going to do this for Joe Smith, the slow, heavy-set guard who can't play. The fact is that the owner of the Topeka franchise has taken an unbelievable personal interest in the case. He is damn-near living with him. Sure, it is because he is such a good player.

"But he also understands that, left to his own devices, this kid might never bridge the gap between failure and success. Maybe it's the greater fool theory. Maybe it isn't."

When Killer walked out of his office after lunch, he looked a bit shaken. Having to deliver bad news can do that to a man. He had just met with Willie Glass. He had just told him to pack his bags.

"Cutting him really bothered me," Killilea said. "He worked so hard. But he just didn't have the size and we just didn't have a spot for him here. He was just in the wrong place at the wrong time."

Down the hall, sitting in a chair, was Lloyd. He had come back from lunch and was talking with the secretaries, killing time before afternoon practice. Killer spotted him. He wanted to rattle him a bit, deliver a scare that might cause Lloyd to work harder. "Youngblood," Killilea called, his voice firm and demanding. "Step into my office." Lloyd grimaced.

"This is it," he said. "I'm cut." Down the hall he walked, looking much like a man headed toward his own execution.

John Killilea was a tough man. He had grown up a slick Irish kid from Quincy, Massachusetts, who knew what from what. He didn't let people get over on him. "I don't like to prejudge anybody," Killilea said. "But in the middle of our first conversation I had to stop him and say, 'Let's stop the street con, okay? Start talking straight.' It was like he was saying everything I wanted to hear. You could see him working for an angle. But after you've been around as long as I have, you can see through it. You almost start thinking three or four sentences ahead."

Though the meeting lasted little more than a few minutes, Killer used the time to explain those theories about hard work and effort. He told Lloyd that, while he had worked hard, he needed to put forth even more effort both on and off the court. He would no longer stand for moments like the one that had disrupted the morning session. He stressed the need for self-discipline. He had hope that, somehow, the message would get through.

"The thing I look for is abnormal behavior," Killilea said. "Is he abnormally tired? Is he screwing things up in practice? Lloyd has not shown any of those signs. But still, I am concerned, because in Lloyd I see the possibility of self-destruction, as well as the possibility of greatness. It is in his lap. But attaining success is more than just saying he is the master of his fate. He still has to learn how to be the master of his fate."

Despite the lecture and the hard-line advice from Killilea, when Lloyd left he was all smiles. "I'm goin' to be here," he announced with pride to the handful of front-office staff. "See, that's 'cause I been workin' hard. I work hard, don't I?" he asked the receptionist, as if to seek out someone who would verify his claim. "I work harder than anybody, right?"

She looked at him, incredulous. Then, with a feigned touch of innocent curiosity in her voice, she asked: "Next to who?"

Lloyd was already out on the court, shooting, when the other players arrived back for the afternoon practice session. But he was hardly serious about it. In fact, he was trying to work a scam. Again, he was limping and soon began to hop on one foot. While doing that he was also shooting jumpers from beyond three-point range. He hit five straight.

"Yo," he said to Cedric Hunter. "Bet you five bucks."

"You kiddin'?" Ced said.

"C'mon, bet you five bucks," he said to Ron Kellogg.

"You crazy, Lloyd?" Ron said. "I ain't betting you."

"Five bucks a shot, c'mon. Bet you," Lloyd said to Calvin Thompson, laughing. All the while, he was tossing shots through the net—just like he had that afternoon back at Andrew Jackson.

Cal pretended to ignore him. Still, on and on, Lloyd went from teammate to teammate until he had gone through them all, no one willing to take a shot at the deal. Finally, Lloyd became bored and went and sat down.

The afternoon practice went without a hitch. Lloyd played well, ran hard and did everything he could. He distributed the ball to teammates. He made his shots. He worked on his defense. He made an effort. Even Killilea seemed impressed. Afterwards, the players attended a team meeting. The next morning the team was scheduled to make the first road trip of the season. As players packed for the trip, Lloyd came across a schedule card. He studied it for a moment, then turned to his friends.

"Look at this," Lloyd said.

"By my name it says, 'School: Vegas, UNLV.' Ha. Check that out. Can you believe that, man?"

"Yeah," Thompson said, laughing. "Can you imagine Lloyd in school? Wouldn't that be funny? Just imagine, Lloyd Daniels in 'Back to School.' Just like Rodney Dangerfield." He began to mimic Lloyd.

Everyone in the locker room was in stitches, cutting on Lloyd. Laughing hard. "Pretty funny, isn't it?" Thompson said.

"Man," Lloyd said. "Me in 'Back to School.' That's funny, man. Me and Rodney. I got that tape, 'Back to School.' Man, can't you just see me?" It was humorous. And, very sad.

With the team about to venture out on their first road trip of the season—the real kind, the kind teams take in a professional minor league; one that would be long and wearisome—Wednesday, November 18, began in the small hours of the morning for the Sizzlers.

The team was to bus from Topeka, catch a flight out of Kansas City, change planes in Denver and then proceed to Casper, Wyoming—all for a game the following night against the Wyoming Wildcatters. From there, it would be a six-hour bus ride Friday morning to Rapid City, South Dakota, to play a game Saturday night against the Rapid City Thrillers.

The following morning the itinerary would be reversed and, late on November 24, a week after leaving Topeka, the team would return—three games into a fifty-four-game regular season.

This would be a new experience for Lloyd. He had traveled before, making trips to Las Vegas and Hawaii with the Gauchos, his club team in the Bronx. But never had he traveled so much in such a short span.

Lloyd was the first player to arrive at the arena for the trip. He was almost an hour early. "Didn't want to be late," he said. Apparently, the talk with Killilea had had some effect. He even brought a newspaper with him. *The Cap-Journal*. It had a page with head shots and bios of each player. Lloyd saw his picture. Even if he couldn't read the copy next to it, he knew what it meant. "Why they pubbin' me?" he asked. "I ain't even played yet. I might ain't goin' to play. How 'bout that happens? You know, here I might don't start. I'm serious. You think I'll play? I say I might don't start.

"So if I ain't, why they pubbin' me?"

Publicity meant expectations and expectations meant pressure. And Lloyd, an insecure, playful little boy at heart, hardly liked it. Worse, there also was an article that quoted Nevada-Las Vegas coach Jerry Tarkanian. As he had before, Tark said Lloyd may be the best he had ever seen. On the bus to the airport in Kansas City, those quotes caused Lloyd undue grief.

Teammates also got on him about the main focus of the article, which reiterated the allegations leveled in *New York Newsday* by sources ranging from Arnie Hershkowitz to Steve Cropper, Ricky Collier, James Jones, Cletus Jarmon to a host of others—all of whose claims indicated Nevada-

Las Vegas had committed several NCAA violations when it recruited Lloyd. Among the alleged violations were the illegal use of a car, as well as the providing of cash, clothes and free meals at hotels in Las Vegas, and the arrangement of jobs for Lloyd and Steve Cropper. Also detailed in the investigation was the guardianship arrangement with Mark Warkentien.

"How 'bout that motorcycle it says you got at UNLV?" a teammate asked.

"I didn't get no bike," Lloyd said. "They made that up."

"How 'bout them pots and pans and that used color TV it says you got?" asked another. "People talkin' shit," Lloyd said.

"Yeah?" Ced said. "I don't think so. I think Tark loves you, man. I think Tark loves you so much he wants to bone you, make love to you."

Lloyd laughed a nervous laugh. His teammates were merciless. He didn't know how to respond. "Yeah," he said finally, trying to act casual. "I done Tark." Cedric laughed so hard, he nearly fell off the seat.

The ironic thing was, in a figurative sense, Lloyd had. The twenty-year-old with the third-grade reading level had bummed up Tark's multi-million-dollar basketball program. On October 21, Nevada-Las Vegas president Robert C. Maxson had announced that an in-house investigation had resulted in a report which included "conflicting testimony" from the parties involved in the incident. The committee had recommended that the matter be passed on to conference officials and the NCAA.

"I think anybody knowledgeable about basketball had to know that the NCAA was going to look into the recruitment of Mr. Daniels," Maxson said at the news conference. Just two days after Maxson released the report, the NCAA had informed UNLV it was doing just that.

Tarkanian and Warkentien maintained that the program was innocent of all allegations. The NCAA, as usual, refused comment.

One administrator at Nevada-Las Vegas said members of the school athletic department wondered whether the program would be forced to "close down because of the Lloyd Daniels Recruiting Violations Investigation by the NCAA. I have never in my life seen anything like this kid and his publicity. Not only does he make every paper from coast to coast for his ability and [his] coke bust, he now creates fury in the basketball department and the NCAA is out to get us." Only time would tell if it would. As of the fall of 1990, the NCAA had still not announced its findings.

After all the laughter died down Lloyd stretched out across two seats and fell asleep. Later, he also slept on the plane. Landing at Stapleton Airport in Denver, Killilea turned to Pat Ditzler, the team equipment manager, who had been assigned to keep an eye on the oft-troubled rookie during the trip, and said: "Did you get Youngblood off the plane?"

"I went back and shook him awake," Ditz said.

"You know," Killer said, "we're going to have to take Youngblood by the hand the first couple of flights. Just to make sure he gets where he's going."

Killilea, after all, knew what he was up against. During his career as an assistant coach with the Celtics, Bucks and Nets, he had seen several players self-destruct, among them Norm Van Lier, John Lucas and Micheal Ray Richardson. Richardson had been banned from the league for life in February, 1986, after testing positive for cocaine use for the fourth time. Sugar, as he was known, was now with the Albany Patroons in the CBA. Lucas, meanwhile, had undergone treatment and made his way back into the NBA with the Bucks. There, he organized a program to counsel players about dependency problems in conjunction with an aftercare program.

It was the strangest of coincidences then that, walking through the airport terminal, Killilea should run smack into Terry Cummings and a few members of the Bucks. Milwaukee, having faced the Denver Nuggets the previous night, was leaving town. The Sizzlers were passing through. As Killilea stopped to talk to a few old friends, Lucas walked over to ask him a question. "Is the kid here?" Lucas said.

Killer nodded. He pointed to Lloyd, then waved him over. Lucas shook his hand, pulled him off to the side and there, in the middle of a crowd racing to catch planes bound for who-knows-where, one recovering addict trying hard to recapture the luster of a faded career took a moment to advise another recovering addict on how to avoid the same pitfalls.

"You and I are in the same boat," Lucas told Lloyd. "I'm going on with my life. You can go on with yours. Lean on people. Call me. I have two years of sobriety. You have a month. But we're both just a day away [from the same old routine]. You have to take it day-by-day."

For almost ten minutes Lucas talked to Lloyd. And, for almost ten minutes, Lloyd stood and listened, intent and genuinely impressed.

"I needed help with drugs," Lloyd said later. "I should admit that, 'cause I had a problem. I had a big drug problem. But now I'm realizin' that. I'm dealin' with it one day at a time. That's what John Lucas was talkin' to me about. He said, 'Just call me when you need someone to talk to. We'll talk.' He said he cared. I appreciate that. I really do."

As Lucas said after he left Lloyd to join his teammates for the flight to Milwaukee, "If my ten-minute conversation can carry him for a week and somebody else can carry him for a week after that, then he may be able to accumulate recovery time. But I could talk to him until I was blue in the face. Until Lloyd Daniels is ready, nobody can make it work."

When John Lucas left, so did Lloyd. There was almost two hours between flights, so, hearing there was major stock on the block—a huge selection of independent ladies, that is—he and Kellogg wandered off to scout the terminal and work a variety of pick-up lines on a variety of nondescript women. Moderately successful, they met a few. Most, unsure of their intentions or merely appalled by their neanderthal approach—more often than not, "Hello" being "Yo babes, wha's up?"—simply walked on by, usually causing Lloyd to fall into a familiar response.

"Yo, *batch!*" he'd yell. In other words, "Hey, bitch!"

Still, when the two did return about a half-hour before flight time, they were a few good names and phone numbers richer for the effort. Standing near the gate as the team waited to board the flight, the two, joined by other teammates, were in a fairly good mood then when they were approached by an older gentleman.

"Excuse me," he asked in a midwestern drawl, his words casting light on his naivete. "But are you fellows some sort of athletic team?"

Ronnie and Lloyd looked at him. Here were more than a half-dozen young men, none shorter than 6-foot-5, save Cedric, who was a tad under six-foot, standing around with carry bags that read "Sizzlers."

"Ah, yes sir," Kellogg said in his most-polite voice, as he tried to suppress a quiet laugh. "We're basketball players. We play for the Topeka Sizzlers in the CBA." The man looked at him. "CBA?" he said.

"Yeah," Lloyd said. "The Crazy Basketball Association."

The man smiled weakly. Everyone else laughed, Killer included.

The laughter subsided moments later when it was announced that the flight was prepared to board. John Harris, a rookie forward from Brooklyn, and Kevin Graham, a longtime minor-league player, had also gone to roam the terminal. Despite having been paged for the past half-hour, the two were still nowhere to be found.

Knowing a good teaching example when he saw one, Killilea decided to broadcast a policy statement. He announced that the pair would be left behind. "Well," Killer said to Ditz, making sure he glanced toward Lloyd in the process, "if they're not back by the time we're ready to leave I guess they'll just have to find their own way to Wyoming."

Lloyd giggled, until he realized Killilea was serious. Until he realized that fines and suspensions were also possible consequences.

"Hey," he said to Ced and Ronnie as he walked out across the tarmac toward the ancient, prop-driven plane that would carry the team on to

Casper. "Know what? John just cut himself. He missed the plane, man. I thought that'd be me, know what I'm sayin'? I thought that'd be me."

Somehow, Harris and Graham managed to make the plane just seconds before the doors closed and the ramp was removed. As they found their seats, even Lloyd breathed a sigh of relief.

When JoJo, Ronnie and Ced entered what passed for the hotel restaurant later that night in Casper, Lloyd and Jerome Batiste were already seated at the table. Their orders had been placed, interestingly enough, since neither was what might be classified a speed reader. Now, kids don't often see the need for being able to read. But just attempt to order a meal from a menu that you don't understand and see what happens.

"Hey, what you guys order?" Kellogg asked.

"We got fish," Batiste said.

"What, like a filet?" Kellogg said.

"I don't know," Batiste said. "It's right here. The waiter said it's good." With that, Batiste pointed to the menu to a spot where it read, "Stuffed Rainbow Trout." It hardly sounded like a filet.

Kellogg made a face. Just as he did, the waiter arrived at the table with two orders of trout. He placed one in front of Batiste, the other, in front of Lloyd. Each looked at the other for a moment, stunned.

The trout was whole. Head, tail. Eyes, included. Quick, Lloyd looked at Batiste and winked, then looked at the waiter, a fair-haired man in his twenties who, it was painfully obvious, had never been outside of Wyoming, much less been face-to-face with a seasoned veteran of the street con.

"Yo, man," Lloyd said. "I didn't order this. I ordered steak. Didn't I order steak?" The waiter checked, then rechecked, the order.

"No, sir," he said. "You both ordered the rainbow trout. See?"

"No," Lloyd said. "I think we both ordered steak. Right, Batman? Didn't you order steak? I heard you order steak. I ordered steak, too."

Batiste nodded in agreement as Ronnie and Ced began to giggle under their breath. Again, the waiter checked the pad.

"No, sir. I think you ordered the trout," he said.

Seeing his plan was not going to work without a few refinements, Lloyd changed his tack slightly. "Oh, but man," he said. "I just remembered I'm allergic to fish. Yeah, I'm allergic. Ain't I allergic, Batman?" Batiste, knowing when to keep his mouth shut, again nodded.

"See, man, that's why I couldn't have ordered no fish. See, I forgot.

I'm allergic. Sorry, but I can't eat no fish. I'm real sorry. But I know you'll do right by me and my man here and bring us the steak. I'm real sorry 'bout that, but I can't eat no fish. I just remembered."

With that the waiter, flustered and blushing over his "mistake" as well as over the stares he was beginning to draw from the other diners and other waiters, agreed to return the trout and get two steaks. Before he left, and as Ronnie and Ced seemed about to burst out laughing, the waiter stopped. He apologized for the inconvenience. As he walked away, Lloyd turned to Batman. "Damn," he said. "No way I was goin' to eat that."

"Me neither," Batiste said. "The thing had eyes."

"Know what?" Lloyd said. "I think yours was still alive, man. I thought I seen the tail move, right on the plate. I thought I seen the tail move."

Later, well after dinner had been served and the waiter had returned with two fine cuts of sirloin steak for Lloyd and Batman, White, who seemed reserved and introspective throughout the meal, began to talk about his time in the NBA. Seeing what had happened before dinner, he wanted to make a point about education and, knowing the players respected what he had done in pro ball, figured they might listen. He spoke about intelligence, about how some people have nothing else going for them, except ball.

He talked about the need to listen and learn. "You know," White said, lapsing into street talk to drive his point home, "some boys that's playing ball got an I.Q. so low that, lose one point and they's a rock." Cedric started to laugh. So did Lloyd and Batman. Ronnie looked on, intent. "They can't read nothing. They can't get by off the court. They don't know how to handle things. Without a ball, they're lost."

The message was aimed at Lloyd. But soon Kellogg, who was both polite and bright, though hardly booksmart, told JoJo he knew just what he meant. Then, he answered with his own tale.

"I'm not the world's best reader," said Kellogg, who shared the same alma mater with Hunter and White. "In fact, in college one time we had to go around to the local grammar schools and talk to the kids, remember, Ced? I went to one class, first grade, and I had to read a book. It was hard. I got to a word I didn't know—I don't know, it was 'vomitizing' or some shit—and I didn't want to be embarrassed, so I looked at a kid in the front row and said, 'Now, I know it's a hard one, but let's see if you know that word' and he told me. I was like, 'Whew, got through that one.'

"I had to read to three classes. So, each time, I read the same book. By the third class, I had it down cold."

No one at the table, least of all JoJo, said a word.

It was only after the table had cleared and everyone had gone back to their rooms, that Lloyd began to talk about his situation, though he was not eager to do so. He never was.

For all of his smoothness in conversation, all of his good-natured humor, his laughter and his curious and inquisitive nature, Lloyd was a notorious introvert when the conversation turned to him. He did not like to discuss himself, his background or the events of his life. For years, he kept from even his closest friends details about how his mother died, details about all but the simplest aspects of his past.

Ask him a question he did not like and he would quit talking, stand up and leave. That world was all he owned. It was a treasured possession. And he was not, if he could avoid it, willing to share it with anyone.

It was with apprehension that he began to speak.

"People," he said, attempting to instill a sense of security and conviction into his words, "they don't know for real about my life. They don't know my life right now is great. They don't know that now my life is smooth. They don't know I'm not gettin' over on that fast life no more.

"Yeah, I messed up a whole bunch of times. I messed up in Vegas, fucked up good, messed up some people. But I think I'm doin' fine right now. I got a real good opportunity here. I met a lot of people in Topeka who want to see a kid like me make it. I'm goin' to get myself right."

"I am," he said, almost under his breath.

His voice, usually so smooth, had begun to falter. He stumbled over a few words, then caught himself for a moment. He started to talk again, but a tear welled in the corner of his eye. He stopped. Only after a bit, did he go on.

"All the shit they's talkin' is nothin'," he said. "The only one I let down was myself, understand? I had my chance. I didn't do what I was supposed to have did. But I can't feel sorry now.

"In rehab," he said, "I was in real tough condition. Ten weeks, I couldn't even touch a basketball. That's because goin' through those weeks in there, I couldn't worry 'bout no basketball. I had to worry 'bout gettin' straight. It was tough. You got temptation everywhere. You got to learn to fight it.

"But, if you want to get high, you'll get high. In New York City or even in Topeka, if you want to get high, you're goin' to get high. Especially, in a small town like Topeka. Everybody knows where you can get it. If you want it, you'll know how to get it. You know who got it. Simple."

Just one week before, Clyde Thompson, the twenty-five-year-old brother of Calvin Thompson, had been shot outside a social club on Sixth Street in Topeka. Everyone had heard about the funeral and that police were checking into alleged drug connections in an attempt to find a motive.

Somehow though, that did not seem to be on Lloyd's mind as he pushed himself back from the table. No, it was something else. Something more personal. A moment later he raised himself from the chair.

"We'll talk later," he said. Then, out he walked.

"The crux of his entire situation," Killilea said over lunch the next afternoon at the Casper Hilton, "is responsibility. What he has to do now is take responsibility for his own actions. What we are trying to do here is to teach him through association. When a person comes out of rehab and goes back into the same environment he was in, it is difficult to keep that situation from happening again. But here, if Lloyd can learn by example and absorb maybe just ten percent of what he sees going on around him, he can improve his situation and take control of his life. And, if he can learn to take control of his life, he has a chance to succeed."

Still, for all his positive talk, Killilea seemed doubtful whether the process would be as simple as he had made it sound. Perhaps it was his own skepticism, his old habit of managing to remain realistic in the face of his own optimism that tempered his outlook and undercut his words. Perhaps it was that numerous others—former Houston Rockets team-mates Lewis Lloyd and Mitchell Wiggins, recently dismissed from the NBA for drug violations, most notable among them—had just failed in their chance at success.

"As far as I'm concerned, Lloyd Daniels is a great talent who has got to learn a lot about things going on in the real world," Killilea said. "He has lived in a basketball world almost all of his life, where he was able to get what he wanted and do what he wanted because of that talent. But he's in the real world right now. He doesn't have maid service. People aren't checking on him all the time. No one is going to go down to the store for him when he needs food. No one is going to write his checks when he needs to pay his bills. Here, you either adjust to things or you fall by the wayside.

"In the NBA they have the three-strike rule. I hate like hell to say this is it for him, that if he doesn't do it now his life is ruined. If he were to falter, you would hope he could get it together enough so he had something else going for him, maybe not just be a basketball player. But, what else does he know at this stage? He has some study habits. He has some social skills. But his interest right now is basketball. Basketball and hanging out on the corner. The harshest thing for Lewis Lloyd and Mitch Wiggins, two better-than-average pro players, was to be put on the street for two years. The point is, you can deny your problems and deny them, but everybody has to know that, if those problems don't get solved, no matter who you are, eventually the roof has to fall in. I saw an end result with Sugar.

"And so you say, 'How many times can someone start over?' After a while, your skepticism grows and grows and grows."

An hour later, Daniels walked into the hotel gift shop, grabbed a deck of playing cards, dropped two dollars on the counter and walked away. Told that the bill was $2.97, he turned to the cashier, pointed to a friend standing near the counter and said, "He's got it." Then he left.

So much for responsibility.

The Casper Events Center is located on a low, barren hill. You can see it from the hotel lobby. In the morning the team bussed over to the arena for a walk-through prior to the game that night. Stuck without a return ride to the hotel after practice, players were forced to scramble down the steep talus slopes of the hill for a mile-long walk back.

Along the way Lloyd, who had not played a game of organized basketball in the year since he appeared in those two games at Mount San Antonio, was asked what the first game of the season would bring. "It ain't no big deal," he said, trying to hide his apprehension. "Ain't no big deal at all. I can't be worried. It's just another game."

Nightfall brought with it a different attitude. Almost 5,000 fans packed the arena before game time, interesting, since this hardly seemed to be basketball country. Casper, after all, was an oil-boom-town-gone-bust. The team, known as the Wildcatters, was even named after oilmen. And visitors often joked that the state motto was "Wyoming, where men are men and women are, too" or "Wyoming, where men are men and sheep are nervous." It seemed that here the real sport for real folks was rodeo.

The University of Wyoming nicknamed its teams the Cowboys. License plates were all adorned with a bucking bronco ridden by a cowboy. Even the Events Center was built for cowboys and indoor rodeo, with basketball as a sort of afterthought—even if the university had created real interest in the sport by reaching the 1986 National Invitation Tournament Championship Game, led by Fennis Dembo. It was almost odd, then, that a large number in the crowd seemed to know of Lloyd. When warm-ups began those people started to get on him. Several fans showered him with obscenities.

"You're a nothing, Lloyd," screamed one man. "You're a fucking jerk."

A majority of the other comments were of the four-letter-or-better variety, replete with the usual assortment of choice accusations. Though his teammates soon began to take notice, Lloyd tried not to let the catcalls bother him. But it was apparent they did.

As he walked to the bench after pregame, one man let loose with a vicious barrage. Lloyd looked at him, said something back, then sat down. "Don't understand?" the man yelled. "Read my lips . . . if you can."

On the public address system, music blared. First, "The Boy from New York City." And then, "Another One Bites the Dust" by Queen.

As Ron Kellogg said afterward: "It seemed like they were trying to tell him something." In fact, he had said as much to Daniels. "Lloyd," Ronnie said out on the court, "you better listen to them songs."

Lloyd started, but he started slow. With Topeka down, 5-0, he hit his first pro attempt, a jumper from the top of the key. Later, with the Sizzlers behind, 9-4, he drew a foul on a nice lean-in move, making both free throws to the crowd's disappointment. Still, it soon became apparent he was doing something he almost never did. He was forcing his game, trying too hard. Adding to the problem was that his teammates could not understand his game. No matter what they did, no matter where they moved on the floor, they always seemed to be a step behind him.

Part of it was that Lloyd lacked structure to his game. He had never really been part of a team, having played only about fifty games in high school and just two in college. Part of it was that, though he and his teammates had practiced the plays for the better part of a month, they were running them as if they were machines—following chalkboard diagrams to the letter, like a competition skater trying to trace a figure on the ice. All the while, Lloyd was going on instinct—reading the defense, understanding where his teammates should be if they really knew the game, knew it like he did. He was passing the ball before they figured out how to get there.

Once, he found Kevin Graham cutting back door along the baseline and hit him in the chest with a pass. It startled him—and bounced off his hands and out of bounds. Another time, it was Kellogg who lost the handle on a nice feed, not realizing until too late that Lloyd had found him open.

By the time the half was over, Lloyd should have had at least seven or eight assists, spectacular ones. Instead, he had three.

He had seen several fine passes go for naught, mishandled by teammates. He also had been burned several times on defense by a variety of players, ranging from the Wildcatters' star, Boot Bond, to A.J. Wynder, a rookie guard from Fairfield University. Worse, Lloyd had gone 1-for-7 from the field. Topeka trailed, 72-57.

The second half began no better. Soon, the Sizzlers trailed by twenty. But then Killilea switched White to the point and Lloyd to shooting guard. And, suddenly, the team came alive. Lloyd hit two straight shots to cut the lead to fifteen and, though he was called for a delay of game warning for tapping the ball out of bounds after a basket—"A damn playground move," Killer called it—and a three-second violation, he lifted the level of his game.

He played better defense, holding the two men he switched off guarding without a basket for the remainder of the contest. He hit five of six shots from the field. His two free throws trimmed the deficit to 108-103 with 4:19 left. And, with time winding down and the score tied at 114-114, the ball came to him. Lloyd moved down on the wing, set and fired a baseline jumper from eighteen. There were twelve seconds on the clock.

In another time, in another game, the shot would have gone. It would have fallen the way it did when he hit the shot from halfcourt to tie the game against Whitney back at Jackson. This time, though, it was off the mark. It hit the rim, fell away. Wyoming won on a basket at the buzzer.

"He made mistakes that a young kid, a rookie, is going to make," Killilea said after the game. "The kind, a kid with four years of college would make. There were times he tried to force it. There was the tech, when he put the ball in, then hit it—a playground thing. But, on the whole, he did all right."

"I don't think he was very pleased with what he did," White said. "He made some mistakes. But, I told him that was to be expected. You tuck it away, you learn from it. Hopefully, he will."

"It was a lot of fun being back there after a year," Lloyd said as he sat in the locker room, his still damp uniform waiting to be removed. "I wasn't never nervous, just happy to be out there again. I think I did all right, all right for a rookie, a young guy. But I could play better, you know that. A couple of times I came down, made mistakes. But I knew it would be tough. I thought, a little tougher." He paused a second. "Damn," he said. "That was a shot I was supposed to made. It wasn't no problem, though. I'll get it back."

The unofficial count had Lloyd with eight assists. The official count was not so impressive, though still not bad. The final result? Daniels, Lloyd: 22 points, 5 assists, 1 steal and 2 turnovers.

Lloyd Daniels was now a pro.

• • •

Back at the hotel bar, Lloyd, Ronnie and Ced were sitting around a table drinking Coronas when John Killilea walked in with Quake. Ced, the rookie, and Ronnie, just in his second season, both saw the coach and, almost at the same instant, each grabbed his beer bottle and slid it off the table and down into his lap—apparently worried about making a bad impression on Killer, even though both were of legal age and the team had no rules against drinking. Ronnie looked at Lloyd, who both he and Ced understood probably should not have been drinking, but who had not moved, his Corona still on the table between his hands.

"Yo, man," Ronnie said. "It's coach."

"So?" Lloyd said.

"Your beer," Ronnie said, motioning with his eyes.

"Yo, be yo'self," Lloyd said. "He knows what's goin' on. You don't have to do that. The man ain't dumb. He knows. Why try to hide? Why not just sit tight?" With that, Lloyd turned to Killer and Quake, who were moving toward the bar. "Yo, coach," he called. "How you doin'?"

Killer nodded in acknowledgment and Quake said hello, as Ronnie and Ced stared on with quizzical expressions.

That done and, having allowed a few moments for his friends to recover from their shock—Ronnie kept telling him, "I can't believe you did that. I can't believe you did that"—the three turned their attentions elsewhere. For a few moments, the discussion among them was about the game. Soon, the conversation turned to women in the bar.

The place was loud and it was packed. A few women were seated at an adjacent table. Lloyd, Ronnie and Ced threw out a few lines, some of them even true. It didn't hurt when they mentioned they were ballplayers. After a few minutes of banter a couple of the girls came over to join them. Lloyd and Ronnie took two and hit the dance floor, but it wasn't long before the two got blown off. Ced, meanwhile, had gone over to the bar and met two women, and he was talking the talk when Lloyd and Ronnie walked over. One of the women claimed she was the girlfriend of one of the 'Catters. Ced looked impressed. Lloyd, however, reached over and palmed her ass. For a moment, she looked surprised. Then, she smiled.

"Like that, uh?" she said. He nodded.

Lloyd turned to a friend and offered a word of advice. "Just watch how black boys operate," he said. Being a pro player was about to pay its first real dividends.

Just moments later, the two girls and a friend were escorted to their car by the trio. They had to go down the road to another bar and collect a few friends, they said. There was a promise to come back in five minutes for a party in one of the rooms. A half-hour later, Ronnie, Ced and Lloyd were still sitting in the hotel lobby, waiting.

At around three o'clock, all three headed upstairs to bed. Alone.

Wyoming is a desolate place, as places go near the end of the Earth, which is what the world here seemed to be to a bunch of basketball players—more than a few from the inner-cities of America—at eight o'clock in the morning on a bus headed across the Badlands from Casper to Rapid City.

There is little to see in central Wyoming. The Rockies—with the Teton, Wind River, Salt River and Absaroka ranges—lie almost due West, well past Hell's Half-Acre and near the Idaho border, their ridges snow-covered and hostile by mid-to-late November. The state's northwest corner is home to Yellowstone and Old Faithful and north, a stretch beyond Hole-in-the-Wall near Sheridan, the Bighorn Mountains rise to meet the blue skies of Montana. South toward McFadden, Rock River and Laramie, where the University of Wyoming is located, the Medicine Bows climb toward northern Colorado and into Roosevelt National Forest and Rocky Mountain National Park.

But here, headed just a few degrees northeast along Routes 387 and 450 toward the Black Hills of South Dakota, there was nothing save a few hundred miles of golden brown scrub flats, about six hours worth to be exact. And, much of it was across the Thunder Basin National Grassland—a god-forsaken place of indeterminable beauty; once home to the Sioux and the Crow, now home only to endless, tireless rolling hills, ceaseless winds and, at last count, one dead tree. This was wilderness. Barren, harsh despite moderate fall temperatures in the mid-sixties. This was isolation.

Few of the team members paid much attention to the view out the bus windows, having opted to catch a few winks. Many stretched out across two seats. Lloyd, who had used part of his $22 per diem to grab a packaged breakfast at the hotel restaurant, ate his meal in silence, staring out the window for a few minutes. "We ain't in the middle of nowhere I want to be," said the citified kid of the untouched land before he dozed off, not quite realizing that he was here of his own choice.

Chip Engelland was a veteran guard and an astute observer. He harbored no illusions of a career in the NBA. When you go undrafted out of Duke and make the Sizzlers as a free agent you come to certain realizations. To him, the life is an interesting experience. That is all. Engelland didn't associate much with Lloyd. He said hello. He told an occasional joke. He sometimes worked with him in practice. That was it. But he watched Lloyd, assessed him. He seemed fascinated with his skills. He seemed fascinated with him.

"I heard he had an amazing amount of tools," Engelland said as the bus from the Jackrabbit Lines rolled along Route 450. "It was just stuff I had seen, read. Just squibs in the papers, old basketball folklore. But I tell you, he is amazing. Magic Johnson can learn things about the game from him. From free throw line to free throw line, his vision is unbelievable. You can see it. He is at home on a basketball court. It is in his blood. It's where he lives."

He paused a moment. The bus was prepared to turn off the road for a rest stop at the Clareton Post Office, an old weather-beaten shack of a place with a bathroom, a sometimes-working soda machine and a half-handful of tired, lonesome employees whose most frequent visitors were no more than just passing through. On the bus, players began to stir.

"Let's face it, this is a major step for him. Being a point guard in pro basketball is like being a rookie quarterback in the NFL. You have a lot to learn. He lacks experience. Right now, he is just making it on his natural skills. But the ones with super talent can make those leaps and not get swallowed up. When he walks on the court, he's the best. Whether it is on a playground in New York City, with ten NBA vets, or in the CBA.

"What he has to understand is that, while he is comfortable now, while he has received some benefits that other people haven't received, you do not get pampered in the CBA," Engelland said, as the bus slowed to a stop on the dirt skirt that surrounded the post office. "Believe me, this isn't a pampering league. This isn't no AAU. He is not going to be anonymous in Topeka. People will recognize him and that will put pressure on him. But he has to deal with that. No one is going to be concerned with how he spends his money or if he is eating three square meals a day.

"He is a professional now. He will always be walking on eggshells. Make a mistake, and it isn't like Lloyd isn't someone who hasn't made previous mistakes, and that might be it. The most important thing for Lloyd right now is to take in as much knowledge as he can. The most important thing for him is to learn, learn, learn. Consider this his education."

Lloyd was working on his education when the bus stopped again, this time about an hour later for a lunch break at Mount Rushmore. He took one look at the faces carved into the mountain, then looked at Killer.

"Yo, coach," he said. "Who's the guy with the beard?"

"Lincoln," Killilea said.

Few on the team had wanted to take a break at Mount Rushmore. Wasted time, they'd called it. When the bus driver turned off the main highway just north of the Crazy Horse Monument—a horse cut into the side of a mountain miles outside of Custer, South Dakota—even JoJo White, the veteran who long ago had grown tired from his share of travel and who wanted more to sleep and get on with business at the hotel in Rapid City, made his wishes known.

"We don't want to see no fucking mountain," he shouted from well back in the bus. Engelland, Ditzler and Killilea all cringed a bit as a half-dozen teammates took up the chorus. When the bus rounded a bend on the winding road leading to Rushmore, however, and a view of the four presidents, their stone-cold faces deep-cut into the rock walls, first appeared, the criticism ceased. Noses pressed against the windows.

"Yo, check that out," Lloyd said to Ronnie. "Ain't one of them guys on the dollar bill?"

You had to wonder how Lloyd could get through the day without getting ripped off by merchants, by teammates. After all, if he couldn't read and wasn't sure which presidents marked what bills, did he understand how to count money and how to be responsible with it? It seemed not. Still, when the bill for the lunch Lloyd purchased in the cafeteria style restaurant came to $3.13, he handed over a twenty. Seeing his acquaintance from the hotel gift shop in line behind him, Lloyd pocketed the bills and left the spare change at the base of the register. "There's what I owe you, man," he said.

"Before, other people was helpin' me through things," Lloyd said when he got back on the bus a little more than an hour later for the final leg of the trip. "Now, I'm on my own. Ain't no one payin' the bills. I pay the bills. I pay the rent. I pay the telephone bill. I'm bein' the man, the way it's supposed to be. Hear me? No one is helpin' me."

It sounded more like a denial than an explanation. But Lloyd gave his assurance that he was sincere. Several times.

"See this coat?" he said, as he pointed to the fine black leather jacket he wore. It was a street coat, the kind the B-Boys wear up on 125th and the big time. The kind dealin' folks wear in the Forties Projects. The kind the cools purchase to mark their success. A motto coat. A coat that, on the streets, sends the message that you are makin' cash money. And how.

"Bought this coat with my own money, I did," Lloyd said. "No one else bought it. Me. I'm workin' hard. I'm doin' what I got to do. I buy my own food. If I spend all my money, I don't eat. I go hungry. If I fall, I fall. No one else. That's the way it is in the real world, right?"

The Rapid City Thrillers were in the process of getting drilled by the Wyoming Wildcatters when, as members of the Sizzlers looked on from the upper deck of the Rushmore Plaza Civic Center, an announcement was made over the public address system. "Tomorrow night," came the voice of a carnival barker, "come see the great JoJo White, the former seven-time NBA all-star with the Boston Celtics, and, also, Lloyd Daniels, the only player in the history of the CBA never to have played in college or the NBA."

Lloyd stared hard at the floor, then hunched down in his seat, as if all eyes in the arena were on him. "Damn," he mumbled to himself. "Damn."

All Lloyd ever wanted to do was just fit in, be just another man in a basketball league doing what he loved to do. But even here, almost 2,000 miles from New York in a metropolis perhaps just two miles square with just two main roads and a population of little more than 50,000, Lloyd could not find a safe retreat. Even here, folks knew of his reputation on the streets of New York. Even here, folks knew about his past.

Even here, he was Swee'pea. And, even here, he was viewed as a sideshow attraction, an oddity.

Seated next to JoJo, Lloyd turned to him a moment. "Why can't them people just leave me alone?" he asked.

JoJo, who knew this world better than anyone else on the team, tried to offer an explanation. Somehow, it didn't seem adequate.

Outside, the night air was brisk. The walk from the arena to the Hotel Alex Johnson was a quick one, just a few short blocks down Mount Rushmore Road to Main Street. It was peaceful here, walking under the stars in the middle of the universe with no smog and no disturbances, just radiant light and cold, clean air.

Within a week, citing his age and his poor performances, JoJo White would again retire—just five games into his comeback. But as he walked toward the hotel that night, White seemed invigorated, almost animated as he talked about Lloyd. "His problem is that his attention span is not that long right now," White said. "His attitude is good, but you don't know how he'll react when things start getting tough. He is the kind of kid who will go right along with what's going on and so, while he's learning responsibility, at this point it may already be a little too late.

"I think people are being so careful with him because they realize that if he breaks a leg right now, what does he have? Zero. They understand that he must get his life together off the court. If you have your life together off the floor, you will have it together on the floor. I don't pull no punches. But I'm not going to beat him over the head with advice. I told him once, point blank, what he has to do. The rest is up to him.

"Right now, I'm just trying to put time in with him because maybe I recognize things that he might not recognize," White said. "He has a chance to do something extraordinary with his life, but he also has the chance to end up with zero. There is a game on the court and a game outside. The game outside is the real world; the game of life. What he has to learn now is that he has to master both."

When he reached the hotel, White headed for the elevator. There was a game the next night. All the travel had taken its toll. He wanted to rest.

Near the side lobby of the hotel, there was a bar. As White walked past it to the elevator he noticed Lloyd. He was inside, drinking Guinness Stout.

Lloyd was out late that night. Still, it was just 10:30 a.m. when he knocked on the hotel room door Saturday. "Hear about Rod?" he asked.

The Rapid City Journal had a short in the morning edition about DePaul guard Rod Strickland, who had been a teammate on the Gauchos and at Oak Hill. Strickland, the paper said, had been ruled ineligible due to academic problems. "How'd that happen?" Lloyd asked. He sounded shocked and his voice had a serious edge to it. "Why'd he get ineligible?"

Responsibilities, he was told. Strickland had not been responsible in meeting his academic obligations. He had missed class. He had not done well in school. He had not remembered the lessons he had seemed to learn back at Oak Hill. The world is not just about basketball, he was told. There is more to it than that. The conversation lasted almost fifteen minutes. When it was over, Lloyd said he understood. "That's why you got to work hard, right?" he said. "That's why I'm takin' it one day at a time. Know what I mean?"

It was difficult to know if he did understand, did comprehend. He was sharp. And, he was streetsmart. But he also was so undisciplined, so naive. It was just about two hours later then, after a brief walk-through in the arena, that Cedric, Ronnie and Cal Thompson began to talk about trade rumors while seated outside the Civic Center. The Thrillers had just acquired Sean Couch, the former guard from Columbia, who had earlier been cut from the Indiana Pacers. Despite having come from the Ivy League, Couch was a terrific guard. Both booksmart and streetsmart, he had learned his skills in the classrooms on Morningside Heights and on the playgrounds of Harlem, where his father, Jim, ran a team called Dyckman.

A season later, Couch, who knew Lloyd through club ball in New York, would be the final cut on the Knicks—almost making a team that had two first-round draft picks at point guard, Mark Jackson and Strickland. Here in Rapid City, someone was going to have to be cut to make room for him.

"Wonder what they'll do," Ronnie said. "They've got to make a move."

Ced suggested one. But Ronnie shook his head. Cal said something. Ronnie and Ced continued to mull options. Lloyd listened for a moment. "Ron," he said. "Mean the guys who start the season ain't the ones who get to finish it? Mean you can get traded?" Thompson laughed. So did Hunter and Kellogg. Engelland almost fell over from where he sat alongside the building. "Mean you can get traded?" Ced said, mocking Lloyd. "Mean you can get traded?"

Lloyd looked at them. "Well, I don't care if they did got rid of me," he said. "I'd just go home."

"I think it's really tough for him," Ronnie said later, as he and Cedric, who were both from Omaha, watched the Oklahoma-Nebraska football game upstairs in their hotel room. "Everyone expects so much from him, everyone is watching him. There has been so much publicity over what has happened to him. He has to realize people are just waiting for him to fuck up. Waiting for him to go bad. But he also has to realize that he has a lot of people looking out for him, a lot of people who care.

"The problem is you can't really tell what he's thinking, what he's feeling. You can't really tell if he is just saying things to keep people happy or if he really believes it. I don't know. I don't think he knows.

"I hate to say this, but if he fucks up this time he is going to end up right back where he started, on the street. And, I would hate to see that, because the boy has so much talent and you know what happens to folks on the street. He just needs maturity. I care a lot for the kid. It is tough, what he's been through. You hope it doesn't happen again. But it is up to him."

As Cedric said: "I don't think anybody on this team is going to be his baby-sitter. You can't say, 'Lloyd, come with me' all the time. He's a grown man. He has to be making his own decisions sometimes. He knows what he should be doing and what he shouldn't be doing, it's just a question of him doing it. He's got to learn to help himself."

Lloyd missed a twenty-five-footer at the buzzer that night. But, it was only at the end of the first quarter, and Topeka still held an easy lead, 35-25. It was one of the few mistakes he made in the quarter. His blind bounce pass to Batman had enabled the Sizzlers to take a 12-9 lead. His basket and two free throws had later extended the advantage to 20-11. His feed to Cal Thompson on a drive was a sight, simple yet splendid, and it kept Topeka in control at 25-20. His off-balance jumper off a pass from JoJo White had made it 35-22 before he missed the buzzer shot.

The most significant thing, though, was that Lloyd seemed comfortable, not uptight. His performance wasn't restricted by his lack of surety, as it had been the previous game. He still lacked the knowledge of how to work within the system. He struggled, at times badly, on defense. He once misread a sideline signal and called timeout at midcourt, when Killilea had simply wanted him and JoJo to switch guard positions. He forced a couple of shots late in the game, when he tried to do too much, drawing criticism from Killer. But mainly, it seemed, his game was one of confidence.

It was with confidence that he took a pass, spun twice off a defender, and, at the halftime buzzer, hit a jumper from the top of the key to give the Sizzlers a 66-39 lead. It was with confidence and skill that Lloyd easily outclassed the opposing guards—blocking former UCLA guard Montel Hatcher, drawing fouls on Brent Timm, who had attended Eastern New Mexico, and Darrin Houston, who had played at Oregon State—all of whom he knew he was better than despite his lack of experience.

And, after a word of advice from Killer—"You're forcing shots and you don't have to. You're not alone. You're not alone," he yelled from the sideline during the fourth quarter—it was with confidence that Lloyd began to distribute the ball in his special fashion. An over-the-shoulder, no-look pass to Thompson for a lay-in, a behind-the-back pass to Graham for a dunk. This was all on unrefined potential. It was Lloyd let loose, like in the park.

When it was over and Topeka had won, 119-102, Lloyd settled into the locker room more as a member of the club. In two games, he had averaged 18.5 points, 6 assists and 1.5 turnovers. And, by the time the Sizzlers would make it back to Topeka, Lloyd would be a star on the rise in the CBA. Just imagine what the kid could do when he learned the game.

12 • Goodbye, Topeka

Lloyd never seemed to learn from his mistakes. He would hint at progress, show glimpses of new-found maturity. Then, with suddenness, he would revert to his old ways. He seemed unable to fight through hard times. When faced with adversity, he usually looked for the easiest way out. It happened on court, where he would be brilliant one game and a non-factor for entire periods the next—blaming poor performances on injuries or on teammates, but never on himself. And, it happened off court, where his personal life continued to hint at a lack of dedication to his responsibilities—something that raised skepticism over whether he could ever reach his pro potential.

There was the span during the eight contests between November 29 and December 20 when Lloyd led the Sizzlers in scoring six times—including three consecutive games, with highs on successive nights against the Charleston (W.Va.) Gunners when he outscored guard Kenny Patterson, the former DePaul star from Jamaica, Queens. There was the night he strafed the Mississippi Jets for 39 points, a sum which proved to be the second-highest single-game total that season for Topeka.

Those games made a good impression on scouts, and lent hope to the thoughts that, somehow, Lloyd might overcome his past and make it. "He was phenomenal in the transition game," Peter Babcock, the director of scouting for the Denver Nuggets, said after he watched Lloyd leave Mississippi burning, having gone 17-for-25 from the field in thirty-six minutes of a 140-119 victory over the Jets. "They got him the ball in the open court and he either scored or found the open man every time." But, as Al Menendez, then scouting for the New Jersey Nets, cautioned: "He still has to prove that he's reliable, that he can exist in the pro environment."

For his part, Lloyd felt he was giving a maximum effort. He tried to be on time for practice, tried to attend weight-training sessions. But, as the season wore on, it became more and more apparent that he still had problems and that they were getting worse. Time and again, he stated "aftercare is more important than ball" to ensure his success. Then, time and again, he failed to attend meetings, substituting phone calls for personal appearances.

"I wake up every day thinkin' about the NBA," he said. But, as Bernie Glannon said, "I don't think Lloyd's ambition is what it needs to be. The guy's plain lazy. When you say, 'Lloyd, you can be a million-dollar-a-year ballplayer or you can be dead in six months,' I don't think he comprehends. Lloyd thinks training is getting up to turn on the TV."

If the message was ever to get through, it figured to happen during the first week of January, when the Sizzlers traveled to Albany, New York, for two games on consecutive nights against the Patroons. It was here that Lloyd, out of shape and making promises to "work harder"—would come face-to-face with what might well be his future.

Micheal Ray Richardson was the best-known member of the Patroons. A four-time all-star in the NBA, Richardson had been voted NBA Comeback Player of the Year following the 1984-85 season, when he returned from his third stint in drug rehabilitation to average 20.1 points, 5.6 rebounds and 8.2 assists in eighty-two games for the New Jersey Nets.

But on February 25, 1986, Richardson, who had managed to make it through the University of Montana despite being what some described as functionally illiterate, became the first player banned for life by the NBA for violating the league's anti-drug rules. After a tour with a team in Israel—one long-standing joke was that Richardson had gotten Israeli officials to spell the name "Isreal"—and a brief stretch with the Long Island Knights in the United States Basketball League, Richardson was working on yet another comeback with the Patroons. He was doing well, too. Richardson would lead Albany to the CBA title, averaging 13.9 points, 4.8 rebounds and 3.1 assists and would be granted reinstatement to the league by NBA commissioner David Stern on July 21, 1988, though he would instead opt to pursue his career with Bologna of the Italian Basketball Federation.

"He came here, paid his dues and did everything we expected of him and more," Albany general manager Gary Holle said of Richardson, who, unlike Lloyd, had attended aftercare on a regular basis. As Richardson said, "If you stick with something, then things will work out in your favor."

Richardson, serious in his comeback attempt, must have put a hundred moves on Lloyd that night in January. And, almost all of them worked. He breezed by Lloyd, made plays, handed the ball off, scored. It wasn't long before Killilea, incensed at the lack of effort, sent Lloyd to the bench. Even Albany coach Bill Musselman, an outspoken sort, had a few words for Lloyd after the game, won by Albany, 121-99.

"He couldn't defend against me," Musselman said. "He couldn't guard a water bucket. He's a worse-than-average college defender. Print that, because I hope he hears it. Maybe that'll wake him up."

Lloyd heard. After he ended pre-game warm-ups the next night he stood and stared at Musselman. Glared at him. He talked trash to Richardson. "He told me, 'You can't guard me,' " Richardson said. "I told him, 'You can't guard me either. What'd we do now?' " More important, Lloyd showed heart. Desire. The problem was, no one knew how long that might continue.

"He's got the talent, but like other guys who didn't go to college, he just doesn't have the maturity," Killilea said. "He reminds me of Bill Willoughby and Darryl Dawkins. They never reached their potential. I hope this kid does." As Topeka forward Bill Martin, who had played at Georgetown, said, "We're trying to get him where he's trying to be. I know talent-wise, he can play in the NBA. But, in the end, that'll be up to him."

In his first nine games, Lloyd averaged a team-high 20.4 points, shooting 55.1 percent from the field. In his next seventeen games, he averaged 12.1 points and shot 42.8 percent. He placed part of the blame on a knee injury suffered in Charleston when he collided under the basket with former Georgetown center Michael Graham. Team officials termed the injury a "slight hyperextension" and said it would have little effect on his performance.

So what was wrong? Lloyd was less effective, was getting less playing time and, finally, by the last week of January, was barely getting into games. He appeared a total of six minutes in three games at Pensacola and Savannah, and was benched in another at Savannah on January 27.

The following afternoon, Killilea was fired and replaced by interim coach John Darr. Asked about Lloyd, Darr had once said, "He has great talent, but there are a lot of great talents around. I imagine, if you go to New York, you'd find a lot of other great talents who aren't anywhere."

That afternoon, Lloyd missed practice. Frustrated, Glannon decided the situation had become critical and said he'd ask Lloyd to undergo urinalysis at Memorial Hospital to determine if he was again using drugs.

"There are rumors and I don't know if they are only rumors," Glannon said. "But tomorrow, I am going to suggest to Lloyd that, if they are wrong, he take a drug test, undergo urinalysis, and prove them wrong. I have seen his caliber of play deteriorate. There has been a lack of defense, a lack of aggressiveness. I am certain he has not been attending aftercare on a regular basis. In fact, I am reasonably certain he has not been doing anything on a regular basis. I just want to find out what the hell is going on.

"You know," Glannon said, "just because he is Lloyd, the rumors will persist all his life. I ask him if there is anything going on and he says no.

He told me, 'I won't lie to you, Mr. Glannon. I won't lie to you, Mr. Glannon.' But, I am going to be hurt very deeply if that is not the truth. It would just mark another victim of the horrible effects of drugs." As Lloyd later said, "An addict got some of the best schemes in the world. They got the best con in America. They can con anyone. And you're talkin' to the best, right here."

What Bernie Glannon did not know, what almost no one knew, was that Lloyd was not only using drugs in Topeka. He was also dealing them.

It had started, Lloyd said, with a midnight run to Kansas City. He and a friend had been in need of some quick cash. The two had contacted an associate and had made arrangements to deliver a package. After a game one night Lloyd and the friend went to Kansas City and collected the package, no questions asked, and delivered it same-day, express mail to Topeka. It was simple. And lucrative. The two did it again. And again. And again.

Soon, it became a regular route. "I was makin' a little money out there," Lloyd said, "[with] a little connection in Kansas City. I was a delivery man. It was mainly like, you know, ounces, half-ounces."

Lloyd had gotten into the business, he said, out of necessity. A CBA salary covers a lot of expenses, as long as a $200-a-day cocaine habit isn't one of them. But that, Lloyd said, was at least how much coke he was using when he played for the Sizzlers. It had started small. He had been clean, had done his job, had submitted to drug tests. He had made the extra effort.

But then Lloyd said that Glannon, convinced he was straight, decided to stop testing him. That provided a window of opportunity. So, Lloyd seized the moment. Once again, he started to snort coke.

"I slipped," he said. "My head got bigger. I said to myself, 'They lettin' Lloyd get over again.' They stopped sayin' I had to go to my drug testin'. They tried to be nice to me, let me have my freedom. That was a mistake. See, when I was first out there, I had to go to my testin' and I was cool. Next thing, Bernie said 'You don't have to go no more.' They didn't want to have to spend no more money, because those tests, they costed money. Then I saw him lettin' me slide, you know. The next thing I know it was like, 'I could go get high, he'll never know.' The disease started comin' back on me.

"I didn't even care 'bout playin' no more," Lloyd said. "I got to be straight with you, I didn't care 'bout playin' no more. You lazy, you tired. I ain't goin' to go out there and kill myself. I just wanted to get high."

One month, he said, he went through $10,000. Soon, even the income from his illicit courier service could not cover his expenses—both personal and business. The phone was disconnected. Creditors began to make house calls. Worse, the drug crew in Kansas City threatened to make a withdrawal, in blood, for cash owed on goods not delivered. Lloyd was living on the edge. "I was Swee'pea," Lloyd said. "A lot of people knew me. They said, 'We ain't goin' to let this punk from the schoolyards of New York City come out here and house-shit.'" Luckily for Lloyd and his friend, the crew decided it was not worth the heat they would take if they knocked off a pro basketball player. Still, Lloyd said, one time the Kansas City crew pulled guns, knives and even a few bats and "threatened to kill us."

The incident should have told Lloyd something, should have sent some sort of message to straighten up. But, it didn't. Because Lloyd decided he still needed coke and cash, and desperate, he turned to yet another scheme. He began to write bad checks. He would go into supermarkets, mom and pop groceries, write a check and get cash. After all, he was a smooth talker. And he was Lloyd Daniels, star of the Sizzlers. He had to be honest, right?

"The people knew me," Lloyd said. "I'm goin' to tell you how sick I was. I was a sick fuck. In fact, I think I need me a couple of smacks. I'd wear my Topeka hat, my Topeka jacket. They already see it's Lloyd Daniels, he plays for the Topeka Sizzlers. And now that's when I really was gettin' over, because they never checked things—it's the Sizzlers, man—so they figured, 'He must have some type of money.' I got to feelin' like, 'Nobody can't stop me.' I was the man. When I get goin', nobody can't tell me nothin'. One night, one place, I went back and wrote three checks, man. Three-hundred here, three-hundred there and three-hundred there. The lady was writin' it down like I was crazy. She didn't know what was goin' on." No one did.

Lloyd submitted to a team-ordered drug test on January 29. Knowing that the team lacked legal standing to force those results to be revealed and knowing that if they were positive CBA commissioner Mike Storen might ban Lloyd from the league, his lawyer, David Chesnoff, declined to release them. Three days after the test and, still without the results,

Glannon placed Lloyd on the injured reserve list and scheduled a meeting with both Lloyd and Chesnoff to see if the situation could be resolved.

"Bernie has told me that there are certain requirements for Lloyd if he is to remain on the team," Chesnoff said, his tone abrupt, during a phone conversation that afternoon from his office in Las Vegas. "I am not yet aware of what those requirements are, but no one has hidden the fact that this young man has problems as the result of his upbringing."

"It is just one big circus," Glannon said. "I have asked the people at the hospital to deliver to me tomorrow, if possible, and Thursday at the latest, a list of what they want him to do with regard to his aftercare. I want them to outline where the meetings are, at what time. I don't want to believe David. I don't want to believe Lloyd. I want it documented—documents signed over to me by Lloyd and David Chesnoff—that Lloyd is being tested and I want to know the results of those tests.

"Right now, I can't confirm drug tests, because I have never been given the results of the tests. I want to know those results. I want Lloyd to report to me daily, so I know that he is at practice, that he has run, that he is going to get into the physical condition he needs to be in to play. Lloyd tells me he is in condition. I said he isn't and I'm the final word. The NBA scouts in over the weekend were appalled at the shape he's in. He hasn't put on any weight since he's been here. He hasn't built any muscle. Until he meets all of the criteria, he is staying on the injured reserve list.

"I've never wavered in my support of him. But I am wavering in my patience. This guy is not in shape, in my opinion, to play professional basketball. He is losing the ball, missing lay-ups. My daughter tried to run three miles with him last week and he could only last half-a-mile before he had to turn back. I know what he can do, I know what he is doing.

"I feel it is about time someone sat him down and got him straightened out. I haven't given up on him. But I am telling people what Lloyd has got to do if he wants to remain a member of the Sizzlers.

"If he does not change, he is not going to stay on this team. I think it's the first time someone tightened the noose a little bit. Maybe we should have done this earlier. But I felt he should be able to exercise some self-discipline. The problem is, he hasn't. I had NBA scouts sit in this office last week and tell me this is the only way this kid's going to make it. He doesn't agree with me. But, right now he doesn't have any choice."

A week later, the situation had still not been resolved. Lloyd, who failed to attend practice in the interim, had still not agreed to submit to routine drug testing or attend counseling sessions. He also had made no effort to attend workout sessions. Left with no other choice, Glannon called Lloyd on Thursday, February 11. He told him he had been cut. "I called him this morning," Glannon said. "He was apologetic to the fans, to me. He said he was sorry. But I told him to pack his things. He was leaving.

"He just never shaped up, as far as I was concerned," Glannon said. "He never gave himself the chance. I don't know what the reason was. I don't understand the thing. I certainly did what I could do, including assisting him with the hospital situation, letting him stay in my home, showing him how to do things the way normal people are supposed to do them.

"But this past week he no-showed a personal appearance with two-hundred seventy kids. Somehow, I can accept him not training. I can, somehow, accept him not going to the hospital, not sitting on the bench during games while he was on injured reserve. But to no-show the kids at a personal appearance—that was the last straw.

"There was a scheduled meeting with the aftercare counselor and he did not show up. His financial responsibility has not been what one would like. I don't know where he has been at night. I don't even know where he has been during the day. There were a lot of indications that Lloyd could not—or was not willing to—adapt to a structured environment.

"We've had twenty-nine scouts through here in the few games he played for us. They told us the talent was there. But, I'm afraid he showcased himself in more of a negative light than positive. To be a professional means you have got to become responsible. It means you have to show up on time, do things properly, the way the coach wants. It means meeting the press, meeting the fans, being a professional. He was just an immature young man. He has to get it together or he'll never succeed."

Before he left the team offices for the ride to Kansas City International Airport, Lloyd stopped for a moment for one last word with Al Quakenbush, the reporter from the *Topeka Cap-Journal*. "I'm upset to be leaving the Sizzlers," he told Quake. "I just wanted to play ball. I'm sorry things didn't work out. Bernie's a good man and he tried to help me out. The Sizzlers were good to me, but I don't think I'll be back. It makes me worried about my future. I don't know if I can get to the NBA now. I got to keep my fingers crossed that somebody will want me. But it's hard to know if they will.

"If I got to go, I got to go. I can't go jumpin' off no buildin's. I'm only twenty years old. There's not that much time, but there's time."

Maybe, Quake thought. And, maybe not.

13 · Waters, Too Strong

Lloyd could not resist the temptation of the streets. The fiasco in Topeka, on the heels of the arrest in Las Vegas, had made that sad fact all too apparent. He was addicted. If not to drugs and to alcohol, then surely to self-destruction. No one in America wanted him on their basketball team, despite his vast abilities. Not in the NBA. Not in the CBA.

So, what now?

He was still just twenty. He had no visible skills other than basketball. He still owed several thousand dollars for his rehabilitation at Memorial Hospital, according to attorneys for a law firm in Topeka. He had bounced several checks. Debt collectors had begun to search for him. He needed a job. The answer to his worries turned out to be as bizarre as his past.

Not long after his dismissal from the Sizzlers, Lloyd boarded a plane and headed for another new start in life. When his trek ended and the plane set down at its final destination, the latest stop on his world tour had left him as far removed as he could be from the streets of New York.

Having considered playing professional basketball in Spain, Puerto Rico and even the Philippines, he instead found himself Down Under. Lloyd Daniels, star of the city playgrounds, was going to be a member of a basketball team in Auckland, New Zealand.

It had been David Chesnoff's idea. John Welch, a former graduate assistant coach at Nevada-Las Vegas, had gone there and liked it and had told Chesnoff it might be a good place for Lloyd to attempt a comeback—despite the fact it hardly was a hotbed of basketball.

There were just ten teams in the First Division of New Zealand's Countrywide League. They played an eighteen-game schedule, all on weekends. Each team was allowed two imported players and, though the locals were not without talent, they were hardly of the caliber common in the U.S. The salary was minimal—$500 a week—though it included the use of a house and a car, as well as airfare to New Zealand, according to league commissioner Ross Williams. Even the attendance, Williams said, was "chickenfeed." In other words, fewer than 2,500 a game in gymnasiums usually owned by the local preparatory schools.

It was the CBA, without perks.

Still, it was basketball. And for Lloyd, it figured to be a haven far

187

removed from temptation. There was, after all, no drug epidemic in New Zealand. You couldn't buy vials of crack on the street corners. Even though Auckland was the most urban part of this island nation located more than a thousand miles off the Eastern coast of Australia—the city, rooted at the narrowest section on the neck of North Island, has a population of about 894,000—when it came to moral corruption, save its "Skid Row" and red-light district, it had nothing on New York and Las Vegas.

As Lloyd noted to the team officials who delivered him from the local airport: "How come the cops here ain't got no guns?"

Because there was no need. Which was exactly why this was going to be the place where Lloyd could get his life in order, once and for all.

In New Zealand, he could get clean. In New Zealand, he could exercise in the unspoiled air—"We're nuclear free, pollution free down here," the locals liked to brag—and build strength and stamina as he recorded stats that would assist him in getting drafted in the NBA. In New Zealand, he could build a track record for being a reliable professional man; one who had become mature, one who had learned his lesson.

"It seemed like a good chance for him to prove himself," David Chesnoff said. After all, even Lloyd Daniels, it was reasoned, could not fuck up in New Zealand. It would be perfect. It had to be.

It was mid-to-late March when Waitemata coach Dave MacCalman asked John Welch if he knew of a player from the States willing to join Waitemata. Welch, himself, had joined the team just the season before. The Runnin' Rebels had been on a tour of Australia and New Zealand, had faced the National Team, and at one of the games Welch had met MacCalman. He told MacCalman that if he ever needed a player, he was interested. Within a week, MacCalman called and offered him a contract.

At the time, Waitemata was in the Second Division. As is the case with most foreign professional sports leagues, teams are placed in one of several divisions and then subjected to promotions and relegations based on their season performances—akin to the New York Yankees finishing last in the American League East and being demoted to Triple-A, while the best team in the International League is promoted to the majors to take their place. It is an odd system, but one that seems to work. And, with Welch in uniform for the remainder of the season, Waitemata went on to win the Second Division title in 1987 and earned a promotion to the First Division for 1988.

Seeing what Welch had done for Waitemata, which had only joined the federation in 1986, MacCalman figured he could use another American. So he spoke to Welch. "I need a rebounding forward who can shoot," MacCalman said. "Do you know anyone?"

Welch said he would make a few inquiries. He called Mark Warkentien in Las Vegas. "He has a player who can shoot, rebound, run the floor and who is so good, he said he is going to be in the pros soon," Welch told MacCalman. "Oh, and he's 6-foot-8."

"God," MacCalman said. "Tell me more."

"Well," Welch said. "There is just one thing Mark wants to know. Is there any cocaine in New Zealand?"

As MacCalman later admitted: "Once his past was explained, it did have me a bit worried. I thought, 'This is a player of high caliber, but he must have had a few troubles.' You don't let a guy of that talent slip through the nets of American basketball if he doesn't have troubles. But perhaps, then, I also thought, as I'm sure everyone else who has come in contact with him has, 'Well, maybe I can help this guy. I'll be the one who shows him the light.'

"Little did I know," he said. "Little did I know."

The province of greater Auckland is divided into four major areas—metropolitan Auckland, the most urban area, North Shore, Eastern Auckland or Manukau, as it was known to the locals, and Waitemata. In Maori, the language of the original inhabitants, it means "strong waters." Rapids.

New Zealand's economic structure is based primarily on agriculture and livestock, with wool, beef, lamb, mutton and produce the chief exports. The bulk of the land is fertile plains with a volcanic central plateau. A western suburb of Auckland, Waitemata was not rural—though its tallest building rose just nine stories. Lloyd had no idea what to make of it. It was culture shock. "Everything was weird down there," Lloyd said. "Like, different. It was strange. I didn't have no idea like how to adjust to things."

In New Zealand, as in other nations once part of the United Kingdom, you drive on the opposite side of the road, a bad sign for Lloyd, who already had enough trouble driving. In New Zealand, as in neighboring Australia, they don't just have dogs and cats—but also lizards called three-eyed tuataras, hawklike green parrots called keas, that sometimes killed sheep to eat their livers, makomakos and kiwis, a flightless bird. In New

Zealand, they talked strange; stranger, at times, than the shit folks talked on the streets of New York. "Even our light switches take some getting used to down here," MacCalman said. "We flick 'em down to turn 'em on, up to turn 'em off."

In an effort to get Lloyd acclimated to his new environment, the first thing MacCalman did was fetch him from the airport and take him to One Tree Hill, the highest point around Waitemata save the Whangarei Mountains to the West. "I wanted to give Lloyd a bit of an idea of where he was and of what it was like down here," MacCalman said.

As the two looked over the landscape from One Tree, famous because it had once been the subject of a song on "The Joshua Tree" by U2, MacCalman said: "How does it feel to be on the bottom of the world, Lloyd?"

"I better hold on, Davie D," Lloyd replied. "Or, I'm'll fall off."

Lloyd had arrived in Waitemata during the first week of April, which is the beginning of fall in the southern hemisphere. It was a week before the season was to begin and, because Waitemata was in its first season in the First Division, the team had still not worked out a lot of its organizational problems. Arrangements were still being made to get Lloyd an apartment and a car. Meanwhile, he moved in with MacCalman and his mother, Aline.

The house was in a well-to-do area of Waitemata. It had four bedrooms in the main house with a swimming pool, pool table and jacuzzi. It also had a separate section for MacCalman, a paraplegic confined to a wheelchair.

MacCalman was twenty-eight. He had attended college in the States, playing basketball at West Hills Community College in Coalinga, California. He spent two semesters at the junior college in the San Joaquin Valley and, on the last day of school, went swimming in a nearby river canyon. He dove in, hit the bottom, and broke his neck. Still, he loved basketball. So, when he returned to Waitemata, he decided to start a professional team.

It was a small operation. "We were without major backing and finances," MacCalman said. "We really weren't as well organized as other teams. When Lloyd came, I think he was expecting a lot different treatment than what he got. He thought it was bush-league and perhaps, to him, it was."

Nevertheless, Lloyd liked living with the MacCalmans. Within a matter of days he had arrived at nicknames for both MacCalman and his mother. "Davie D," he called MacCalman. "And he started calling my mum 'Mumsy,' " MacCalman said. "It was kind of funny, really. But he had a natural way with people. He had us laughing. He was just fun to have around." At least for a while.

There were four teams based in Auckland. On the day before the season began, members of each team marched in a parade down Queen Street, the main street in the city proper, and then gave a basketball demonstration on a temporary hoop in Queen Elizabeth Square. The parade, which drew supporters of the teams—Altos Auckland, North Shore, Ponsonby and Waitemata—was followed by a press conference.

Lloyd was more than willing to march in the parade and shoot baskets. In fact, a photo of him driving in for a lay-in before a host of onlookers in the middle of the square appeared the next morning in the *New Zealand Herald* with a caption that read: "New Yorker Lloyd Daniels shoots for goal."

Still, Lloyd had had too much press in the States. And so, even though he talked to a reporter from the *Dominion Sunday Times*—"I just want another chance," he said. "God gave me a gift. It's up to me to use it. That's why I'm in New Zealand"—Lloyd decided he was not about to go out of his way to attend an interview session. MacCalman did. He was asked the first question. "We've heard about this Lloyd," said a reporter from one of the local papers. "His reputation precedes him. What about it?"

The question caught MacCalman off guard. He understood that Lloyd had uncommon talent. He had seen glimpses of that skill during the first practice. But why should anyone care in New Zealand?

"Lloyd came from the depths of New York," MacCalman told those at the news conference, though he admitted later that he really had no conception what that meant. "A world away from New Zealand. He is here to improve his skills, to work on his chances to reach the NBA. Any reputation, things about Lloyd, should be left behind. Give him a clean break."

Later, after the press conference had ended, MacCalman thought more about the question. "I got the message," he said. Lloyd might be more well known than he first realized, and his situation might be worse.

Waitemata opened that weekend in Wellington, a city of almost 600,000 located on the southernmost tip of North Island. It was about a two-hour flight in a forty-seat plane that dipped and darted in the infamous wind currents that enveloped Wellington, which is surrounded by mountains that are home to a few active volcanoes.

The Exchequer Saints, having won the league title the previous season, were the top-seeded team in the First Division. Waitemata, its players being "rookies" as they were called, was seeded last. No one gave Waitemata much of a chance. No one, except Lloyd.

In the first minute of the game, Lloyd drew a foul and made both free throws. Two minutes later, he sank a three-pointer. With eight minutes gone, Waitemata was still close, down 22-18. Lloyd had scored fourteen. He had 22 points at halftime and Waitemata, thought to be a sure victory by many in the crowd of 2,500 at Madgwick Stadium, trailed, 52-46. Basketball in New Zealand would be a breeze, so it seemed to Lloyd.

But little more than twelve minutes into the second half, Lloyd was called for his fifth foul with Waitemata behind, 86-72. "It was a little push foul," MacCalman said. But Lloyd lost it. He began to yell. As Lloyd argued, his face inches from the face of referee Robin Milligan, a woman in the stands who was with Lloyd began to scream. "Spit on him, Lloyd," the woman yelled. "Spit on him."

As Lloyd said, "I was like, 'You son of a bitch.' *Pth, pth.* 'You motherfuck.' *Pth, pth.* I was cursing him, sprayin' him."

"We couldn't believe it," MacCalman said. "It was a bad call. Lloyd had been in the country only about five days. He didn't know how to react, so he argued it. But here was his girlfriend telling him to spit on the referee. I didn't think he actually did spit on him, but there was a reporter there who wanted to make a name for himself and he wrote a story. The next day the paper had a headline, 'Lloyd Daniels Spits on Ref.' It made him look bad, though Lloyd actually did admit to me later that he had a way of talking and spraying at the same time."

From there, the situation just got worse. Around the house, Lloyd had done what he was told. Dishes, his chores. "My mum wouldn't take any shit from Lloyd," MacCalman said. "And he listened to her. Toward the end, he was telling me she reminded him of his grandmother."

Lloyd moved out of the house after the trip to Wellington and began to share a place about a half-mile away with Warwick Meehl, a guard on the New Zealand National Team known as "The Ice Man of New Zealand," sort of the New Zealand version of George Gervin. It seemed that after all his past problems, after having worn out his welcome in so many places, Lloyd should have learned his lesson and made an effort to work—and work hard. But in his new residence, Lloyd had free rein. And there, left to his own devices, he began to run afoul of MacCalman and his team.

It started with the usual M.O. Lloyd claimed injuries in practice, then said he could not run. He would be sent to the trainer, but the trainer would not be able to find anything wrong. Soon, he began to miss practice altogether. He missed one. Then, another. MacCalman could not understand it.

"I said to him, 'Lloyd, you're down here to get yourself on the straight and narrow. The letters "NBA" should be a neon sign to you.' But he would just show up, touch his toes twice and go, 'Okay. That's it coach. I'm ready.' Then he would pull-up lame and go see the trainer. He was out of shape. He refused to run, lift weights, do the extra things he needed to do. He wasn't trying hard enough. We had a few run-ins at practice because of that.

"I'm a taskmaster," MacCalman said. "But he made it hard for me, a real test. I'd tell him, 'You have to do more than just show up.' "

"I told him the competition sucked down there," Lloyd said. "No ones had no kind of game that could touch me. Why should I have worked? It wasn't nothin'. Besides, I told Davie D what type of player I am. I said, 'I'm not 'bout bein' a practice player, Davie D. I'm a game player.' But, over there, they wanted me to work. You believe that?"

"The question is, 'Does Lloyd want to improve himself?' I know he wants to be an NBA player. But I don't think he can rationalize what it takes; the commitment, the sacrifice. He likes to win. He doesn't like to work hard. His work ethic wasn't where I would have liked it."

After the loss to Wellington, Lloyd led Waitemata to victories in its next two games. He had twenty-three as the team won by three at Nelson, located on the northern tip of South Island, and had a game-high thirty-six as Waitemata handled Altos Auckland, 94-84, in the opening of Chase Stadium, that team's brand-new 3,000-seat arena.

Off the court, though, his actions were becoming more and more distressing. He was having problems with one girlfriend, who was disturbed over allegations that Lloyd was seeing not one, but two other women, MacCalman said. As Lloyd said, "There was all these 'Kiwi Girls' who ain't never had no black boys before and they loved me. How could they not? They had to love Swee'pea. They wanted to ride me. The 'Kiwi Girls' was all over my dick."

Then, there were the drinking problems. Drugs are scarce in New Zealand. But beer flowed like water. Lloyd was going out to local bars on a regular basis with A.J. Tuitama, a twenty-one-year-old forward from Waitemata. The two would have two, three beers at a bar, then two or three at another. Before long, MacCalman said, Lloyd was bringing the beer home—usually a few cases a week. Before long, MacCalman realized he had a problem.

"He was drinking too much beer," MacCalman said of the situation, which would almost be ironic if it weren't so sad. After all, imagine a man drinking too much beer in a nation often teased for its beer drinking? As MacCalman said, "We like to drink our beer and we really don't like to hold a man down when he is having a few. But when it begins to affect his work, well, you have to ask him to stop. I never saw him so drunk he couldn't stand. But it got to the point where he was drinking enough that it became a concern."

Not that the New Zealand Basketball Federation had not seen its share of Bad Boys from the U.S. Just the season before, there had been a player from Los Angeles who robbed a local service station the night before he was to leave for home—as if a 6-foot-6, bald-headed black man would be difficult to identify in Auckland. He was arrested the next morning at the airport. Another player, loaned furniture by his club, turned around and sold it to some locals. "Twice," MacCalman said.

Still, no one had seen anyone like Lloyd. "He took New Zealand by storm," MacCalman said. "Here he was, 6-foot-8 and out of New York, a young man who knew how to hustle people. New Zealand is a back lot. We were curious, fascinated by a person like Lloyd and very susceptible. So, Lloyd was able to do whatever he wanted in New Zealand.

"He charged videos from the local shop to other members of the club. He rang home quite a few times, made toll calls, and charged them to other people. There was a liquor store about two-hundred yards from his place. He had a tab going there. He had run amuck."

After the Auckland game, Lloyd went to a team-sponsored party, known as an "aftermatch." He wasn't supposed to stay long, because the team had a game the next day. MacCalman told Lloyd to arrive early, that there was a pre-game run-through. "He swore on his mother's grave he would not let me down," MacCalman said. "To me, that was a fairly solemn vow. But he never arrived for practice." Waitemata lost by three to New Plymouth. Lloyd had just twenty-one. "That was when I lost all respect for the man."

The two met the next afternoon. MacCalman told Lloyd he was wasting his time. Lloyd said he wanted to go home. "It took us about five minutes to reach a decision," MacCalman said. Lloyd was headed stateside.

"I can't believe Davie D said it was for too much drinkin'," Lloyd said. "He knows in his heart that wasn't what it was. I left there because it was borin', because there wasn't nothin' for me to be doin', at least nothin' that I realized at the time. I was homesick, far away from home for the first time. The competition was weak, know what I mean? It wasn't nothin'. And, there was a lot of other things I could've did, except that I was a city kid and I didn't know how to appreciate them then. So, I just went to Davie D and said things wasn't workin' out. Then I just went home."

Still, as Warwick Meehl drove him to the airport, Lloyd began to have second thoughts. "Should I go?" he asked. "Think I should go?"

Meehl wanted him to remain. Deep down, so did MacCalman. But both knew it was best for him to leave. Warwick told him, "Yes."

"You know, he reminds me of Billie Holiday or Charlie Parker," MacCalman said. "He just had a sad beginning, and he doesn't seem able to shake off the scars he carries. People tried to help him. But Lloyd always seems to know all the answers. It is the life he has chosen. People have given him other options. He has looked at them, stayed with them a while. But, in the end, he always goes back to that life. He needs a crutch and his pursuit of that crutch is what has brought him down.

"We took sort of a gamble. We were told Lloyd was a bit of a time bomb and that, at some stage, he would blow it for himself and for the team. But we felt that New Zealand would be a good place for Lloyd. It turned out that it was just too much of a backwater and too much of a culture shock for him. We weren't sociologists and we weren't in a position to change him.

"I just wish it could have been under other circumstances when he was here. I wish Lloyd could have been not so Lloyd Daniels."

14 · Cracks in the Concrete Dream

The gymnasium was bathed in a dim, almost yellow light, the kind you find in most high schools, the kind that makes a place seem old and worn. The two banks of bleachers, one on each side, were full now. And the kids seated in them screamed loud as they toyed around, being rowdy, being kids. John Salley, standing under one basket, stepped to the microphone.

It had been a while since he had last been here, though he tried to make it back at least once a year, sometimes more, just to stay in touch, just to remember where it was he had come from. Just to let the kids know that someone out there, no matter how successful, still cared about them.

"Yo, Canarsie," Salley yelled over the microphone to the kids from Canarsie High School in Brooklyn, the place where he first started on a road he only dreamed would take him to the NBA. It was February, 1990, and Salley had come home for the NBA All-Star Break. He was wearing sweats and a pair of sneakers—Osaga Spiders, his own brand—and, of course, his hand was adorned with the gold, red and blue NBA Championship Ring he had won the previous season as a member of the 1989 World Champion Detroit Pistons. "Yo, Canarsie," Salley yelled again. "I'm not foolin'. Listen up!"

The noise died down. Attention turned to him. "Now," he said, "what I've got to say may not penetrate everybody. But I have one job. And my one job is to get through to one person. And, if I get through to one person, then my trip here was necessary." He paused. "I came here to talk about drugs."

Students groaned. "Yeah, I know," Salley said, as he laughed. "You figure this is going to be one of those speeches, like, 'Yo, you shouldn't do drugs. You should stay in school. You shouldn't do this, you shouldn't do that.' And then you'll turn around and the person who said that, they're being picked up for using drugs. One thing you're never going to see—and, if you do see it, you might as well call *The New York Post* and tell them they're lying again—is me using drugs. But I didn't come here to talk like that. I came here to talk to you. I came here," he said, "to talk about the future. Your future."

Salley began with a few jokes. He set the tone. He got them to listen, lured them in like a tall—and, at a shade under seven-foot, he was tall—Arsenio Hall. He laughed. He made fun of them, made fun of himself. When he finally had the crowd where he wanted them, in the palm of his hand, the man known as "The Spider" set the trap. He told his stories, issued his message. He talked about drugs. He talked about responsibility. He talked about school and the future, about hard work and effort. He talked about success.

"You know," he finally said, beginning his story, "one of my best friends got killed because of drugs back when I was in college. Another one of my friends got killed because of drugs since I've been in the pros. One of my other friends, he used to be a real good friend, too, has an occupation that I don't believe in. Hear me. Hear what I'm trying to tell you."

The kids listened as Salley spoke. His friend Don Washington had been a disc jockey at a party somewhere in Virginia. He had been working at an event where illegal drugs were being used. Someone who was high decided to rob him. When Washington fought back, the man stabbed him. He had been killed over a gold chain. The other friend was named Lloyd Harrison and he was killed back when Salley was at Georgia Tech. It had happened during the season. Harrison and some friends, who were back in New York, had allegedly gotten high and gone into a laundromat to do some clothes. A man there had crawled into a dryer. Harrison had laughed at the man, who, angered that Harrison made fun of him, shot him in the chest. In the heart. It was about as senseless a murder as murders go in New York. Yet, the drug overtones, the actions and reactions without thinking of consequences, had all the unmistakable signs of events in a drug environment.

Salley was distraught, he said. He had gone to Georgia Tech coach Bobby Cremins, asked him for a plane ticket to New York. "I know that it was NCAA violation," Salley said. "But I asked Bobby Cremins for a ticket home. He said there were three games coming up, but I said, 'I don't care, because my friend got killed, and when we find the guy who did it, we're going to shoot him.' Cremins gave me a one-way ticket. I said, 'What's this for? How am I going to get back?' He said, 'I figure if you kill the guy, you'll be a murderer, too, and won't be coming back—so it won't matter.'

"I gave the ticket back, because I realized then that this guy didn't kill my friend, but that drugs killed him. If there wasn't a drug atmosphere, none of that would have happened. I hate drugs, because that is what killed my friend." The kids in the bleachers had long grown quiet. "Bad associations," Salley said for emphasis, "spoil useful habits."

The streets of New York City are filled with bad associations. Sometimes so many that they become impossible to avoid. Associations that come in the form of life-long friends and acquaintances, people who once seemed good and honorable and who sometimes, when you least expect it, turn out to be drug dealers and muggers and murderers. Bad associations that turn out to be neighbors and relatives, turn out to be people you played ball against in the parks and on the playgrounds. Associations with people you said hello to, people you grew up with, people you knew. Or, thought you did.

And, because of that, what happens is the lines in judgment often become twisted and bent. Become corrupted. Or worse, forgotten.

It was a lesson that Holcombe Rucker had tried to teach kids in Harlem back in the days, when, in the Fifties, he laid the foundation for what would become the Rucker Pro League. Rucker understood the value of associations, of education, because he realized that he, too, could have succumbed to the streets. He had, after all, dropped out of high school to join the Army during World War II, and it was only after he came back from the war in 1946 that he went on to earn his high school diploma and a degree at City College.

Rucker saw basketball as a way to reach kids who had been unreachable, using it as a hook to teach them sportsmanship, to encourage education, to steer them toward opportunities in business—like Saul Lerner had tried to do with Lloyd. You couldn't play in one of Rucker's youth-level games until you showed him your report card. That led to the formation of an organization called "Each One, Teach One," which has working professionals—from teachers and guidance counselors to police and firefighters—who advise kids on issues ranging from health education to career options and drug abuse. But, the world that Rucker tried to make a better place has changed much since his death in 1965; the problems worse, the drugs more prevalent, the moral fiber that once bound community more corroded. It's more difficult to stay focused, more difficult to find success.

"I think it's hard to do sometimes," Mark Jackson said, "but you do have to learn to be strong and understand the road you have to take if you want to be successful. It boils down to environment, your upbringing, who you're with, the type of family you have. Those are all key factors, because there's a lot of great players that haven't made it because they became sidetracked and there's a lot of ones, who maybe aren't as good as those guys, who stayed on the right path and became successful. You've got to remember, there's a lot of legends on the streets of New York City."

Jackson was sitting in the Knicks' locker room in Madison Square Garden, getting dressed for a game against the Dallas Mavericks. He knew of what he spoke. He had played both with and against many of those legends—Lloyd, Ron Matthias, Richie Adams, Red Bruin, Pearl Washington, Walter Berry and Kenny Smith, among others—while growing up in the Hollis-St. Albans section of Queens. He had seen a few reach the level he had. He understood that more than a few of the folks who never got there, never made the NBA, were better than some of the players he would face soon outside on the court, better than more than a few he faced every night.

Jackson knew because back when he was a student at Bishop Loughlin High School in Brooklyn, he was perhaps the third best guard in the city—behind both Washington, who became a national sensation at Boys & Girls and Syracuse, and Smith, an all-American at Archbishop Molloy and North Carolina. Jackson went from there to St. John's, where he gained respect as a good player who could sometimes be outstanding. But he was not considered great despite being selected one of the two best players in the metropolitan area as a senior at St. John's.

Mark Jackson had something a lot of players didn't. He had determination. And, that determination allowed him to focus in on one goal—the NBA. It allowed him to move on while friends around him fell. It allowed him to bypass the streets. Because, even though he still had a few bad associations and sometimes ran with the wrong crowd—in the summer of 1989, he had to be subpoenaed to testify as a character witness for an old neighborhood acquaintance, Thomas Mickens, who was on trial in Brooklyn federal court on charges related to his alleged cocaine trafficking and money laundering operations—he usually knew when it was best for him to move on. It forced him to become image-conscious, knowing that, even in college, he was a role model; knowing that kids wanted to emulate him and knowing that to be a success he had to be positive about himself, about the future.

Despite being labeled as too slow, too sporadic, and despite being selected eighteenth overall in the first round of the 1987 NBA Draft, he went on to become the first rookie ever to average double-figures in assists as he was voted 1987-88 Rookie of the Year. Despite his critics, the following year he was named to the East squad for the NBA All-Star Game.

Not that Jackson hasn't had problems. He has had a few. There was his publicized dispute over having to share his position with Rod Strickland, a dispute which, some said, contributed to Strickland's being traded to the San Antonio Spurs. There was what some viewed as whining over his treatment in the press, as well as negative reactions toward fans who booed his poor performances. And, there were his shortcomings as a player, most notably that he had a hard time defending almost everyone in the league.

Still, Jackson had made it a lot further than most people ever thought he would. He made the NBA. And, what allowed him to do this, he said, was family. Family who had stuck by him, believed in him. Friends who had lent their support. "I was very fortunate to have good backing, as far as my family was concerned," said Jackson, who had even lived at home during his rookie season. "That backing was a very influential part of growing up. It kept my priorities straight. It helped keep me away from the wrong people, helped keep me headed in the right direction, helped me with academics, everything. It helped me to stay strong. It helped me to be smart enough to know when to say, 'Yes,' and when to say, 'No.' I'm glad that I had that, because, when I go back to the neighborhood and I see some of the guys still playing, I realize that it's really unfortunate they didn't have that, too."

Unfortunate, because kids without that guidance often never got a chance to become like John Salley or Mark Jackson—or, even to become a success merely by becoming good citizens. Instead, despite their best efforts, they often get caught up in "situations," as problems are called on the street, their careers passing them by the way Lloyd's was; their lives complicated by the lack of foresight when choosing friends. Bad associations are like that. Just look at what they did to the worlds of Shorty Black and Greg Vaughn.

Shorty Black hadn't liked the call, it having gone against his team, and so angered, the witness alleged, he decided to do something about it late on that summer afternoon on the asphalt courts of Baisley Park. His teammates had protested to the referee and had made it known that he had made an inappropriate decision when he disallowed a basket with about a minute left in the contest and the other team ahead by just two.

But the ref said he was not going to change his mind, was not going to reverse his call—a call which, police and several street-level informants said, may have cost the game for The Supreme Team.

Too much had been riding on the outcome. Police said as much as

$50,000—the sum allegedly placed on the game, allegedly sponsored as a "community service" of sorts by local drug dealers. And so, Robert Whitfield testified before Justice Lawrence J. Finnegan in New York State Supreme Court, Shorty Black hit the referee.

It had happened in an instant, too fast for the referee to react in self-defense. Shorty Black, whose real name was Earl Byam, had come from the bench, his fist drawn as a lethal weapon, Whitfield testified.

A bad call can cost a man and his team a lot in the parks and on the playgrounds of New York City. And, though no one other than Whitfield seemed sure who threw that punch, when it was thrown that warm July afternoon and it landed firm, landed sound, it also cost Greg Vaughn, the man on the receiving end of the blow, his life.

Shorty Black, charged with manslaughter, pleaded his innocence. He had not been the assailant, he said, but had been the victim of mistaken identity. A few witnesses testified that perhaps that was not true—one, Hassen Pinchback, a law clerk who lived in the neighborhood and who had served as the time-keeper and alternate referee for the game, agreed to take the witness stand despite alleging death threats had been made against himself and his family. No one, however, could offer proof to substantiate the accusation against Shorty Black and no one, other than Whitfield, claimed to have seen him throw the fatal punch.

In fact, other witnesses—including one named Darrin Hall, who said he had watched the game from a point outside the chain-link fence that surrounded Baisley Park—told the court it was not Shorty Black who was involved at all on the afternoon of July 30, 1988. It had been someone else, Hall said. A fact which, some street-level police sources said, was true.

Under cross-examination, Assistant District Attorney John Scarpa had asked Hall, "Are you positive that Earl Byam did not throw that punch?"

"Yes," Hall said, having added that his view was such that it was "clear enough to see it wasn't Earl."

Neither he nor anyone else seemed to know who, though, had delivered the blow during the fracas that had evolved after the call. The first law of survival on the streets, after all, is to forget a man's face and his name in due haste when hard times come to call.

And so, Shorty Black walked clean, and rightfully so, since there had been no proof of wrongdoing by him. An eleven-man jury—the twelfth juror had nearly had a nervous breakdown during deliberations and was excused three hours prior to the delivery of the verdict—found in favor of acquittal on charges of first-degree manslaughter, second-degree manslaughter and second-degree assault on the afternoon of June 20, 1989.

"Lord! Oh, God!" Shorty Black had yelled when the verdict came in, having grabbed his attorney, Howard Meyer, and hugged him for dear life. "Thank you. Thank you, God. Oh, God. Oh, God. Oh, God. Thank you."

Greg Vaughn, relatives said, had no idea that the game he was to referee might be run by drug-lords. He would not have done such a thing, they said, had he known. Vaughn, after all, had spent a great deal of time preaching the perils of drug usage to local kids and his stature, both as a teacher and coach and as a man, was of assistance in getting his message through.

"He was always against any kind of drugs—beer, crack, heroin, cocaine," one former player, Bryan Cromwell, said. "He told us that if anyone ever came in smelling like beer, he'd take him into a room and beat him like if his own son had done it." His kids, both his students at P.S. 140 in South Jamaica and his players, respected that attitude. It meant he cared.

Vaughn was 6-foot-6, 235 pounds, and had been a basketball star of sorts at Queens College, a Division II school just off the Long Island Expressway in Flushing, Queens. He had become the all-time leading scorer and rebounder in school history, scoring 1,873 points and grabbing 989 rebounds. His uniform, Number 44, had even been retired during a ceremony in 1986.

After his graduation, he had become the assistant and then head basketball coach at Medgar Evers College. Later, tired of having to drive across Brooklyn from his day job to Medgar Evers where his job, which was part-time, paid little, he resigned from that position to become a junior varsity coach at Prospect Heights High School in Brooklyn. It was more convenient.

The basketball team at Medgar Evers, a Division III school with few resources when it came to finances, was often bad. Vaughn, a man who knew how to remain in good spirits in the face of hard times, tried his best to take it in stride. Even when his team once headed into the post-season conference tournament with a record of 2-20, he kept his sense of humor. "I've got my strategy all figured out," he said. "First, I'm going to go out to a restaurant, sit there all day and eat until I put on a hundred pounds. Then, I'm going to get me a pair of glasses and a white towel.

By game time, I'll look like John Thompson and maybe my team will play like Georgetown."

He took life for what it was. And, he was having fun. As Shawn Woods, who had been a forward for him at Medgar Evers, recalled after his death, "He could make a guy laugh at a funeral on Christmas Day."

Despite his jovial nature, and despite his fear of what drugs could do to a neighborhood and to its residents, Greg Vaughn was caught on a battleground—one through which, despite his stature, even he could not safely tread; one which, despite his background, perhaps he did not fully understand. After all, the battle-lines often are unclear in neighborhoods like South Jamaica, Queens, where drug dealers and thugs may appear to be average citizens and where average citizens may turn out to be of the criminal mind. Sometimes, it is just too hard to tell.

Some said Vaughn must have known what kind of game he was working, especially since he was paid for his time and especially since Baisley Park, located on Foch and Guy R. Brewer Boulevards near the back of the Baisley Park Houses in South Jamaica, is known as "The Sniff Bowl." Whether he knew of the element that joined him in the park that afternoon and looked the other way because those people had once been friends and neighbors, or whether he had no idea, proved, in the end, to be a moot point.

Struck in the head by an unidentified assailant, he fell face first into the ground that afternoon and wound up in a comatose state—left in the arms of Hassen Pinchback, who had been his friend, as all the other bodies, devoid of souls, scrambled out through the gates of the park and into the recesses of the neighborhood. Five days later, Greg Vaughn died another victim.

He was thirty-three.

On the streets, they call them "vics." They know no colors, no sexes, no ages. They are victims. Innocent, involved by happenstance. They are hurt, maimed, changed for life. That's if they're lucky. Usually, they just die.

Barbara Chiles had been a "vic." Which had a lot to do with the emotion her son was feeling when he took the court at Columbia University that night in March, 1989. Tony Chiles, Jr., who had been on Riverside Church and who knew Lloyd quite well from club games and from games in the parks, wore a white headband that night as he drew a heartfelt ovation from the crowd. Across the front, in hand-drawn letters, he had written a simple dedication. "Mom," it read, the same inscription also written on his left wristband.

Just a week earlier, his mother had been found slain in her apartment in the Kingsbridge section of the Bronx, handcuffed with two other women and shot twice in the head, execution style. One of the other women also died. Police, seeing the situation, called the double-homicide a drug-related hit. It was a simple explanation, one that seemed to fit the scenario. Except, Tony Chiles said that night, it didn't. Instead Chiles, a senior political science major at Columbia who later would become a basketball agent, said it was just a case of his mother being in the wrong place at the wrong time—another innocent victim in a city already filled with too many innocent victims.

"My mother was a good person," Chiles said, soft spoken, as he stood in the hall outside the Columbia locker room, drained from the emotion of the game—a 92-85 overtime loss to Yale, the first since his mother's death. "She had nothing to do with drugs or those situations. If you had listened to the story the police told or read the ones in the newspapers, you would think that my mother was the queen of crack in the Bronx. It wasn't anything like that."

It would take more than a year for police to learn just why Barbara Chiles was murdered. Strange as it seems, the full picture became clear only after the then still-unsolved case appeared on the television show "America's Most Wanted." It turned out, police said, the assailants had allegedly kidnapped one of the women, nineteen-year-old Sarray Watson, and another woman, named Rita Faulk. Watson, Tony Chiles said, had been a casual friend of his brother's girlfriend. She had been to Chiles' home once, but knew that Barbara Chiles worked at Chemical Bank and kept the books for a store owned by his relatives. Accosted less than five blocks away, Watson had panicked when the robbers demanded money from her and Faulk. She took them to see Barbara Chiles. And Chiles and Faulk wound up dead.

"It was a situation that got out of control," Tony Chiles said, later. "She was a young girl. She panicked. My mother died. She was an innocent bystander." Unfortunately, in New York City, such situations are not uncommon.

Drug games, too, are common in New York City. Almost as common, in fact, as drugs and violence on the playgrounds, though often much harder to find. While crack vials litter the streets in most neighborhoods, for the most part the games go on unannounced to all, except the participants, who are hired to perform while bets are placed between rival factions. The usual payment to key players, who appear because the money often is just too good to pass up, is said to range at times into the low-to-mid four figures. For organizers of these games, the stakes are said to often be much higher.

One playground player tells of a game scheduled to be held one summer in a park buried somewhere in Harlem. The call went out to some real talent, the player said, some of the best known to both high schools and colleges, and even a few former members of the professional ranks.

"This homeboy, called himself 'Robocop,' who I think was a real cop and who sometimes worked a few games here and there as a referee, was supposed to work the event," the player said of the game. "It was to involve some top-shelf folks. Robocop showed and met this dude pulled up in a Benz. He opened the back lid and there it was, a hundred-and-fifty grand, in cash, just sittin' there in the trunk. Players was each going to be gettin' like five-grand to appear. They offered Robocop two-grand to call the game.

"He said, 'Think I'm crazy? If I make a bad call, the bullets'll be flyin'. I could make myself dead.' " So he turned down the assignment and the game never came off that afternoon. "The thing was, he was right," the witness said. "This was some dangerous folks. Some serious shit."

Often, witnesses said, games are run in parks and playgrounds that are inaccessible to all but the slickest of the slick and only "known" viewers are given a chance to watch. Watchdogs stand armed with undergarment Uzis and are usually dressed to the *nines*—in this case .9-millimeter automatics or "M&Ms with peanuts," the gun and its bullets—those being weapons of choice. On the streets, it is called "goin' illegal."

And, illegal, those guards stand their ground to keep curious folks, the "unwanted element"—that is, cops and coaches and, yes, reporters—out and away from the action, which, witnesses claim, often includes bets being taken out in the open. One afternoon, the action might be at The Sniff Bowl, another afternoon at Ajax Park in Queens and another, still, at The Mecca in Brooklyn or Mitchell Houses in the Bronx. Or, anywhere.

"A lot of kids play in drug games," Stan Dinner, the old Ben Franklin coach, said, stressing that, for many, the work beat working a minimum-wage job. "It's an easy way for some of these kids to earn some money. You can pick up a few hundred bucks if you have the right connections."

"Hundreds, maybe thousands of kids have played in those type games," Ron Brown said. "Some get a few bucks. Some get more than a

few bucks. It's attractive because it's easy money. They don't think about
what it really is, so they just don't turn it down. They figure, 'Everybody
does it.' "

"Everybody in New York knows about it," said Tiny Archibald, who
was raised in the environment and who knows people who play in these
games. "It involves high school kids, college kids. There's a lot of people
getting paid. People in the front row are handing out money. Some of
these kids are driving cars you and I can't afford. You see it. Some guys
get five-hundred, a thousand a game. The drug dealers, they're buying
players. They tell the folks they're betting against, 'I'm gonna bust you
by eight. I'm gonna bust you by ten.' They set the line and decide how
much to bet. The kids get paid, are getting stuff, on the basis of how they
can dictate the outcome of a game."

But there is more to those games than money and bets. Because,
scarier, drug games and drug tournaments are often "sponsored events,"
run by neighborhood power brokers who use them to both improve their
stature and gain respect in the community. "You know how McDonald's
is into community relations?" said one local basketball scout who is familiar
with the games. "Well, your drug dealer maybe would like it to be known
that he is willing to give back to the community, too, because it's good for
business. So, maybe he sponsors a tournament for the kids. Maybe, he
buys some shirts for the players. Maybe, he buys some trophies or some
sneakers and hands them out. It improves the way folks view him.

"Think about it. Why did people always protect the Mafia? Because
they were scared, but also because the Mafia looked out for the community."

Like bad associations, those contributions often skew the line between
right and wrong. What with all the positives and negatives of the situation,
sometimes it is difficult to make out all the angles. Though it sounds
cliched and stereotypical, dealers are often viewed as successful people
in the community and, despite the dictums of common sense, are often
held in high esteem. It goes back to having juice, back to making cash
money and to having something that others want.

And, the view of those community people is perverted even more
when dealin' folks put back into the neighborhood some of what they
take out, if not in blood, then at least in a material sense. Politicians often
ignore their needs. Police, too, more often than not. "Folks in inner-city
environments are constantly faced with poor housing, poor sanitation,
high unemployment rates," said Bob McCullough, Sr., who served as
commissioner of the Rucker League. When someone shows interest in

lending a helping hand, even someone of questionable moral fiber, it is not often rebuffed.

A few years back, Earl Manigault, who had tried to heed the advice of people like Holcombe Rucker, decided to run a tournament for little kids in Goat Park. Called "The Goat Tournament," it had, as its goal, to teach the kids to steer clear of drugs and the streets and to place an emphasis on education. It is frightening. But to fund his tournament Manigault turned to dealers, getting from them the money he needed to purchase shirts and uniforms for the kids. "I told them dealers," he said, "You have to put something back into the community. They couldn't argue with The Goat."

A long-time associate of Manigault, Gene Williams, who worked with the Rucker League and "Each One, Teach One," argued with the logic. But he had a hard time arguing with the results. After all, he said he disliked the notion of dealers funding tournaments. But he admitted that, sometimes, it is hard to dissuade folks from accepting their assistance for something positive.

"It takes money to run a tournament and, if the parks department cannot run the tournament, these people feel someone has to," Williams said. "It's bad. It gives dealers exposure and gives some legitimacy to what they do. I don't condone it. But what can you do? The message is there, anyway. And, it does lend itself to having activities in the community."

The problem, of course, is that despite all the uncertainties on the streets of New York, there always remain certain constants. One is the basic law of the streets: You get what you pay for. Unfortunately, on the playgrounds and in the streets, the phrase sometimes takes on a perverse new meaning.

Vernon Harton was in his office at Jacksonville College when the phone rang. It was early August, and Harton was sweltering in the heat of another Texas afternoon. Still, his mind was on basketball. The fall semester would begin in a month at Jacksonville, a small junior college in Jacksonville, Texas. Basketball season couldn't be far behind. So when Harton lifted the phone and heard it was Malloy Nesmith, a returning player from Monroe High School in the Bronx, he was estatic. For a moment, that is.

"He said, 'Coach, did you hear the news?' " Harton recalled. "I was like, 'No. What's going on?' Then he told me."

What Nesmith told Harton was that Karlton Hines, Jacksonville's star recruit, was being held without bail in the House of Detention for Men on Rikers Island. He had been charged with second-degree murder.

"Malloy said, 'You can forget about Karlton because he's in the slammer,' " Harton said. "I said, 'He's in the slammer?' and Malloy said, 'Yeah, they said he killed somebody.' As you can guess, it came as a shock. I couldn't believe it. I never had anyone who couldn't come to school because 'maybe he killed somebody.' It's terrible, a guy with all that ability. We heard he couldn't find the classroom, that he didn't always want to go to school. But we hadn't heard whether or not he had ever been in trouble. I guess he is now. After all, they got him for murder. We've crossed him off our list."

Once, Hines had been selected as the best player in Manhattan. That was back when he was a sophomore at Manhattan Center High School—which had once been Ben Franklin—and back when he was on the Gauchos. From there, he had tried to get out of the city, spending a season at Maine Central Institute, where, courtesy of tuition paid by Lou d'Almeida, the 6-foot-5 swingman averaged 25.1 points, 7.6 rebounds and 6.2 assists and was offered a scholarship to Syracuse. But, you know the old cliche: "You can take the boy out of the city, but you can't take the city out of the boy." And Karlton Hines, well, he couldn't leave the streets. So he left Maine Central.

According to Edward McCarthy, spokesman for the Bronx District Attorney, Hines's arrest stemmed from what was believed to have been a drug-related altercation in the Bronx on July 30, 1989. The incident ended, McCarthy said, when Hines "took a broken bottle and slashed the throat" of 30-year-old Edwin Santos in an alley behind a building on East 156th Street, near Yankee Stadium. Santos was pronounced dead on arrival at Lincoln Hospital.

Hines, who was just nineteen, claimed self-defense. He said Santos had pulled a knife on him. Still, here he was, a tragic figure. Selected a preseason high school all-American by no less than *Street & Smith's*, Hines, who had lost his scholarship earlier in the year when Syracuse heard he had dropped out of classes at Adlai Stevenson, was now charged with second-degree murder, as well as second and third-degree assault and resisting arrest.

But Hines got off. "It was alleged by the defendant that the other man had pulled a knife on him and that, in self-defense, he took a broken bottle and slashed the throat of the other man," McCarthy said, as he tried to explain the decision reached by a grand jury in Bronx Criminal Court. "The grand jury believed that and refused to indict him."

"That afternoon," Tony Chiles said, "Karlton came up to 155th Street and was playing ball like nothing happened. He came straight to the park. He was like, 'Ain't no big thing.' He scored something like thirty-five, I think."

And so, when Harton answered his office phone in late August, 1989, and heard the news, he decided to change his stand a bit. After all, like most coaches, he knew talent when he saw it—questionable association or not. "Karlton got off, did he?" Harton said. "Hey, well that's no problem then. I mean, well, if it was only self-defense, I can live with that then. As long as he didn't murder anybody, well, then, I tell you partner, he can still play here if he wants to."

Hines never did make it to Jacksonville. At last word, he was still in the Bronx.

John Salley had a desire to bypass the streets that had swallowed up the likes of Earl Manigault and Red Bruin, that were swallowing up the likes of Lloyd, Greg Vaughn and Karlton Hines, that had swallowed up his own friends—friends who, like him, had once had a future. Friends who, instead of finding the road to success, had become dead or as good as dead.

What Salley did, what he was telling the kids at Canarsie to do, what he told kids all over the country to do in his role as a guest speaker, was to find a way to avoid trouble. He told them to be strong, to avoid the easy way out. "My mother," he said, "always told me there were two paths I could take in life. She told me there was a straight path toward your goal and a crooked one. She asked me which one I wanted to take. I said, 'The straight one.' She said, 'No. You want to take the crooked one. The straight one means you're taking shortcuts to get there, cutting corners. The crooked one may take more time. But you learn to play by the rules, learn to overcome obstacles and, in the long run, learn to be a better person.'"

It was not an easy thing to do. Then again, Salley said, "If making it was easy, everybody would do it. That's the truth. I didn't have talent, as much talent as some people, but I had determination and hard work."

It was true. Salley was not much of an athlete back in high school. Just a bit over six-foot, he had to make the Canarsie basketball team as a walk-on—the seventeenth man on a seventeen-man roster. He was under-recruited in high school, a pencil-thin 6-foot-7 forward who had raw ability and heart, but an uncertain future as a major-college player. Georgia Tech took a chance on him because he had potential and because he was the type of kid who would work his hardest to bring that potential to fruition.

He was someone who was able to see the future, the way he had when he attended Canarsie—"I got in trouble back then, but only for standing out by the door talking to the girlies," he told the kids at Canarsie. "But I came to class"—and the way he did at Tech, where, by the time he left school, he had grown to seven-foot and become a first-round draft pick in the NBA. Even when he fell twelve credits short of graduation, he made them up in summer school after he had reached the NBA. As he said, "That degree was important to me." He was the first black player at Tech to have his jersey retired.

Still, Salley knows that things could have turned out different for him. He saw bad things happen to his friends back in the Bayview Houses, which overlook Jamaica Bay, a complex hardly as bad as areas like the Bronx and Harlem and East New York. But still, an area that had its trouble.

"As far as living in a certain environment, a lot of times you're born to fail, if you know what I mean," Salley said later, as he sat in the coaches' offices at Canarsie. "You're in a situation where you're not going to win—I don't want to be that negative—but, where the system doesn't want you to win. Still, sometimes people slip out. I just happened to be the one to slip out that time. See, if you grow up your whole life looking at people pimp, you're going to be a pimp. If you grow up your whole life looking at drug dealers, sometimes that's the way it goes for you. My environment was that I watched my father get up at four-thirty in the morning and not come back to the house until five o'clock at night. He'd watch Walter Cronkite and go to sleep. He drove a truck. He worked hard. He did the same thing his whole life.

"In other words, I had a positive example. I had a family. But, what I try to tell these kids, kids who might not have that, is that what you have to understand when everybody's running around and patting you on the back—or, when people are running around putting you down—is that, in the end, it's only going to be you. Yourself. When you were born, you were born by yourself. When you die, you will die by yourself. And, if you want to be a success in life, you have to do it by yourself. No matter what your situation is, no matter how it was that you started off in life."

That Salley now tries to be a role model for kids is because he had seen others, other pros, do the same when he was younger. He had sat at clinics and listened to Bernard King, then with the Knicks, talk about success. King, after all, came out of Fort Hamilton High School near the Verrazano Bridge in Brooklyn to find both trouble and success at the

University of Tennessee and the Golden State Warriors. Yet, King had managed to overcome his problems. And he told kids that they could do the same.

Salley listened. He listened to King and to others like World B Free, who had come out of Canarsie with Geoff Huston to make the NBA, yet who still came back to give clinics and talk to kids about success. "You know," Salley said, "those guys gave me hope. They made me think about things."

They made him think about life, about the world. About himself. As he said, "People ask me who my idol is and I tell them, 'Malcolm X.' They ask me why and I tell them it's because he went from a negative to a positive. He was in jail, he was a bad person. He took drugs, he sold drugs. He was, at times, a pimp for women. He was put in jail for his negativity. He went to jail, educated himself, read every book that he could possibly read to the point where he had to wear glasses. He came out, took a religion that he felt was of his feeling and conscience. He took people from what you would call the gutter to become upstanding human beings and I think that's important. He told people, 'Follow your conscience and let it be your guide.' "

Michael George still lives in the neighborhood where he came up, around the St. Nicholas Projects—St. Nick to the boys on the block—on 131st Street in Harlem. He still has the same friends, what few are left, and still takes his runs in the same park where he played ball as a kid. He accepts the area for what it is: A home to working-class folks, some struggling to make it 9-to-5 and others, still, looking to make it on the shortcut.

Back when, he was a player. Not a known one, but one who got his share of time in the neighborhood parks. He teamed in the same backcourt with Steve Lappas, the former assistant coach at Villanova who later became the head coach at Manhattan College, to win the 1970-71 Public Schools Athletic League "B" Division City Title at Bronx High School of Science. After college, he became a sports reporter for *The New York Post*.

He also once was a member of a drug team. It wasn't nothin' at the time, he thought. A few locals, people he had known all his life. Parkies. It began one day, when they were approached by a summer-league coach named Darryl, who needed players. Mike and his friends agreed to play.

Darryl had a fine team and one of his best players had once been a starter in the Atlantic Coast Conference. Darryl also turned out to be a drug dealer. But he treated his team right, whether it was members who worked for him in the field, or just ones who were on his team to play a little ball. And so, the kids thought, it was easy not to mind his occupation.

"You could always go to Darryl and borrow five-hundred for new sneakers," George said. "Know what I'm sayin'? He took care of his crew. He wanted us to be the best. To be respected. Now, some of us wasn't about drugs. But that didn't affect the way he treated you. His team was a reflection on him, on his business. Things had to be done right.

"When we went to games, we went in a black pearl limo. Darryl would send over three limos to take his team to the games. We used to go from Manhattan over to Brooklyn, pull up at maybe eleven o'clock at night in front of these projects, and pile out this limo—steppin' out in style to play our game. We would intimidate people just because we played for someone who could afford to send us in limousines and have them wait around for us while we played the game. It was a whole social thing. There were guys who couldn't play for Darryl and guys who wanted to."

To some of the crew, the impressionable ones who didn't have their head, the lifestyle was one they then chose to follow. Not only did Darryl use his team to enhance the reputation of his drug business and earn a little side cash with some well-placed bets on the games, sometimes even betting against them—but he used his team to recruit new employees, who became street-level dealers. Of course, the one constant understood by Mike George and not understood by most young kids on the street, was the consequences of making such associations—which is why George eventually quit the team. There was the brutality of street-level corporate takeovers, which happened when you least expected them, when things were going good or bad. They were swift, messy and always very deadly. They ruined your future, like they did to a player named Razor, who was shot in the head—just like Darryl.

"Darryl got killed," George said. "And the set-up was that Darryl probably got killed by someone on the team, this guy named Hilton, and everyone knew it. See, Darryl got killed in his apartment. Darryl was the kind of guy who always came to the door with his gun cocked, because of the nature of the business. But Darryl didn't have his gun when he got two in the head. He left it in his desk drawer. So everyone figured it had to be someone he knew. Hilton lived in the building. Hilton wanted to move up in the organization. And, Hilton was the guy who was crying loudest at the funeral.

"But it wasn't long before Hilton got set up, too," George said. "He was in the community center hangin' out when someone came runnin' in and said, 'Hilton, there's someone outside needs to see you.' Hilton went outside and took three in the chest." In other words, choose your friends well.

But perhaps it's because it is difficult to tell the good folks from the bad that a game between the Rastafarians—a posse whose trade was alleged to be in marijuana—and The Supreme Team—a crew, as members of a drug gang are known on the street, whose business was alleged to be in crack cocaine—came to be refereed by Greg Vaughn. Perhaps, that was how Boo Harvey, then the point guard at St. John's, also came to be a participant.

Harvey told St. John's athletic director Jack Kaiser he had considered the contest to be "a pick-up game." He also denied knowledge of players having been paid, though it seems unlikely a player of Harvey's stature—someone who grew up in the infamous Forties Projects in South Jamaica—would not have known the game was funded by drug dealers and that certain players would receive money. "There's always heavy betting on these games," one police source said, "and [gang members] probably would want to let bettors know it's going to be happening. Players would have to know."

Some street-level informants even told police that Harvey, who had performed for The Supreme Team, had been paid for his appearance. "A drug game?" the police source said. "Fifty-thousand? Someone was paid. You know the 'name' players must have gotten some cash to be there."

Harvey, who refused public comment on the situation, denied he was paid. And, as Kaiser said: "I'm not Sherlock Holmes. I have to believe my man. We did have a special session with Boo and he steadfastly said he did not get paid and said he did not know if anyone got paid. I asked questions, he gave me answers. Boo was very candid. He said that, at the time, he did not consider this to be a big thing. He was in his own neighborhood, on his own playground. We told him there was this necessity to watch acquaintances and friends and where he hangs out. But these are probably people he has known all his life. Kids, you know, can easily rationalize."

"You hear rumors and you read things in the paper," St. John's coach Lou Carnesecca said. "Drugs, gambling. It's all conjecture. This referee was a nice guy. He must have thought it was all right to be there. Boo did, too."

Though the NCAA eventually suspended Harvey for one game for having appeared in what was termed "an unsanctioned summer-league game," in reality, the suspension was irrelevant. Of importance, really, was what his participation illustrated: That money, drugs, violence and basketball are inextricably linked in the inner city. They are part of.life, part of death.

Like Mike George and Greg Vaughn, Harvey was only dealing with people from the neighborhood, a neighborhood in which he had received mixed messages all his life. Chances are, as Kaiser said, he had known most of those people since childhood and never once questioned their motives or their business. To him, to Mike George, to Greg Vaughn and to others they were acquaintances, people to play ball with. That some might be drug dealers or doctors was not a factor. To him, to them, they were just folks.

And, perhaps that was why, when folks in the middle-class neighborhood of South Jamaica got together to hold a three-day memorial tournament at Baisley Park in an effort to raise money for a widow, Robin Vaughn, and her six-year-old son, Darryl, more than a dozen uniformed officers from the housing police had to be called in to patrol the area. It seemed someone reported that local residents had been seen placing bets on the games.

All this, John Salley said, was why it was important for little kids to see him, to see he was, as he said, "tangible." It was important that they see other positive role models. People like his teammate Vinnie Johnson, who had come out of the city and now talked to kids about success. People like Rolando Blackman, who graduated from Grady High School in Brooklyn and became a four-time NBA all-star. People who had turned their lives around like Bernard King and Chris Mullin. People who provided positive examples, like Len Elmore, who came out of New York City to have a fine NBA career, then went to work as both a television commentator and an assistant district attorney in Brooklyn. People like Ricky Sobers and World B Free and Kenny Smith and Kenny Anderson. People who made it, were making it.

"You know," Salley told his audience that afternoon at Canarsie, "when I was in school, like the fourth grade, I had a friend in my class named Darryl Littles. When we got to the fourth grade, Darryl Littles couldn't read. Now, it wasn't the school's fault. You can't say it was his parents' fault. It was Darryl's fault. We was in a science class and the teacher said, 'Darryl, read this paragraph.' Darryl said, 'I don't have my glasses on. I can't see.' Good trick, right? The next time, the teacher called on Darryl and Darryl had his glasses, had his glasses on and, when he was asked to read, he said, 'I can't. I got a headache.' Everybody was going, like, 'He can't read. He can't read.' And Darryl was like, 'I can read. I just got a headache.' I said, 'Darryl, you didn't know the word, did you?' He said, 'I knew the word. I knew the word. I just didn't feel good.' Let me tell you something. When Darryl finally told me he couldn't read, he was embarrassed. My mother helped him learn how to read. I helped him learn how to read. Darryl's a sergeant [in the military] now. And you have to read if you want to make sergeant, because you have to take tests. What I'm trying to say is that, if a brother like Darryl can make a change in a little bit of time, then anybody can change—if they want to."

As one kid from Brownsville, a member of the Canarsie basketball team named Dwayne Carter, said when Salley was done, "This meant a lot to me. I can understand, relate to it. A couple of my friends have gotten shot. One got shot in the head. One got shot in the back over a girl and another was shot 'cause of drugs. It means a lot for him to come down here and tell us that it don't have to be that way. Maybe it will make a difference."

For the sake of those whose futures hung in the balance and had yet to be decided, you could only hope he was right.

15•Van Nuys, ASAP

To be eligible for the NBA Draft, college underclassmen had to declare, in a written letter to the league, their intentions to leave school. The same was true for other players—in college or otherwise—whose senior class had not yet graduated. Once having submitted the appropriate forms, the names of those players were then placed on a list of so-called "early entries."

The list for the 1988 NBA Draft contained twelve such names—most of them expected—when the league disclosed the identities of the eligible underclass draftees on May 18.

Guard Rex Chapman had decided to leave Kentucky. Tito Horford, the 7-foot-1 sophomore center whose controversial enrollments in Houston and Louisiana State had once been nullified by the NCAA, had announced he would leave Miami. Jerome Lane was going to leave Pittsburgh and Charles Shackleford had said goodbye to the folks at North Carolina State. Guard Rod Strickland, the junior from New York City whose college basketball career had been best described as checkered, had thrown in the towel at DePaul.

But one name on the list caught most people by surprise. Lloyd, whose well-chronicled past was already being heavily scrutinized by a host of curious-but-cautious NBA officials, had declared himself eligible.

"I'll go to an NBA camp," said Lloyd, not sounding like someone who was worried about his past and what it might mean to his draft status, "and, if it doesn't work out, I'll come back to the CBA. No harm done."

"There's no question he can play in the NBA," said David Chesnoff who, acting as an agent, had in March filed the letter which stated the intentions of his client to enter the draft. "It's just a matter of his learning to accept discipline—making games, making practices. It's called maturity. That has to come from him. He knows what the score is now. All he wants is a chance to show what he's got. He realizes this could be his last chance."

With former Houston Rockets guards Mitchell Wiggins and Lewis Lloyd banned from the league for a minimum of two years for drug violations—and, with Micheal Ray Richardson still awaiting reinstatement, Chris Mullin having just completed treatment for his admitted alcohol abuse and Nets forward Orlando Woolridge having become a recent guest in the Alcohol and Substance Abuse Program in Van Nuys, California—it seemed there was little chance that Lloyd would be selected in the 1988 NBA Draft.

A high-ranking official had said NBA commissioner David J. Stern might even warn all league teams that a contract with Daniels would not receive automatic approval, as had been the case three years earlier, when the Cleveland Cavaliers selected Tulane star John (Hot Rod) Williams. Implicated in the point-shaving scandal at Tulane, Williams did not have his contract validated until he had been acquitted on sports bribery charges—one year after he was drafted by the Cavaliers.

Still, though some scouts and general managers remained skeptical that Lloyd could ever straighten out his life—as Peter Vecsey, the viper-tongued columnist for *The New York Post,* wrote, echoing their concerns about his drug problems: "Lloyd Daniels entered the NBA Draft because his life-long ambition is to receive an expense-paid vacation to Van Nuys"—several teams continued to express at least a marginal interest in him.

"I see a few teams giving him a chance," said Indiana Pacers general manager Donnie Walsh, following the NBA Draft Lottery at the Museum of Natural History on May 20. "I would give him a chance. He has to get himself squared away, but I see someone drafting him. No one will waste an early pick, but I think someone will take him. We will consider it."

"I think that, with his previous background and his involvement in things, teams will think about it seriously before they bring him in," said Phoenix Suns general manager Cotton Fitzsimmons. "But I think someone will bring him in, take a look at him. I would question that he might go in the first three rounds. But he'll probably get invited to a camp."

Gary Wortman, the head scout for the Seattle SuperSonics, said that while he believed most underclassmen weren't quite mature enough to survive in pro basketball and also questioned whether Lloyd was "ready for the rigors of the NBA," he also said that he had seen Lloyd with the Topeka Sizzlers and thought the Sonics would consider taking a chance on him. "It's difficult to say where he'll be picked, but I think he could even be a first-round pick," Wortman said. "It'll be interesting."

Said one general manager, who asked not to be identified, "If Daniels showed up at the Chicago pre-draft camp and showed that he could play NBA-caliber basketball, teams would be interested. We wouldn't scratch him off our list because of his problems."

Other officials were less sure. Some said their teams, in the interest of self-protection, would avoid all contact with Lloyd. As Dick McGuire, the director of scouting for the New York Knicks, said bluntly: "We have no interest in him. None at all."

"I think it is a little too early to assess his situation," said Nets general manager Harry Weltman, whose team had lost Richardson and Woolridge to drug problems within the course of the previous three seasons. "I am not positive Lloyd can play in the NBA and people will have to take a strong look into whether he has made any advances in dealing with his life."

Still, the draft remained more than one month in the future. There might be time for the jury to reach a favorable verdict on Lloyd—for teams to weigh the positives against the negatives, take a chance and select him in the draft. But with his past, it would remain a risk. And, considering the disaster that followed the 1986 Draft—Len Bias died and draftees Chris Washburn, William Bedford and Roy Tarpley all found themselves in rehabilitation for substance abuse—it might be one most teams would elect to pass on.

As Marty Blake, director of scouting for the NBA, said: "There's only so many strikes you can give a guy. At one time, I assumed Lloyd Daniels had talent. Now, I haven't the vaguest idea where he might be drafted—if he gets selected, at all. It's a tragic case."

Lloyd was not selected in the 1988 NBA Draft. Rumors and reports of his personal problems in both Topeka and New Zealand, in addition to his well-documented background, caused teams to avoid him. His only chance now was to be invited to a rookie camp somewhere, though, after all this time, he would still have to prove that he was clean—and, had the ambition necessary to make it in professional basketball. So he headed for Los Angeles and joined a team in the L.A. Pro Summer League.

Lloyd held his own in the L.A. Summer League, where he went against folks like Orlando Woolridge, Benoit Benjamin and Reggie Miller. He became friends with UCLA guard Pooh Richardson. He also received some favorable reviews from scouts who had seen him there and liked his game. But, the scouts also noticed that Lloyd still seemed to have problems.

As his teammates said, Lloyd sometimes arrived at games "high" and "reeking of alcohol," something he later admitted.

The subsequent lack of interest of teams in signing Lloyd to a free-agent contract sent another warning signal to Mark Warkentien and Sam Perry, as well as David Chesnoff, who now was acting as Lloyd's agent.

"Lloyd was preparing to go to the CBA," Warkentien said. "But he was not ready. We brought him to Las Vegas and proposed he enter rehabilitation. Me, my wife, David Chesnoff, Sam Perry—we all sat in my living room until all hours of the night until we convinced him to re-enter rehab."

"For a while, it seemed he was getting real healthy," Chesnoff said. "But soon you could see he was getting lazy again. I said to him, 'Lloyd, I get the feeling you've been disregarding your health.' He said, 'Ches, I really want you [guys] to find the best program you can.' He realized he was strung out. That he wasn't playing to his full potential. He was worried about his health. He was staying up late and partying. He said he had had enough."

As Lloyd said, "I didn't think I had a problem. I thought I could do it on my own. I was in denial. I thought I could still get high and play ball. But you know the old sayin', 'You can't do two things at once.' You got to pick one thing. If you goin' to get high, you just got to get high. You got to say, 'Can't play no ball no more.' If you want to play ball you got to say, 'Can't do drugs no more.' I couldn't do that. I tried, but I couldn't do that. I knew I needed to get me some help. I knew I could have been better in L.A. if I wasn't gettin' high. I finally realized that drugs and basketball don't mix."

On October 24, Lloyd, who had suffered relapses after two previous stints in drug rehabilitation, entered the Alcohol and Substance Abuse Program Treatment Center at Van Nuys Community Hospital in Van Nuys, California. Otherwise known as ASAP/Van Nuys, the center served as rehab central for the NBA—with fourteen players treated there for dependency problems over the course of the previous four years. Not able to get into the NBA, Lloyd had still managed to become a member of its most exclusive club.

For the next three months Lloyd served as the cornerstone for what could have been a solid franchise in the NBA in 1988-89. Forget the Lakers. Forget the Pistons. At various times, Lloyd was in Van Nuys with Duane Washington, Dirk Minniefield, David Thompson, William Bedford and Roy Tarpley. Lloyd Daniels, the self-proclaimed new Chris Washburn when he was at Laurinburg, even got to meet the original model at Van Nuys.

Chris Washburn was his roommate.

"We was all addicts, all addicts," Lloyd said. "But, how'd you like to coach that team? We had the All-Van Nuys Team. All of them was my boys. Chris Washburn's my boy. Roy Tarpley's my boy. We was all lovely together."

• • •

The ASAP Family Treatment Center had become associated with the NBA in 1985, when Dr. David Lewis, the program's founder and director, signed a contract to serve as an exclusive "rehab and detox" facility for the league's players—a situation that would enable his program to administer to the specific needs of addicted athletes. There had been a growing concern among NBA teams, as well as the rest of the business community, that the use of "recreational" drugs was having an effect on the ability to conduct business. Publicity generated by revelations of drug-addicted athletes threatened the league's future success, tarnishing its most marketable asset: its image.

What ASAP/Van Nuys offered was a chance for self-help. A positive. A chance to come clean and come back. And, part of its attraction was that the program offered a chance for basketball players to play basketball while they submitted to more conventional treatment—something which seemed to make that treatment more palatable. "We're the only drug treatment center in the country with NBA-approved breakaway backboards," Lewis once said. It was rehabilitation and rebounds. "Physical exercise is helpful in recovery," he said. "It is a perfectly good addiction."

Of course, part of the rehabilitation at Van Nuys remained traditional. The twelve-step program developed by Alcoholics Anonymous—a program in which an addict must first admit he is powerless over drugs or alcohol—was used. Part of the treatment program required daily sessions with counselors, all of whom were themselves recovering addicts. Days were structured to allow patients about an hour-and-a-half free time, though players, who often awoke at 6:30 a.m., spent as much as three hours a day playing basketball and volleyball, riding exercise bikes and swimming laps. There also were nightly counseling sessions, as well as group therapy.

Patients began rehabilitation on the east wing of Van Nuys Community Hospital, where they slept in hospital rooms with hospital beds. There were no televisions and no telephones. Only after they had shown progress toward their recovery were they moved to one of the six bungalows—"Clean and Sober Houses," as they were known—on the hospital grounds, which were surrounded by a six-foot-high fence.

The average stay at ASAP/Van Nuys lasts about 45-to-48 days at a cost of about $500 a day. In Lloyd's case, some of the bills were paid in advance by David Chesnoff—with the remainder of the more than

$20,000 to be charged either to Medicaid or against Lloyd's future earnings.

"If you willin' to work it, it works, man," Lloyd said of the program. "All you got to do is take one day at a time. If you want to work they program, it'll work. It's up to you. You got to be one-hundred percent clean. You got to say, 'I need help.' That's the only way you goin' to make it in life. It's just a mind over matter thing. You got to realize, say to yo'self, 'Do I want to come out of here with nothin' or do I want to be somethin'?' That's what it is."

The problem was that, at times, Lloyd did not seem to approach Van Nuys as something therapeutic, as rehabilitation that could start him on the road to success, to the NBA. Instead, there were more than a few times when it seemed that he saw the entire experience as one big party, as the "expense-paid vacation." After all, the afternoon Lloyd entered the hospital, the first person he saw was Duane Washington, the Nets' guard—not to be confused with Dwayne (Pearl) Washington, the former all-American from Boys & Girls High School in Brooklyn who also played with the Nets, as well as with the Miami Heat. And, the first thing Lloyd and Duane did when they met in the hall was exchange high-fives.

"Here," a witness said, "you figure this is going to be a serious thing. Then, you see that. I've got to tell you, it made me wonder."

Wonder all you want. But, at least, Lloyd now had a chance. What was the alternative? To end up like Micheal Ray Richardson, Mitchell Wiggins and Lewis Lloyd, banned from the NBA because of not being able to conquer their drug problems? To end up like Earl Manigault, Joe Hammond and Fly Williams, never having had a chance to succeed at a pro career because of drug problems? To end up like Len Bias, dead because of drugs?

To wind up like Richie Adams, dying a slow death?

Flora Adams spoke with a heavy heart, the kind you get when you are forced to watch your son make a shambles of his life. Once, she said, back when her son Richie used to be regarded as one of the best basketball players in New York City, she used to think that someday he would make the NBA. He was that good, had that much talent.

"He had a future," she said, thinking back to the old days. "Know what I'm saying?"

She was in her apartment in the Andrew Jackson Projects near the Grand Concourse in the Bronx, no more than a few blocks from Yankee

Stadium. It is a neighborhood where the landscape, cratered with the battered hulks of burned out tenement buildings, eerily mimics the tattered dreams of local residents. It is the neighborhood that gave her son life. The neighborhood where, years before, he first headed down the road to ruin.

It was a simple beginning, she recalled of that time. Junior high school. Some wrong-minded friends. A mugging out there on the Concourse. Later, it became more complex. Drugs. Muggings to support a bad habit. Some stolen cars. A few armed robberies. "I don't understand," she said. "I raised four kids. I have two daughters and they were never in trouble, never did no drugs. My baby is nineteen years old. I never had no trouble with him.

"But in this building I'm in, mostly everybody is on crack. Everybody my son Richie hung out with is on crack. All the girls, the young girls, is on crack." She paused a moment. "You know," she said, "he's not a bad child. If you knew him, you'd like him. You would. Evidently, he was just weak. One of the weaker ones. He was a follower. He trusted everyone."

These were painful words. Words of anguish. As she spoke, her eldest son, the drug addict, was across the East River, in a jail cell on Rikers Island.

There Richie Adams, the former star forward from Benjamin Franklin High School and Nevada-Las Vegas—the man once known as "The Animal"—sat in a jail uniform awaiting sentencing in New York State Supreme Court, First Judicial District, following his guilty plea on May 16, 1989, to a count of robbery, first-degree, and two counts of grand larceny, fourth.

According to Colleen Roche, a spokeswoman for the Manhattan District Attorney, the twenty-six-year-old Adams had been arrested after he tried to steal money "by placing a gun to the jaw of a woman at a cash machine" in Manhattan on September 25, 1988. Then, fifteen days later, she said, he "snatched a purse" from a woman in an apartment building in Manhattan. On April 30, 1989, Roche said, he was arrested while out on bail; caught stealing the purse of a sixty-eight-year-old woman in Grand Central Station.

As if to document how much of a wreck he had made of his life, Adams, who is 6-foot-9, 210 pounds and who has no front teeth, grabbed the purse at 5:04 p.m. in the middle of a rush-hour crowd. He was wearing a UNLV sweatshirt. As Roche said, "He wasn't real difficult to identify."

And so, now Adams sat in Rikers, declared a predicate felon due to his numerous offenses, facing 4 1/2-to-9 years in the state penitentiary.

"I told him," Flora Adams said, " 'You know, you are one of those people out there in the street that I'm afraid of.' He just sat there and gave me the strangest, saddest look. What could he say? I told him, 'That was somebody's mother you robbed.' It was all quite disappointing to me."

On the basketball court, removed from his penchant for self-destruction, there seemed little reason ever to be disappointed in Richie Adams.

Despite his thin, wiry frame, he could dominate games. Intimidate people. Be strong. Make his own decisions. The right ones. Back then, he was a man to be feared, a player's player. The kind who owned the park.

"If Lloyd Daniels is Magic with Larry Bird's jumpshot," Orlando Magic forward Sidney Green said, "then Richie Adams was a smaller Bill Russell. That's the only comparison I can make. That's how much of a great player Richie Adams was. I would have to put him high on the charts of all those I have played against. No problem, he could play in the NBA."

The first real glimpse of just how good Adams might be came in eleventh grade when Gary Springer, then a senior at Franklin, got hurt prior to a game against Charles Evans Hughes High School. Hughes featured shooting guard Steve Burtt, who later starred with Springer at Iona College and spent a year with the Golden State Warriors, and Kevin Williams, who starred at St. John's and later played for the New Jersey Nets. "Richie came in and had something like forty-two points with twenty-two rebounds and eleven assists," said Stan Dinner, the Franklin coach. "It was, without a doubt, the greatest performance I've ever seen in high school, college. No, anywhere."

"The ball would come off the rim," Springer recalled of that game, "and he just was going over everyone. Once, Richie threw it down so hard they had to stop the game until the rim and backboard stopped shaking."

But, off the court, another pattern began to emerge. Not only did Adams "borrow" Dinner's car. And, not only did he arrive "high" for the playoff game against Stevenson. He also began to steal things from local stores, began to steal things from his own friends and teammates. Sometimes, friends said, he stole to help people, sort of a latter-day playground Robin Hood.

Dinner recalled the time when a girl in school told Adams she had been without food and was hungry. "She was pregnant," he said. "She said, 'Richie, I got nothing to eat.' Richie went out to the supermarket and loaded up just like that. He put it all under his coat and came back."

But sometimes, Adams just stole. "I think he was a kleptomaniac, maybe, he would steal so much," Springer said. "He was good at it, too. He'd walk into a store and come out with soda, cookies, crackers—anything anyone wanted. But there was a time me and Lonnie Green was sitting with him in a pizza place and the guy put Lonnie's change on the counter. We turned around for a second and, when we turned back, it was gone. Richie had taken it. He gave it back when we asked. He said it was all a joke. But I think he was calling out for help, though. I really think he needed some serious help."

Like Lloyd, Adams had started smoking marijuana when he was just ten. He started snorting coke at eighteen. He became moody. One minute, he'd be laughing. The next, he wouldn't talk to anyone. Often, he mingled with people he should not have associated with. He refused to listen to good advice.

"Intellectually, he was smarter than anybody we had," Dinner said. "Now, I don't know what that means, but he wasn't a dumb kid. This kid had some brains and he wasn't a bad kid. Richie would give you the shirt off his back. He just didn't listen to the right people. He was self-destructive."

Because of his bad attendance record, dating back to his days at Alfred E. Smith, Adams failed to graduate from high school. He later earned his General Equivalency Diploma and attended Massachusetts Bay Community College. Then he went to Nevada-Las Vegas. But the team had Green, then a senior who played the same position. So Adams rarely played as a sophomore.

Sitting behind Green made Adams jealous, according to Joe Bostic, who runs a private elementary school in Bedford-Stuyvesant and is a longtime friend of Adams and other players from the city—including Lloyd, Mark Jackson and Walter Berry, all of whom played at one time or another for his summer-league team, The Wiz. "In his heart, Richie knew he was better than Sidney," Bostic said. "He knew he should be starting, should be playing. It hurt him, bothered him. He couldn't be patient. He started to act stupid."

Danny Tarkanian, the coach's son and a player on Nevada-Las Vegas, was perhaps the closest to Adams during that time. "More than once," Tarkanian said, "he told me that he was a manic-depressive. During some practices, he would just go sit in the corner and not talk to anyone. I mean, he wouldn't move. Guys would say things to him. Dad would try to get him onto the floor. But Richie just sat there. It was like he was in another world."

The situation became worse after the season. Adams' grandmother died. Days later, so did his girlfriend's mother. Distraught, Adams, who had gone home, refused to return to school. He refused even to leave his room, often sitting in bed for hours with shades drawn, smoking joints. "You couldn't talk to him," Flora Adams said. "He was in his own world."

By the time he did go back to Las Vegas, he had missed too many classes and was forced to sit out the year as a redshirt—which was fine with Jerry Tarkanian. Adams had become so much of a problem, he and his coaching staff did not want him back.

Danny Tarkanian convinced his father to give Adams another chance. His father did. And Adams responded, not only on the court—he was named conference player of the year two straight seasons, averaging 15.8 points and 7.9 rebounds with 45 blocks as a senior—but also off it, where he showed a remarkable ability to work with children.

"He'd prop his hat sideways," Jerry Tarkanian said, "and sit with the kids. The other guys would have taken their showers, left the arena and he'd still be there laughing, signing autographs, talking to the kids. The other players would leave with their girlfriends. Richie would leave with the kids to go get ice cream."

The problem was, Adams was a lot like those little kids. He was a follower, one who always seemed to follow the wrong people; one who always seemed to make the wrong decision every time his life neared a crossroads.

Touted as a legitimate pro prospect, he joined the Long Island Knights in the United States Basketball League—a sort of semi-professional league run during the summer—to earn some money before the NBA Draft. Then, just after he was selected by the Washington Bullets it was discovered that he had been arrested earlier that morning in the Bronx, driving a stolen car. "He had gone out to Long Island to pick up his paycheck from the Knights," Flora Adams said. "He said the cab didn't wait for him and he didn't have cab fare to get back. He knew he had to get to the draft."

And so, Adams took a car from the parking lot outside the gym. "It was wrong," Flora Adams said. "But that is the way he is. He didn't mean no harm."

"The amazing thing," Tarkanian said, "was that the police gave Richie a polygraph test and he passed it. He wasn't lying. He really believed that he had just borrowed that car. To him, he hadn't done anything wrong."

Given probation, Adams went to rookie camp with the Bullets in

Princeton, New Jersey, but eventually was released. It seemed no one looked highly on the fact that he snuck out of camp each night and went home—one time leaving pro camp to go to the Bronx to appear in a drug game for $100.

"Some of his friends came out to see him at the hotel," Springer said. "His get-high buddies. Richie climbed out the window, actually hung out on the window ledge, and went with his so-called friends." Said Flora Adams: "Every night, his friends would go over and get Richard and every day the coaches from the team would come here, pick him up and bring him back."

After that, Richie Adams bounced around for a while. He played for two years in Argentina on a team that Springer was also supposed to join. "But," Springer said, "the guy mailed my plane ticket to Richie and Richie cashed it in—a twelve-hundred-dollar ticket. That's when I knew Richie was off the deep end. It really hurt me."

Jerry Tarkanian also sent him a plane ticket, one to Las Vegas, where he had several jobs lined up for Adams—one, as a valet at an exclusive club, the other as a bartender, a job Tark said would earn Adams a minimum of $50,000 a year. Adams cashed that ticket.

Later, Tarkanian sent a non-refundable ticket. "I was supposed to meet Richie at one for a four o'clock flight," Joe Bostic said. "All I had was a phone number of the place we were to meet. I called at one. No Richie. I called at two. No Richie. I called at two-thirty. No Richie. Three. No Richie. Finally, he showed up at the place and called me and said, 'Joe, come get me now.' It was three-fifteen and, of course, there was no way we could make it."

Even Dinner arranged for Adams to play with a pro team in Yugoslavia. "I called a representative of the team and said, 'I'll meet you tonight at eight o'clock with Richie.' Richie met me at 11 a.m. and was with me all day. Around 7 p.m. he says, 'Coach, I'm hungry. Give me some money and I'll go get a sandwich.' I said, 'Great Richie. Go get me a coffee, too.' I gave him a few bucks. I didn't see him again for four months."

"You know," Tark said, "it's hard to understand this drug thing, what makes these kids do this. Why can't these kids reason? Why couldn't Richie reason? Why couldn't Lloyd reason? Why can't any of these guys see what they've given up when they do this? Why can't a guy who's making a million dollars a year in the NBA reason? I don't know. I don't understand."

"Sometimes," Bostic said, "these guys just don't have the internal strength to say, 'No.' It's just like Swee'pea. If tomorrow, you could take

Swee'pea out of his environment, change his mentality, Swee'pea would be a pro within a year. There is no doubt in my mind that there aren't fifteen ballplayers in the country better than Swee'pea. I'm talking about the pros, anybody. There is nobody I've seen that Swee'pea is not, offensively, equal to or better than as far as making something happen—including Magic, Joe Dumars, any of them. But people like Swee'pea, people like Richie, people who find this kind of trouble, they just don't understand the ramifications of what they do. It's just that, for all of them, the siren's song of the streets is stronger than anything you can tell them. It's stronger than anything you can say."

The games were incredible at Van Nuys—sort of like out-takes from an NBA "jam" session—except that these stars were patients, and the games were played on the confines of the undersized, outdoor court. Sometimes, Lloyd would go head-to-head with Tarpley, the seven-foot center from the Dallas Mavericks, at times dunking on him, or embarrassing him with a move that would cause him to tell Tarpley, "Yo, go get your sneaks, man." At times, Tarpley would return the favor. "Showin' him some," Tarpley said.

Sometimes, Lloyd and Tarpley would get smart and make sure to be on the same team, the two of them going against Minniefield and Thompson, both of whom were smaller. Sometimes, Lloyd and Washington would go against Minniefield and Washburn. Other times, Lloyd would go one-on-one with Washburn or Washington. But, almost always it seemed, Lloyd came out on top. "What used to get me pissed off," Lloyd said, recalling those games, "was that they would say to me, 'Don't worry, Lloyd, you be in the NBA one day.' I knew I should. They all knew I should, too.

"Like Chris Washburn. He was dookie, hear me?" In other words, he said, Washburn wasn't shit. "He couldn't stop me. And Duane Washington? He had one hand. Naclerio is better than him. I told him, 'I can't believe you made the NBA.' And, even if, like, David Thompson could still jump, I still had a better all-'round game than all of thems, hear me? I was better than all of them guys.

"Like, Roy Tarpley is supposed to be the 'Player of the Nineties.' Right? He's the 'Player of the Nineties.' That's what they call him. Well, I used to serve Roy Tarpley. Ask him. I used to serve him all the time."

"He did," Tarpley said. "He tricked me a couple of times, put a couple of playground moves on me. But I told him, 'Life isn't all about basketball.' "

Not that Tarpley had a right to talk. He had grown up in Brooklyn and Queens and had moved, first to Mobile, Alabama, and then to Detroit before he attended the University of Michigan. There he became an all-American and led the team to consecutive Big Ten titles. Selected seventh overall in the 1986 NBA Draft, he fast became a force in the league, winning the NBA Sixth Man award over Thurl Bailey of Utah for the 1987-88 season—finishing among the league's rebounding leaders despite being a reserve.

But off the court, Tarpley had major problems. In the summer of 1987 he had been admitted to Van Nuys for treatment of a substance abuse problem. On January 5, 1989, when Lloyd was nearly finished with his rehabilitation, Tarpley was readmitted to Van Nuys—his second NBA violation.

Still, Tarpley understood he was weak, that he had a problem. He admitted that he had stumbled several times, and said he was now working hard to overcome his addiction. But he couldn't say the same about Lloyd.

"We played against each other all the time," Tarpley said. "He was fun and I really had a good time with him. I really got to know him, we got to know each other because you're all on the same level in there, have the same sickness, disease. He's a very talented guy. He's got all the physical ability in the world. But there's a question of maturity, being responsible, being responsible for yourself and making the right decisions.

"In order to make it," Tarpley said, "you have to be dedicated, willing to go that extra mile. I didn't see that from him. I don't think he wanted to work that hard. His biggest problem was maturity. There comes a time when you have to be mature. Some people take longer than others. It is tough. I know it's been hard for me. But, you've got to want it. And, you have to want it bad. He wants it one day and the next, like, it's no big deal. You've got to want it all the time. It's not an easy process. It's a one-day-at-a-time thing. He got a great sense of humor. He got a nice personality. But he can get carried away with it sometimes. He doesn't know when to stop. You know, like, a joke is a joke. Like okay, man, enough is enough is enough. He likes to make people laugh. But you can only laugh so much and then it's time to get serious. And, a lot of times, when people tried to get serious with him, he was still there fooling around. It seemed like it never sunk in."

The man on the phone was talking about his life, about how he had never learned to get serious, about how far he had fallen.

"Some of the sergeants and guards here like me," he said. "They watched me play in Vegas."

Richie Adams—inmate No. 89T2957—was calling from a pay phone at Bear Hill Correctional Facility in Malone, New York. He was laughing about a move he'd made earlier in the week, a 360-degree tomahawk—the kind he used to do on national TV, the kind once pictured in *Sports Illustrated*. "They gave me a job working in the gym," he said. "I'm still the same. I still got it."

He had been in so deep that even the high-priced lawyer Danny Tarkanian and his father had hired couldn't get Adams off. He had gotten the maximum—4 1/2-to-9 at Bear Hill, a medium security prison in the Adirondack Mountains, so far north in New York State that it was almost in Canada—and yet, Adams sounded as if he didn't seem to mind. "I feel like I used to when I was in Vegas," he said. "Even though I'm locked up. I know that I'm locked away from society and not able to do the things I used to do."

This was rehabilitation for Richie Adams, rehabilitation for him and a million other addicts in America. Playing ball, biding his time until he could get back on the streets. Still, you had to wonder how much different it was from the rehabilitation Lloyd was going through at Van Nuys. Sure, Adams didn't have the counselors. Certainly, it didn't cost as much. But would rehab change Lloyd, cure him? Would prison change Adams?

One of the reasons Nevada-Las Vegas had implemented its drug-testing program in 1985 was because of Adams. The coaching staff had suspected he was using drugs—specifically, cocaine—and wanted to catch him, get him treatment, Jerry Tarkanian said. But the program, then in its infancy, lacked the teeth that would allow the school to take formal action. The first positive test would result in a meeting with the violator. Counseling was optional. A second violation meant the coaches would meet with the player's parents and counseling would be mandatory. The third time a player tested positive, he'd be suspended. Two tests were given that year. Adams failed twice.

"In college," he said, "I used a little cocaine and smoked a little marijuana. I did it in my apartment." He even exchanged tickets to get the drugs.

"We had a meeting about the testing," Adams said. "Tark brought all the players in one-on-one. He gave a speech about it and said if we used drugs we could be suspended from the team. If they did find drugs in our system, they would call our parents. Mom didn't come because she knew about it. She just said that whatever Tarkanian wanted to do, it was up to him. He brought me in and if he wanted to suspend me, he could suspend me."

But, partly because he lacked leverage and partly because he couldn't afford to lose his best player and still win basketball games, Tarkanian never suspended Adams. After all, Nevada-Las Vegas was headed for a 28-4 finish in 1984-85, after going 29-6 with Adams in 1983-84. Nevada-Las Vegas was headed toward its second straight conference title.

Instead, what Tarkanian and his staff did was sit Adams for parts of games. "I sat in some games," Adams said. "I might not have started or only played twenty-five minutes instead of thirty-eight."

Then again, Adams wasn't about to listen to anyone—not Tarkanian, not his assistants, not counselors—who offered advice on how to get a handle on his drug problems. All of which explains why, after all these years, he was in prison for drug-related robberies; why he never sought treatment.

"I didn't have to rob," Adams said. "I just did it because I was stupid. I'm still the same Richie. I did stupid things 'cause of Richie. But you lose your mind so much, it makes you go out and do some stupid things. Drugs make you so unaware of things. It made me crazy, to go out and rob someone in front of fifteen-thousand people. I was walking down the street, saw an opportunity to rob somebody. I just went out and did it. You think, 'If police chase me, I'm going to get away. If they catch me, I'll get out soon.'

"To me, I make problems for myself. It was my problem. Now that I'm getting older, I realize this thing was hurting me. It is hurting me. I said I would stop some day, and this is what it got me. I went to jail."

"You know what the sad thing is?" the basketball scout, Tom Konchalski, said. "It is that we know and care about Richie Adams because he is 6-foot-9 and a great basketball player. That is not his fault. But there are so many other guys upstate, in prisons, who aren't 6-foot-9, who aren't great ballplayers, who might not have that talent, whose stories are just as sad, who had the same tragedies befall them—sometimes through no fault of their own—and we don't hear about them, read about them, or care about them. We only hear about our guys. The players. But it isn't just them."

Flora Adams sits in her apartment in the Jackson Projects. She is fifty-two years old now, having worked much of her life to make a better life for her children and grandchildren, two of them—Richie Jr. and Richelle—Richie's children by two different girlfriends. She always made sure there was a roof over their heads. She always made sure there was enough to eat. She made sure their clothes were clean. And still, this happened.

"You know, the first time he ever got arrested, I was ashamed," she said, trying not to sound guilty as she explained that she still speaks with her son on a regular basis, except that now it's always by phone. "I was embarrassed. I used to visit him. But I felt like the criminal, so I don't go no more. It still hurts me, knowing that it's my child who did these things. I never thought I would have a child who would do things like this."

The last time she saw Richie, she said, he looked better. His face, once drawn and gaunt from self-abuse and drugs, had filled out. Even though he was still missing his front teeth—she had found his dentures, broken, while cleaning his old jacket earlier in the week—she said, with a certain touch of irony, "Richie always looks better when he's locked up. He looks healthier. He looks fatter. It's sad to say, but I told him he looked like my child again. I mean, you wonder what made it all go wrong with him."

She and her son's friends—the real ones, the ones like Sidney Green and Stan Dinner and Joe Bostic and, yes, even Jerry Tarkanian—often wonder just what will happen when Adams eventually does get out of prison. It is difficult for them to admit, but they're skeptical about his prospects.

"Richie's history," Dinner said. "You hate to say it, you really do. But he's twenty-six years old and he's history. He's yesterday's news. I mean, what can you do with him? What are you going to rehabilitate him to do? What can you teach him to do? You're going to teach six-foot-nine Richie Adams to do what? Tell me. He has no skills. He don't have a degree. He's a basketball player. What can a basketball player do with no education? What?"

What indeed? After all, how can you treat a person for a problem when a major part of their problem is their environment, a factor over which you have no control? How can you treat a person who doesn't want to be treated?

All her life, Flora Adams tried to lead her son down the right road and couldn't. She tried to save him from himself, and couldn't. He had always fallen prey to his weakness, to his environment.

"I always ask myself," she said, " 'Was there anything else differently I could have did?' But I did the best I could for him. My children were never hungry. They were never dirty. They always had a roof over their heads. I think I did good by these kids. It worked with three of them. But Richie, he lacked the strength to make it, to keep away from the streets.

"You know, when he first went to Rikers he would call and tell me to bring over all these clothes. I would bring him some and a few days later, he'd call again. More clothes. I finally said, 'What are you doing with all these clothes? You're in prison. What do you need them for?' It turned out he was taking them and giving them to all the guys. 'Ma,' he said. 'But they don't have no clothes. They need them.'

"See, I'm not blaming nobody. He has his own mind. But he is free-hearted. He was not a leader. He was a follower. People outside can fill his head. And that was how he got into trouble. The people he thought was his friends really wasn't his friends. He never understood that. He thought everybody was his friend.

"Sometimes, I ask him, 'Richard, don't you wish you could start over again?' and he'll say, 'Yeah.' I still love him, but I am disappointed. If anyone could have made it, it could have been him."

Lloyd still had a chance to make it. Even he knew that much. So he tried hard to heed the advice of the counselors at ASAP/Van Nuys. In the house, where each patient was assigned chores—sweeping, cooking, cleaning—he always tried to do his on time. "There was days I had to sweep the floors," he said, "and days I had to do the dishes. It wasn't no big deal. It was what you had to do."

When the patients met at night for their group therapy sessions, Lloyd tried to be open and explain how he felt, explain why he was the way he was. "You had to share thoughts with the other people," he said. "I told them how I used to be out on the streets, how I got a problem. The idea was to get your feelings out. You'd see guys break down. I cried one day. I'm not ashamed. I cried. You realize things when you do that, you really do."

Perhaps the person who tried the hardest to make Lloyd understand his situation was David Thompson. Once, back when, Thompson had been known simply as "The Skywalker"—the guard who leaped over centers and other mere mortals in a single bound. An all-American, he had soared to spectacular heights in college and in 1974 carried North Carolina State to the NCAA Championship. He had gone on to become an all-star in the NBA, once, one night back in April 1978, scoring 73 points in the final game of the season while trying to win the league scoring title. He didn't. But it was the second-highest single-game total ever, behind the 100-point game of Wilt Chamberlain.

But Thompson was a cocaine addict, a cocaine addict who also liked to drink. When his career ended in 1984, he was left with nothing—no wife, who left him, taking their children; no house, which he lost to the Internal Revenue Service, which took all his possessions in lieu of the $810,461 he owed to forty-one creditors, as well as in back taxes; no self-esteem, which he had lost long before he lost his material possessions; and, no employment. He filed for Chapter 11 in 1986.

Thompson eventually took a job with the Charlotte Hornets, where he addressed groups of kids and adults, as well, and spoke to them about the dangers of substance abuse. Having failed to heed his own advice, Thompson slipped in the fall of 1988. On December 15, Thompson, like the others, found himself a patient in ASAP/Van Nuys.

"He told me straight up, as a man, 'Hey, look at me,' " Lloyd said. " 'Look at me. I been there. I got an NCAA ring. I played in the NBA All-Star Game. And, now I got to work for the Charlotte Hornets. In the office.' We'd talk 'bout life, personal life, me an David T. We'd be talkin' every night. He'd say, 'Look at Chris Washburn. Look at these other boys. Is that how you want to end up?' He told me, 'Lloyd, live a wrong life and you'll be back. Either you'll be back or you'll be dead. Remember that,' he said. 'Remember that.' "

Of course, Lloyd told him he would. "The thing with addiction," Thompson said, "is you can feel that you want to do it, get yourself straight. But, while you say things that you genuinely mean, the second you go out with the wrong people, take that first drink, do that first drug, it all goes down the tube. I think Lloyd really wanted to stop. But one thing he had to realize was that alcohol is also a drug and would lead him right back into all his problems. See, but he didn't want to give things up, give it up completely. You've got to be willing to change your playmates and your playgrounds. Because, if you go out with your old buddies, you have to realize that they're going to persuade you to take a drink or do drugs before you persuade them not to. But it seemed Lloyd could never come to grips with that.

"The idea is to do it one day at a time," Thompson said. "You can't say, 'I've got to stop for the rest of my life.' You just have to say, 'One day at a time.'

"It becomes as hard as you make it. The center is a lot like going to school. You learn the medical reasons behind why you drink or use drugs, then you learn the physical and the emotional aspects of your dependencies. But it also becomes one addict talking to another, learning to understand what another person has to say about it. If you can identify with what another addict has to say, then you can get rid of your guilt, the negative feelings. A lot of people who use alcohol or drugs have done things that they regret and they have to be able to forgive themselves before they can move on toward recovery. But, you have to be honest to go forward. Honesty. That's the key. You have to be honest, open-minded. You have to be teachable. You have to be willing to go to whatever lengths to do what you have to do to stay sober.

"Rarely has anyone failed who followed the path. But you have to want to be sober for you. Not for basketball, not for your family, not for your kids. But, for you. And that means you have to be honest about it. I don't think Lloyd ever understood that."

Lloyd was in ASAP/Van Nuys for eighty-five days, from late October, 1988, until near February, 1989. Then, he spent a few weeks in a halfway house near Sherman Oaks, California "He was a much-different guy," Chesnoff said. "He was much more mature, much more goal directed."

Jodie Tarkanian, Tark's daughter, recalled how Lloyd came to visit her for dinner while he was in the halfway house. They went to basketball practice at UCLA—"We went to talk to Pooh," Jodie said. "He was like, 'Pooh, my man. Pooh, my man' "—then made a spaghetti dinner and went bowling.

"He said he was doing good," she said. "He came in, helped with the dishes. He had even tried to help me cook. He was talking about the NBA. He said, 'This is my last chance. I have to do well this time.' I kind of got the feeling that he really wanted to do well. But he just didn't know how."

"In my opinion, he had to stick with ASAP and with the halfway house, play in the summer league again, spend a whole season in the CBA and, maybe the next year, an NBA team would pick him up," Chesnoff said. "But he would have to really live and work hard. And I don't think he could do that." Instead, Lloyd decided he wanted to go back to New York. "Against my advice, he went back. That was a problem. That's not exactly an environment best-suited to staying out of trouble. I've been in that neighborhood with him. They sell crack on the street corners, not baseball cards."

"I went back," Lloyd said, "and in 'bout a month I had some problems. I didn't follow no aftercare. I got big-headed, said, 'Yeah, you could smoke a joint. It ain't no big deal.' Everybody thinks, 'Oh, I could drink, as long as I don't do cocaine' and 'Oh, I could smoke as long as I don't do cocaine.' Well, I didn't do no coke for two weeks. Then, I had a relapse. People tried to help me. But I didn't have the sense to realize what it meant to stay clean." He didn't have the sense to do what was necessary to ensure his future.

16 • The Entourage

Ronnie had let Lloyd off at The Entourage Cafe close to midnight. They had just come from Madison Square Garden and Ronnie was tired and not feeling well and so wanted to get home. But Arnie Hershkowitz and some players were supposed to be there, so Ronnie decided to give Lloyd a ride.

The Entourage sat just outside the boundaries of midtown. It was sort of a preppie hangout, frequented mainly by kids in their early twenties home on vacation or just out on the town. It had become a hangout for Hersh and Ronnie and their summer-league teams because Hersh knew the manager, a guy named Dave. The players, most of them in high school, never drank. But they ate there after games. Sometimes, Ronnie and Hersh paid the bills. Other times the manager, Dave Liss, picked up the tab.

When Lloyd walked in, Hersh was sitting at a table. Jamal Faulkner, the all-American from Christ the King, one of the best high school teams in America, was there. So was Syracuse-bound center Conrad McRae and Future Pollard. "Yo," Lloyd said. "What's up?"

He began to talk and the conversation had just gotten started when in walked Mike Tyson, then the undisputed heavyweight boxing champion. "Yo, Mikey Boy," Lloyd said, seeing Tyson. "Hey Lloyd," Tyson said, as he walked over—Jamal, Future and Conrad looking on in apparent disbelief as he and Lloyd did high-fives, low-fives, shakes, smiles. They hugged and started to talk like long-lost homeboys. "It was like old-home week," Hersh said.

The two had met earlier in the year through a mutual friend and, knowing that they both came from the same area of Brownsville, began to hang around together. Tyson had been through his divorce with Robin Givens, his world was in turmoil and Lloyd represented the old days. He was someone from the 'Ville, a time when life was simple. A time when he could be himself. So the two would sometimes get together, go to clubs, go drinking. They were the new Odd Couple, the rising star and the fallen star. And, yet, they were two much the same people.

"Mikey and me is B-Boys," Lloyd said. "We got history."

But, Hersh said, "Tyson thought Lloyd cared about him, because of where they were from, you know, as friends. But Lloyd looked at Tyson as money for Lloyd. Lloyd looks for the next guy he can cling on to. He'll parasite off anybody. Tyson just happened to be the richest anybody he knew."

Despite his alcohol and substance abuse problem, Lloyd spent a lot of time at The Entourage—most of it, drinking, Hersh said. The rest of the time, Hersh said, Lloyd was busy trying to bum money, the way he did back when he was coming up. But now there was a difference. Back then, back when he and Sam Perry and Ronnie and others were all too willing to slip meal money and carfare to a kid whose star was on the rise, Lloyd was considered nothing more than another streetwise kid looking out for things. It was almost cute. Now, Hersh said, it had become an annoyance. After all, Lloyd was a has-been or a never-was. His act had grown old and tiresome.

Still, one last time, Hersh decided to make a deal with Lloyd. Lloyd had asked, as usual, for twenty dollars. Hersh said only in return for a favor. Conrad, Future and Jamal were at The Entourage that night. They needed a ride home. Hersh asked Lloyd to take them. He gave them the keys to his car. "I told him, 'Be back in an hour.' I figured he'd be back in about three."

Of course, he would be lucky to get it back at all. Lloyd, who may have been the world's worst driver, was driving on the Brooklyn-Queens Expressway heading for Long Island University in Brooklyn, near where Conrad lived. Conrad was in the back seat with Future, who lived near Boys High. Jamal was seated in front. But Lloyd didn't know what exit to get off and, since Conrad, Future and Jamal didn't drive, neither did they. "Hey, where you get off? Where do you get off?" Conrad yelled to Lloyd from the back seat. "I don't know, man," Lloyd said. "I ain't sure."

"What's the matter?" Conrad said. "Can't you read the signs?"

"Yo, man. Don't play me," Lloyd yelled. "You don't know me well enough to play me. Play me and I'll kick your ass. I mean it."

"Ah," Conrad said. "You can't read, can you, man?"

He started laughing and making fun of Lloyd. All of a sudden Lloyd turned around, reached into the back seat and began to fight with Conrad, in the car, on an elevated section of the BQE—going well over fifty-five miles-per-hour. "What'd I tell you, man?" Lloyd said. "What'd I tell you?"

Jamal had to grab the wheel.

At six-thirty the next morning, Hersh called Ronnie. "Ron, you're not going to believe this," he said. "Lloyd stole my car."

It was three days before he got it back.

• • •

Lloyd had blown his chances in high school, in Las Vegas, in the CBA, in New Zealand and, now, he was laying waste to the strides he seemed to have made during rehabilitation at ASAP/Van Nuys. But, while Lloyd was hitting bars and searching the neighborhood for crack cocaine, back in Queens the kid who once earned himself "a little name" in a few of the local gyms and parks had finally reached his senior year—and fulfilled his promise.

Kenny Anderson was now 6-foot-2 and, though still a willowy 170 pounds, had been the most sought-after high school recruit in America. The previous fall he had narrowed his college choices to five schools: Syracuse, North Carolina, Georgia Tech, Georgetown and Duke. Then, after much suspense, on November 9, 1988, he had announced he was signing with Georgia Tech.

Word on the street suggested that schools had offered six-figure payments to entice Anderson to sign with them. But Georgia Tech coach Bobby Cremins, as well as Pierre Turner, Vincent Smith and Anderson all laughed and said that, at best, suggestion of such a figure was preposterous and, at worst, it was scandalous. Still, such rumors served to confirm Anderson's status as the most-recruited player in the nation, just as his selection of schools was confirmation that "Team Anderson" had been successful in taking a kid with raw talent, a kid who was immature, and guiding him safely home.

After all, when Duke announced it had signed Bobby Hurley, Jr., a guard from St. Anthony's in Jersey City, New Jersey, which would be selected as the 1989 national high school champion by USA Today, Anderson, who had shown mainly cursory interest in playing his collegiate ball at Duke, was able to pick another school. And, when Georgetown coach John Thompson failed to recruit Anderson in person—the Hoyas eventually signed Andrew Jackson guard Dave Edwards, who played one season before electing to transfer to Texas A&M—he was able to eliminate Georgetown from consideration.

When Joan Anderson decided that Syracuse coach Jim Boeheim was "too cold," her son simply chose another school. And, when Anderson decided he didn't want to attend North Carolina, he was able to give his own reason: "I don't want to be another horse in Dean Smith's stable," he said.

Anderson later apologized for that remark. But still, the point had been made. Kenny Anderson had had a choice, had been given a chance to decide his own future. He had options, and his options had been not only five of the most prestigious basketball schools in America, but also five respected academic institutions. The Kenny Anderson who began life near the Forties Projects had a limited future, despite basketball. The Kenny Anderson who would come out of Archbishop Molloy with a B-minus academic average and 2,621 points—at the time, the highest total ever in New York State—had the world at his feet, which probably explained how he wound up his senior season as the *Parade Magazine* National Player of the Year.

And, it partially explained why, upon his graduation, Kenny Anderson's high school jersey was enshrined in the Basketball Hall of Fame.

Even Tom Konchalski, the scout, said when asked how Anderson ranked as a basketball player and a person: "There are only three people that Kenny Anderson ranks behind. The Father, the Son and the Holy Ghost."

"If it wasn't for them, for that support network, there's no telling where I could have been," Anderson said. "I might have tried to get over on people, I might have gotten sidetracked. It was hard. It was a lot of work. But you have to make a sacrifice to avoid temptation. You have to realize that there is a lot of bad out there. I think those people helped me realize that. I think that it helped me stay focused on what I had to do."

Of course, the shame was that most kids never learned that lesson, never had anyone to help them learn it. Because they weren't as talented as Kenny Anderson, or because they didn't receive such good advice or didn't listen, instead they often wound up not like Kenny Anderson, but like Lloyd or Richie Adams or Earl Manigault. Cast adrift, their futures bleak.

Hersh had given up on Lloyd, written him off. Like everyone else, he had grown sick of his headaches. So, in a deft move, Hersh passed Lloyd off on Ronnie. But Ronnie was also tired of the aggravation. He couldn't deal with the constant headaches. The only reason Lloyd ever called him was because he needed something. And so, Ronnie decided to find someone who could put more effort into working with Lloyd than he could; someone who could bring new perspective to the situation. That person was Kevin Barry.

Kevin had met Ronnie through mutual friends. Because Kevin ran the Give a Kid a Chance Foundation, the non-profit organization to assist under-privileged children, he was more than willing to take a chance on Lloyd. Kevin had been dealing with kids like Lloyd forever, it seemed. All the way back to his friendship with the old boxing trainer, Cus D'Amato, which was how he had met Mike Tyson. Barry was the person who originally introduced Tyson to Lloyd. Now, he was going to try to save Lloyd.

"This guy was mesmerized by Lloyd," Hersh said. "He really felt he could make the difference. But he was getting conned by Lloyd."

Kevin insisted it wasn't that at all. Yes, he did let Lloyd move into the house with him and his sons in the Marine Park section of Brooklyn. And, yes, he did buy clothes for Lloyd and try to get him straightened out. For a while, Kevin said, it worked. "I was teaching Lloyd things like how to brush his teeth, how to change his clothes," Kevin said. "No one had ever shown him the right way to do those things. It was like he was twelve years old. It was like he was 'Rain Man' or something."

Hersh, meanwhile, cut his losses—so to speak—and ran. The incident with the car had said it all and he no longer wanted to deal with the situation. To him, Lloyd was beyond help. He had become yesterday's news.

"He's at an age where, if he can't take care of himself, I don't want to be a part of him," Hersh said one night in late April at The Sports Page, the bar in lower Manhattan run by former Ben Franklin coach Stan Dinner. "This kid is twenty-one years old and he is finished. People I know told me that he has been blackballed from the NBA. For life. The Knicks and the Nets said they are never going to touch him. I don't want to see the kid die. But I don't want any part of him. He came in the other night. He was all drugged up. He was drunk. He was like, 'Let me have some money. I'll pay you back as soon as I make it. I promise.'

"But, the things we allowed him to get away with when he was young—the things like, 'Give me ten dollars, give me twenty'—we won't let him get away with any more. Back then, he was a celebrity. And, you want to be associated with celebrities. But to me the kid is poison now. Double-X poison. You know what I mean? To me the kid is poison."

Two weeks later, Lloyd got shot.

17 • Operation

It had been a rough night. And now, on a bench near the elevators, a few anxious relatives gathered and sat, motionless, not quite sure what to make of the situation.

They had been summoned to Mary Immaculate Hospital in the early-morning hours and, what with the operation over, the sun already reaching toward the noon sky and nothing much else to do, it was here they now sat and waited for the latest word on Lloyd.

It was difficult, the waiting. Just down the hall, behind a set of ominous wooden doors with wire-reinforced windows, Lloyd, heavily sedated, slept in the Intensive Care Unit. There was a blandness to the room. It was an awful, sick-feeling place. A place where patients hovered, in limbo, between life and death. A place where nurses whispered. A place where the monitors used to record vital signs emitted a steadfast, but monotonous beat—the rhythm an eerie sort of background music for the host of inward, silent moans that seemed to be exuded from the very souls of the residents.

For all their nuisance, those machines confirmed that Lloyd was, indeed, alive. Still, he didn't look so good. A drainage tube, filled with blood-tinged fluid, protruded from the wound in the left side of his neck, another from the wound to the right side of his abdomen. Gauze covered the wound to his left shoulder. At one point that morning the detectives had even come to Lulia Hendley and asked to take the clothing Lloyd had worn when he was shot.

"They said, 'Just in case he dies, we need it for evidence,' " she said. "Then, my heart sunk. I said, 'No, not Junior. This is my oldest grandchild.' I thought then he was gonna die." She was not alone.

Downstairs, a television crew waited out the morning. The local all-news radio station—the one that said, "Give us twenty-two minutes and we'll give you the world"—reported the shooting on its broadcasts. A few reporters and at least one photographer spent part of the morning and much of the afternoon in the hospital searching for tidbits of information.

The severity of the situation became apparent around mid-morning, when a wearied, bleary-eyed man walked through the front door of Mary

241

Immaculate. He seemed a bit shaken as he moved toward the front desk. He wanted news, he said. He wanted it now.

"I'm his father," the man said, as he rubbed his work-swollen hands. "I'm Lloyd Daniels, Sr."

Many years before, he had abandoned his son and, in the process, had perhaps condemned him to this fate. But all that seemed forgotten as he stood at the desk and asked his question. "Is he alive?" he said.

Yes, he was told. But, no one knew for how long.

Annie Sargeant was slow to walk down the hall. She walked as if she was tired, as if it hurt her feet to do so. She looked worn. The green cloth coat she wore and green kerchief thrown over her still uncombed hair did nothing to help her appearance. It was apparent she had been up all night—or, most of it, anyway. She had just come from a visit to the I.C.U.

"He was in pain," she said. "You could tell he was in pain."

She had her hands in her pockets as she searched for a tissue, but found none. She was near the hospital doors now. There, she stopped for a moment as a reporter asked her a question about the shooting. Early reports, he said, were that it had been drug-related. Sargeant had raised Lloyd back on New Jersey Avenue. When drugs were mentioned, she became defensive.

"It wasn't no drugs," she said, adamant in her denial. "It wasn't no drugs, I can tell you that. He was robbed. Somebody robbed him. He didn't mess with that stuff. He didn't mess with no drugs. It wasn't no drugs."

"Mama," said her daughter, Barbara Stephens, who had moved to her side. "Mama, c'mon. Don't talk to these people. You don't have to talk to them. Just shut your mouth and let's get out of here. Now. C'mon, mama. Let's go."

As the pair walked out through the main entrance, another relative, who asked not to be identified, shook her head. "I don't know why she said that it wasn't drugs," the woman said in a serious voice. "You could have predicted this would happen. Anyone could have predicted this would happen to him. It's because of what he be into. It's what he be into that caused this."

The implication was clear. "Why did this happen?" Ron Naclerio said. "Because he was reading Shakespeare and his tutor didn't like the way he was reading it. Come on. In that neighborhood, who knows why? It could be anything. But you have to have a pretty good idea. It had to be drugs."

It was, of course, related to drugs. But the incident that led to the shooting and the actual shooting itself had not happened the way relatives had first explained it, the way it was reported in the papers and on the news.

In reality, Lloyd said, he had been drinking Olde English with his aunt, Sherry Baptiste, and had decided he wanted to get high. So he went out on the block and, down around the corner of Francis Lewis, he found a young kid, maybe sixteen years old, selling crack. Lloyd walked over to him and demanded his goods. When the kid refused, Lloyd, who had done this several times before, beat the shit out of him—and stole his crack, about $100 worth.

Angered, the kid and his partner, who was also a juvie-wise ass, decided to follow Lloyd home. They did. They found him. And, they shot him.

"I know these jokers will kill you," said Lulia Hendley, who had seen the assailants come to the house and had seen her grandson, seen Junior, get shot. "If you take they crack, I know they'll shoot you. I know they will kill you. They'll kill you. They really doesn't care. They give it to you one way or the other, whether you live or die, they don't care."

Word on the street was that there was a contract out on the shooters. In fact, Hendley said, when the triggerman found out who he had shot, he sent word through the grapevine. "They said to say he was sorry," she said. "But, you can't change something that's been done."

As one person said, "You know how many drug dealers who knew Lloyd have also put the word out, 'Get this kid.' The kid's dead who did this." As another said, "Hey, they shot Lloyd Daniels. They shot Swee'pea. These guys had a better chance of living if they had shot a cop."

Not many of the folks who knew Lloyd were surprised at hearing the news that he had been shot. Most reactions were similar. After the initial shock, whatever emotion had been evident soon vanished. Such news, after all, was perhaps inevitable.

"You know, it's sad I tell you," Lou d'Almeida, the businessman who ran the Gauchos, said when informed of what had happened. "God damn. I saw him earlier this week. He stopped over at a game and said, 'Hello.' He told me he was working on getting a tryout somewhere. He was on his way back, I thought. I told him, 'When you're ready to do it, when you have some good news for me, give me a call.' And, now this."

"We've been waiting for this call every day since he left," Kristi Gillam, the daughter of Topeka Sizzlers owner Bernie Glannon, said when told the news. "Tell you the truth, we kind of expected it."

"You can say it was the path he was walking," said Waitemata coach Dave MacCalman, when he got the call. As Ronnie said, "It's like if your father is ninety-nine years old and has been terminally ill for ten years. You know what's going to happen. But, it's still a shock when it does."

"It's too bad," John Killilea, the assistant coach for the Houston Rockets who had been his coach in Topeka, said. "As a basketball person, you say it was certainly a shame because of his ability. But, to hell with his talent. It's too bad for this to happen to anyone. But this is a problem with society. The educational system didn't do a bit of good for him. The culture didn't do a bit of good for him. He wasn't prepared to step out of his environment, didn't have the ability to sever that bond. But I also guess you couldn't force him to do what had to be done, either, so he became just another one of those guys in the trenches. You knew nothing good was going to come of it."

"I was hoping nothing like this would happen," said Dave Jones, a Gauchos coach who first met Lloyd when the player was fourteen. "You always hear things on the street. I just hoped the street life would never catch up with him. You know, he was here last week working out, working hard because he wanted to do this. He watches NBA players and knows he's better than half the guys he sees. He just listened to a lot of the wrong people."

As d'Almeida said, "When I watch all these playoff games on television, sometimes I think, 'Hey, I'd like to see what Lloyd would have done here, what he would have done there.' People always say he is the most incredible talent they have ever seen. I see Magic Johnson. I see Michael Jordan. Then I see Lloyd. Boy, oh boy. It's sad. You know, it's unbelievable how many wrong turns he's taken, especially when you consider how many good turns he could have taken. They say a cat has nine lives. He may have one left."

Laid out on the stretcher in the back of the ambulance, Orlando Antigua figured he, too, had one life left. And unfortunately, he thought, it was in the process of coming to an end. He had been shot in the head. Maroon-red blood was pouring out of the corner of his left eye socket, streaming down the side of his face. All he could think about was dying. And, he thought as he stared at the ambulance ceiling, the worse part was he didn't know why.

It was Halloween night, 1988. Antigua and his friends had been walking along the Grand Concourse in the Bronx. There was a commotion at a discount appliance store down the block. Some kids were arguing with some store employees. Antigua stood on a car bumper to get a better view and, as he did, someone behind him—someone he did not know—threw an egg that landed in front of the store. The next thing he knew, Antigua said, the store manager had drawn a gun and shot him in the head. "I guess he thought I did it," Antigua said. "He pulled a gun and shot me. I hit the hood of the car. Blood was just coming out. I was panicking. I ran up to him and said, 'Mister, why'd you shoot me?' He just looked at me. He was like in shock."

Some victims of violence turn out to be like Lloyd. Not really victims, but rather folks who are involved—and, in some way, responsible for what they get. Others, like Barbara Chiles, are real victims and don't deserve their fate, and, don't get a second chance. But sometimes, though not often enough it seems on the streets of New York, real victims catch a break. They live. They go on to lead productive lives. They turn out like Orlando Antigua.

Just three weeks after the shooting, Antigua made his varsity debut for the basketball team at St. Raymond's High School in the Bronx. And, by the winter of 1990, the 6-6 junior forward had blossomed into one of the most promising players in the city. He still has fragments of the small-caliber bullet imbedded in his head, near his left temple.

"It's hard to take in," he said. "When I saw the X-ray, it really hit me." All the same, despite the occasional headaches he can live with it. He can even live with the kidding from his teammates. "They called me BH," he said. "For Bullethead."

Because of the type of person he is, Antigua can even accept that the man he alleged had shot him was cleared of all charges. Four witnesses testified the store manager, who had no criminal record, shot Antigua. Five said he did not. The gun was never recovered.

"Orlando was just checking out what was going on," Bronx assistant district attorney Robert Kelly said of the incident. "He stood on the bumper of a car, seeing what was happening. An innocent bystander. I don't get witnesses like that in the Bronx. Usually, they're involved in some way or are criminals. But he was a good kid. He wasn't causing any trouble. Half the kids in the city should be as good as Orlando. It's tough here in the South Bronx, and Orlando is doing good for the situation that he's in."

"When I do think about it now, it hits me," Antigua said. "When I start to talk about it, I think how close I was to dying. It changed my attitude. Now, it's like a second chance. When something goes wrong in my life, it's just a small thing compared to that situation."

That Lloyd survived was due to circumstance and coincidence, as well, it seemed, as to the luck of the draw.

It seemed the night Lloyd was shot an ambulance crew just happened to be on a meal break in the area and, once the call was made, arrived on the scene in under five minutes. It also seemed, according to Dr. Walter F. Pizzi, Chairman of the Department of Surgery of the Catholic Medical Center of Brooklyn and Queens—the organization which ran Mary Immaculate—that once the crew arrived Lloyd received immediate and proper treatment from the paramedics, who also knew to transport him to Mary Immaculate, the only hospital in Queens with a Level One Trauma Unit.

Then, perhaps, there was the most incredible twist. Dr. Pizzi had implemented plans for the trauma unit after lessons learned during his association with a former colleague, a renowned thoracic surgeon named Dr. Emil A. Naclerio—whose son just happened to be Ronnie.

The elder Naclerio, who wrote six books on medical techniques during his tenure at Harlem Hospital and who once operated on Dr. Martin Luther King Jr. after the civil rights activist was stabbed in Harlem in 1958, had been a pioneer trauma surgeon and an advocate of specialized emergency trauma care units before his death in 1985. "He was a distinguished chest surgeon, one of the first to promulgate trauma care in New York City hospitals," said Dr. Pizzi, who, based on some of those lessons, established the trauma center at Mary Immaculate less than a year before Lloyd was shot.

"It's a small world," Ronnie said, when he met Dr. Pizzi for the first time after Lloyd was shot. "A very small world," Dr. Pizzi told him.

"You know how close this kid was to death?" Naclerio said, later. "A high school overtime period away. That's why I find this incredible."

"It is because of that center that Lloyd is alive," Dr. Pizzi said. "He was the right patient for the right hospital at the right time. He had the right care from the scene. The paramedics did all the right things. There was a team of trauma surgeons ready for him. Everything happened perfectly and the system worked." As Ronnie said, "I'm glad it did."

Lloyd was asleep when Ronnie went to visit him that afternoon. "How're you doin'?" Ronnie asked him, when he finally opened his eyes.

"I don't know, Ron," Lloyd said, in a whisper. "I don't know."

"You're going to make it," a nurse, standing near the bed told him. Lloyd tried to force a smile, but couldn't.

"Ron," he said. "I screwed up big-time. I'm lucky to be alive ain't I? I was real close. I almost died. Maybe God still wants to see me play."

"God and the Devil were fighting for you," Ronnie told him, trying to cheer him. "They were choosing up a game." Again, Lloyd tried to smile.

"He didn't look good," Ronnie said, later. "I mean, he looked like he was going to make it. But you could tell he was bad. He had all these things in his nose. He was attached to all these machines. He was in pain. He was scared. He told me he thought he saw the world, his life, pass before his eyes. He said he saw his mother. Hopefully, this struck a nerve. He said it did. I think he finally realized he's not invincible."

"It was a major thoracic wound," Dr. Daniel L. Picard, the Director of Surgery at Mary Immaculate and the doctor who operated on Lloyd, said, still later, as he stood in an office down the hall from the ward. "One bullet hit him in the right side and penetrated his right lung. Two other bullets struck him in the left side of the neck and the left shoulder.

"The damage was pretty extensive. It was close to the vital organs. He lost about six pints of blood. But he was lucky. The prognosis for recovery is good. I will make no prognosis, however, for his sports career."

Dr. Picard didn't have to make a prognosis, because back in St. Albans, folks on the streets had already begun to form their own opinions. It was the afternoon after the shooting. And, as Lloyd continued to recover in his hospital bed, down in Jamaica Park, where he used to play ball, kids talked about the legend who had become, in their words, a "bum."

"He was still the best out here, the best ever in this neighborhood," said Anthony Johnson, a seventeen-year-old who had often played against Lloyd. "He could shoot from anywhere, pro three-pointers like they were nothing. But he didn't seem to care anymore."

As another player, nineteen-year-old James Stanton, said, "He wasted his talent, hanging out with the wrong crowd, the wrong people, the wrong influences."

Down at the corner of 203rd Street, a young man wearing a New York Giants jacket and selling five-dollar vials of crack offered an assessment that seemed to summarize the entire situation.

"We knew him here," the man said. "He came around a lot. He was a basketball player. Once."

A basketball, autographed by Michael Jordan, a Brooklyn native, sat on a table near the bed in Room 613. Lloyd, shadowed by the rack that held his I.V. solution, was standing at the window. There were flower baskets there, including one from Jerry Tarkanian and the basketball staff at Nevada-Las Vegas. It was a little more than a week since Lloyd had been shot. Already, he was up and walking around, walking the halls, waiting to get out.

"You want to know how dumb I was?" Lloyd said. "I saw the gun and still I came out on the kid, like I was a gangster or somethin'. The kid was like, 'Where's my money? Where's the shit?' He wasn't goin' to let me house him like that. He wasted two bullets in the air. Then, when I didn't hand it over, he shot me. I came rushin' at him, we was tusslin' and then he shot me two more times and I went down. I was so surprised to be shot. I was scared. That's what I remember, bein' scared. I was like, 'Don't let me die, God. Don't let me die.' All I could remember was like how in 'Starsky & Hutch' when the bad guys got shot and like when they closed their eyes they was dead. I was like, 'You got to hang on, hang on. Don't close them eyes.' I thought that, like, if I closed my eyes, I was dead. So I never passed out.

"I should be dead," said Lloyd, whose recovery was called a "medical miracle." "I know that. God always say that if you do crazy shit, you goin' to get it back some day. Well, man, I tell you, that happened to me. Because of that, all I watched the first few nights here was them God shows, one service right after another. Today, I feel a little better. I may watch some wrestling today. I don't want to mess up no more."

On the table, next to the basketball from Jordan—it read, "Get well, Lloyd. All my best, Michael Jordan"—there were letters and get-well cards, hundreds of them. In fact, it seemed they were working overtime downstairs in the hospital mailroom to keep even with all the cards and letters that had come in from around the country.

There were letters about Jesus, letters about God. There was a letter to inform Lloyd that he had been enrolled in the "Priests of the Sacred Heart." There were letters from ex-addicts, who advised Lloyd to "be strong." There were letters from ex-addicts who told Lloyd it was not a crime that he had been weak. There was a letter from a girl who wanted Lloyd to come live with her in Toledo, Ohio.

And, there was even a letter from a girl in Queens who identified herself as the president of "L.L.D.A."—the "Leave Lloyd Daniels Alone" Society, which felt Lloyd was "being exploited by the media."

He received a letter from a woman who wrote, "I don't know you, but I am going to say it like it is: 'Are you crazy or what? Are you?' I never met you personally, but I heard of you through newspapers and T.V. 'Are you a man or what?' You, with such talent . . . and such beautiful height. "If I was able to travel—and, I'm not rich that I can afford to go by cab, you see I'm sixty-six years old and homebound—I know I would slap your face and probably do it a few times! What right do you have to ruin your life? Have you no value on your life? I will say this to you, Swee'pea, and remember this. Picture yourself deep in a grave turning to bones for the rest of your life while worms eat you up! I care—and your family cares, the world cares. Do you give a damn?"

A former police officer wrote to tell Lloyd that he once had a drinking problem, but was now sober. "I haven't had a drink for eight years," the man wrote. "Not one drink and not one drug. No pot. No speed. No beer. No hard stuff. No nothing, and I feel good about it."

The man went on to explain to Lloyd that he could get clean, too. All it took was work.

Perhaps, the most heartfelt letter came from an athlete who had been there before, who had suffered a relapse of his addiction, and was again fighting hard to overcome it. It came addressed on the official stationery of the Charlotte Hornets. It included an official team hat.

"I'm sorry to hear about your present situation," David Thompson wrote. "I hope that you will be okay and will come through this just fine. I am very concerned about you and your future. God sometimes puts people through things to make them realize just how precious and important life is. I hope you take this situation and make it a positive one for you.

"Things in my life are so much better today because of me staying clean and sober. Today, I am celebrating five months sobriety.

"Lloyd, you know if I can do it, so can you. You have a lot of people that care about you and want to see you make it. It's still not too late! You have really got to try and get your life in order before it is too late! If I can help in any way, don't hesitate to call. You need to get out of New York.

"Enclosed is a Charlotte Hornets hat. Keep this hat and use it as a motivating factor. If you are serious enough, you can be there or with some other team. You've got too much talent to waste it on the streets. God was with you this time. Lean on him. He won't let you down."

"You know," Lloyd said, later, "people still love me. They still want to see me do well. But God, he don't like ugly . . . I keep gettin' these lessons in life, but I ain't never learned. I want to learn now."

"Lloyd, you're just a lollipop," said Ronnie, sitting nearby. "What are you gonna do with this chance?"

"I stay right, now," he said.

"Whether that will wear off in a month or two, who knows?" Ronnie said, as he stood outside the hospital after visiting hours. "Now, he just has to do what he says. Sooner or later you have to get up on your own two feet and do what you're supposed to do. He still has a chance. I know this sounds stupid. But maybe those three bullets saved his life."

18 · Con Man

The television was on. Lloyd was stretched out on the couch in the living room. Kevin was seated on a chair near him and it was there he fought, without much success, to hold back a yawn.

It was almost midnight. In the old days, that would have meant it was just about time for Lloyd to hit town in an attempt to "break the night"—to stay out 'til dawn in search of liquor, in search of crack, in search of a good time. Instead, here he was, inside the house as the night struggled to escape its youth, his body drained and wearied—not from self-abuse and drugs, but rather from a long, hard day of work.

Leaning back, Lloyd stretched his arms, sighed. "Yo, Kev, like, I'm exhausted," he said. "It ain't easy, all this workin' out stuff."

Kevin laughed. "Welcome to the real world," he said, drawing a grimace from Lloyd. "No one said this was going to be easy, Lloyd. You know this isn't going to be easy. But you can do it. You know you can."

Lloyd nodded. It had been just three weeks since he had been shot, just a week since he had been released from Mary Immaculate. Yet, he had just spent five hours running, lifting weights, working to get back into shape and had even gone out and beaten Ronnie in a game of one-on-one. The scars that remained on his neck, chest and abdomen served as a brutal reminder to how close he had come to death, but he sat and talked about the future, once bright but now, at least, salvageable.

"It ain't easy," Lloyd said, a firmness, a sense of conviction reflected in his voice, in his words, and intimated in his intonation. "Ain't nothin' in life is easy. Gettin' shot ain't easy. But, whatever happens before, happens. I just got to say, 'I fucked it up.' But, like, we all fuck up. Hear me? I can't take back my past. All I can do is make a future. It's up to me now to make a future, know what I'm sayin'? No one else. It's up to me."

He pressed himself back into the couch, turned away for a moment. He was thinking about his situation, about just how hard it had been. How had he come to this place in life only to find himself in such dire straits? Could he ever do what was necessary to make things right? He didn't know.

"I'm goin' to do it this time," he said, when he turned back again. "I got to do it. I ain't Superman now. I know that. Can't take no more

251

bullets. I got to get well now. No bullshit this time. I want it. I want it bad. Those who help theyselves make it. You know, that's what they say, 'Those who help theyselves is the ones who's goin' to make it.' You heard that, right? So I got to take it one day at a time now. One day at a time. I learned that. I think I learned that. Gettin' shot helped me learn it."

"You know," Kevin said, after Lloyd had gotten up and gone inside to go to bed, "I think now the true person has come out of Lloyd Daniels. Every night, he prays to God. Every night. He has been working hard. And, I mean really hard. He knows he is on his last legs. You know what they say, 'You have to hit the bottom before you hit the top.'

"Well, just a couple of weeks ago, I would have told you it was over," Kevin said, as he clicked off the television. "But, I think he has hit bottom. Now, you would hardly believe the turnaround."

Most mornings, Lloyd woke at 11 a.m. and then headed to a local gym—the Brooklyn Health & Racquet Club—where he would lift weights for two-to-three hours under the supervision of trainer Joey (Boy) Fortunato, whose job it was to make sure Lloyd got back into competitive shape. Fortunato would work him on the leg machines, have him bench weights, run him on the track and have him ride an exercise bike to increase his strength and stamina. After a break for lunch and a late-afternoon rest of an hour or two, Lloyd would return for a night session.

"The guy was soaking wet every day," Fortunato said. "People couldn't believe it. It was every day. I'm serious about it. No drugs, no beer, no alcohol. You could not believe the resilience in this kid, the convalescence in such a short amount of time." It wasn't long before Lloyd had begun to regain much of the weight he had lost after the shooting.

Where once he had been accused of drinking a case of beer a day, Lloyd, whose weight had dropped to 177 pounds in the hospital, boosted his weight to 190—each day drinking a case of a high-calorie, high-protein nutrient mixture. "That's fifteen cans to each case," Kevin said.

Kevin, Ronnie and Tom Rome, the agent, even made plans to enroll Lloyd in an out-patient drug and alcohol rehabilitation program and, until all the logistics could be worked out, formed a network that enabled them to keep someone with him "24/7"—twenty-four hours a day, seven days a week. "Team Daniels," they called it. "He is constantly, constantly, constantly occupied," Kevin said. "That's so important right now." As Ronnie said, "You know what they say about horses? Well, we're leading him to water."

There were positive signs that their efforts had managed to affect the situation. When Ronnie made a mistake and ordered a beer at dinner one night with Kevin and Lloyd, Lloyd just looked at him and said, "Go ahead, Ron. I know I can't have no beer."

"He went out for a run around the block one night," Kevin said, "and all these little kids started running along with him. It was like a scene out of 'Rocky.' Except Lloyd was telling them, 'Don't do drugs.' People come up to him on the street and say, 'Hey, we want to see you play again.' You cannot believe it. This is amazing, the change."

One night Lloyd picked up a doll of the Popeye character Swee'pea that Kevin had bought for his son, John. Ronnie was there. "Yo, Ron," Lloyd said. "We got to ask Tom. When I make the NBA, can I still use 'Swee'pea' or do we got to get permission? We'd be stealin' it, right? He had it first."

The moment was good for a laugh and, it showed that Lloyd did still want to make the NBA. Still, as usual with Lloyd, it remained to be seen just how long the good times, the sober, drug-free times, would last. Would it be long enough for him to make a serious run at professional basketball? Would it be long enough for him to just get on with his life? Would it be an hour, a day, a week, a month, a year? No one, it seemed, knew for sure.

"I just feel so confident that this could happen this time," said Kevin, for better or worse, an eternal optimist. "I know it could. The past, we can't change. Now, it's all the future. All the future . . . all the future. This could be the time it happens, the time he makes it."

"I'm keeping my fingers crossed," Ronnie said. "If you didn't think you could win this game—had no chance of winning—you'd forfeit. Walk away. But, look at this kid. He was shot in the neck and the bullet just missed the jugular. He took one in the chest and it just missed his heart. If the ambulance broke down on the way to the hospital, he was dead, anyway. And here he is out of the hospital and playing ball. You have to believe there is a reason. Maybe, this time, he finally got the message."

It sounded so familiar, the refrain.

The kids surrounded Lloyd just outside the entrance to the subway stop near the park at West Fourth Street. "Swee'pea," one said. "Give us your autograph?" One after another, Lloyd signed, scrawling his name, almost illegible. And, he continued to do so as he walked toward the park and later, even as he changed out of his street clothes along the fence.

Lloyd had come to Manhattan to get a few runs with some serious folks—just to see where he stood. With word out on the street that he might show, the kids came, too.

In New York City, performance reviews more often than not are rated on fan appreciation—appreciation of a dunk, of a shot, of a pass, of a move. With the crowd lined four deep in places along the fence, Lloyd understood full well that, this afternoon, the critics were out in force. He wasted little time, then, showing them just what he could still do.

The court at West Fourth is a box and games there are more often like a steel cage match than basketball. Rules are that there are no rules. Dunks, jams and flagrant fouls are what happens there. It is body-on-body.

But, on an afternoon when the mercury soared into the nineties and he, himself, had a temperature of 102—the result of a bout with the flu—Lloyd raised the game to an art form at West Fourth.

While others dunked, he shot. While others shot, he passed. While others looked on, he hit shots they dared not attempt. And, while others stood awaiting his next move, he made passes they believed could not be made. When he was done, he had amassed 21 points with 24 assists. "Bullets don't stop my man Lloyd," someone in the crowd screamed. Said another: "He's had more chances than the law allows. But the man still got it."

Indeed, he did. One night, that summer, he dropped forty on Ricky Sobers. Another night, on a team that featured Syracuse-bound Conrad McRae, as well as a host of other local high school and college stars—Jamal Faulkner, Shane Drisdom, Wilfred Kirkaldy, Future Pollard, Effrem Whitehead and Duane Causwell, among them—he hit seven consecutive three-point jumpers in the second half of a game to be voted the most valuable player at a tournament in New Cassel, Long Island.

Soon, Tom Rome received new interest in Lloyd. The Harlem Globetrotters wanted him to come to camp in the fall. A team in Greece offered a contract worth over $100,000. A team in Spain wanted him. A team in the Italian Basketball Federation offered to outbid the team in Greece. Several NBA teams even made preliminary inquiries, according to Rome.

"A lot of people are interested," Rome said. "But it has gotten to the point where the kid has got to do it himself. He has just got to go to a camp and do it, show what he can do. It's not such a big leap for him."

"All I need is a chance," Lloyd said. "I can't even think about failin'." Asked what he was doing different to ensure success this time, Lloyd issued a straight-forward answer. "Workin' hard and pissin' clean," he said.

It sounded good. The problem was, as usual, it wasn't true. Lloyd had been enrolled in an out-patient substance abuse program and had been asked to submit to urinalysis. But, according to Rome, Lloyd often failed to attend the aftercare meetings. And, he proved unwilling to submit to drug tests. As Kevin Barry said, "Why is it every time he's supposed to take a drug test, he's nowhere to be found?" The answer was soon apparent.

There was a meeting with Dr. Pizzi in June when Lloyd agreed to submit to urinalysis. But, later that afternoon when Lloyd appeared for the test to be administered, he had changed his mind and refused to take it.

"The idea was for him to start proving that he was clean so he could build a good track record," Ronnie recalled. "And Lloyd agreed to take the test. But then when we got down there, he said no, he wouldn't take it. I was really pissed off. We got into an argument over it. I told him, 'You piece of shit. Why are you going back on your word?' He said, 'C'mon Ron. Don't you trust me?' I said, 'No, I don't trust you. Why should I trust you?'

"He said he felt there was no reason for him to have to prove that he was clean, that he should be trusted. I started yelling and told him, 'Look, if you're not going to do it, let's get the fuck out of here, because I don't want to have to deal with none of your bullshit.' He tried talking to me, but I said, 'Just shut the fuck up. No more of your shit. Get in the fuckin' car, I'm dropping your ass off at Kevin's. I can't deal with any more of this.' He kept on telling me, 'Yo, I'm clean, Ron. I'm clean.' "

The problems were sporadic. For a week, Lloyd would be fine. He would work out, meet his obligations and all would go well. Then, one night, he would leave the house and not come home. "You know what they say about the monkey on your back?" Kevin said. "Well, it's almost like he has this monkey inside him and that monkey sleeps almost all the time. But, when he feels the need for a mind-altering drug, the monkey goes berserk."

Kevin thought the best solution might be to get Lloyd out of New York. He took him to the Sugar Ray Leonard-Thomas Hearns fight in Las Vegas. For Lloyd, it was like going home. He saw David Chesnoff, his former attorney, and his former guardian, Mark Warkentien.

There, arrangements were made for Lloyd to join a Dutch basketball team on a ten-game tour against teams from the World Basketball League—a professional league for players under 6-foot-5. Two of the games on the tour were scheduled to be in Las Vegas, where the team, Meppel-Computerij of Meppel, Holland, would face the Las Vegas Silver Streaks, who were owned by Bernie Glannon, the former owner of the Topeka Sizzlers.

"The pay will be minimal," Glannon said. "But it'll be the opportunity to play ten games. I'll encourage that if I'm convinced Lloyd is straight."

League commissioner Steve Ehrhart, who said Lloyd could appear because opponents on non-league teams faced no height restrictions, said, "He claims he has straightened out and we are giving him a great opportunity to prove to people that he has done that. He approached us. He was very open about his background, his ups and downs and his problems. This seemed like a fair opportunity for him to either put up or shut up. The American public will now get a chance to see what he is all about." And it did. Because, arrangements made, Lloyd never arrived at the first practice session.

Perhaps, that was no surprise, considering there were many indications that he was also having problems in Las Vegas—among them, according to at least one source, that he had been seen at the Leonard-Hearns post-fight party draining drink glasses, all while warning the partygoers in a slurred voice, "Don't do drugs. Drugs'll kill you. Don't do drugs."

Ronnie Lott, the all-league defensive back from the San Francisco 49ers, pulled him aside a moment. "Do you know how much money they'll pay you if you only stay clean?" Lott told Lloyd. "You could have a good life." Everson Walls, the defensive back from the Dallas Cowboys, also offered some advice. "You've got to come through this," he said. "You could do so much."

Finally, Pooh Richardson, the guard from UCLA who had just been drafted by the Minnesota Timberwolves, walked up to Lloyd and said, "Lloyd, be real. Wake up and see what you're doing to yourself."

But the advice, like with those folks back at I.S. 59 in Springfield Gardens after the death of Len Bias, fell on deaf ears. Once back home, the trouble continued. And one afternoon, an undercover policeman spotted him in Roosevelt Park off Houston Street near the Bowery in Manhattan.

"We make about five-hundred, six-hundred collars a year in that park," the officer, Detective John Kanovsky of the Manhattan South Narcotics Unit, said. "It's a park known for drugs. If you're there, you're not there to play ball and you're not there to meet friends. I saw him milling around. He was wearing a red sweatsuit. I walked over and said, 'Hey, Swee'pea. How you doin'?' He looked at me, realized that I was a cop, and said, 'Oh, okay.' He made believe he was dribbling and shooting. Then, he walked away."

So much for rehabilitation.

It was around midnight when Kevin, Ronnie and a friend reached Gerard Avenue. They had just come from an affair at the New York Athletic Club and, dressed in suits, to the people that lined the streets that time of night, they more resembled narcs than a couple of people in search of a friend.

The block was a shambles and the element of danger all too apparent. Just a block or two from Yankee Stadium, it was in one of the worst sections of the Bronx. It also was not at all the environment for a man with a bad habit to be in. Yet it was here Lloyd had come to live with a cousin.

Ronnie stopped the car in front of the building on Gerard. Fearing it might be stolen, he and Kevin got out—and locked their other friend inside.

"You got to see this street," Ronnie said. "It was the middle of the night, but everyone was out, drinking, doing drugs, selling drugs. It was the type of block you could get killed on and, here we are, we got suits on and people are looking at us. I mean, this was shady. We walked into the building and these two addicts are standing there and they see us and figure we're cops, so they start to run. We walk over to the elevator and hit the button, but this woman comes over and, in Spanish, she says, 'No trabaja.' In other words, it don't work. So, we walk the six flights to the door and, when we get there, we knock. We're knocking, knocking. We hear noises inside the apartment and Kevin goes to me, 'I hope we got the right one. I don't want to die.'

"With that, Lloyd steps out and shakes our hands. He goes, 'Yo Ron, Kev. Word up. How you guys doin'?' No sooner does he say that than two gunshots ring out in back, in the alley outside the window—and, I mean, this ain't no bullshit. They were gunshots."

"I'm like, 'Lloyd, get your stuff and let's get the fuck out of here,' " Kevin said. "But Lloyd was like, 'C'mon, that's just the way it is up here.' "

Back in the car, the four drove a few blocks to the Stadium, where Kevin, Ronnie and Lloyd got out and talked alongside the outfield wall.

"Is this what you want to do with your life?" Kevin asked Lloyd. "If it is, then keep doin' it and I don't want to hear from you no more." Lloyd looked at him and, as Kevin later said, "He gave me a bullshit story."

"No, Kev," Lloyd told him. "I don't want this. I was just checkin' it out for a few days. Really, I was just checkin' it out."

As they stood there under the el—the elevated IRT subway tracks—cars, trucks and even a few buses went by them. And, as they did, a few people leaned out the windows. "Hey, Swee'pea. Stay clean," one driver yelled. "Yo, Lloyd," yelled another. "You can do it." It was a strange kind of sad.

Lloyd came home the next afternoon. But, as Kevin said, he wasn't quite sure whether that was because he really did care what happened or because Mike Tyson had left tickets for him, Kevin, Ronnie and Joey Boy for his fight that night against Carl (The Truth) Williams and Lloyd didn't have a ride to Atlantic City. Whatever the case, the four headed to Atlantic City and arrived to find that the fight had ended just moments before—another knockout by Tyson.

In the lobby, Kevin ran into new Kentucky coach Rick Pitino and began to talk. "How are you Lloyd?" Pitino said when he saw Swee'pea, whom he and his staff had scouted when he was at Providence. Lloyd talked to Pitino, who was holding a beer, his first, then pulled aside Kevin. "Damn," Lloyd said. "The man should watch his liquor and stop worryin' 'bout me."

The post-fight party was held in the Convention Center. LeRoy Neiman said hello to Lloyd and told him he had seen him down at West Fourth Street. "I'll be out there drawing you soon," Neiman said. Heavyweight contender Evander Holyfield stopped over to speak with Lloyd. "You look good," Holyfield told him. "Watch those bullets."

For a while, Lloyd talked with Charles Oakley, Charles Barkley and Benoit Benjamin. But then Kevin ran into Linda Taylor, the wife of Lawrence Taylor, the all-pro linebacker for the Giants. Kevin had met Taylor at a golf outing with Fran Tarkenton. He had met Linda through her husband. He thought that, since Linda had suffered through the drug addiction of her husband, maybe she could talk to Lloyd about his problem. "She was like, 'Let me give you a lecture,' " Lloyd said. "She said, 'I understand what you're goin' through. My husband, you know, he's workin' his problems out. It's tough, but hang in there. Take it one day at a time.' " But Lloyd wasn't listening.

Instead, he seemed to be more concerned with his celebrity status. As he said, "Hey, everyone was admirin' that night."

From there, it got no better. Too many nights, Lloyd did not come home. When he did, Kevin said he either smelled of beer or appeared to be high. A few times, Kevin locked Lloyd out of the house. Other times, the two sat all night talking about his problems—which included, according to Kevin, much more than drugs and alcohol. "The kid was a con man," Kevin said.

There were the phone charges, which were all to hot-line numbers. Kevin thought Lloyd was calling the sex phone or something. But he wasn't. "The bill was one-hundred-and-fifty dollars," Kevin said. "They were 'Freddie' bills, you know, Freddie Krueger from 'Nightmare on Elm Street.' Can you believe that? I thought it was sex calls and it was 'Freddie' calls. It's like he's twelve years old."

Then, there was the twenty dollars Lloyd "borrowed" from the paper route run by Kevin's son. There was the twenty-five dollars he "borrowed" from the local pizza boy. "He told him, 'Oh, don't worry. Kevin'll pay you back,' " Kevin said. And, then there was the ten dollars he "borrowed" from the kid who lived next door to Kevin.

"He told the kid, 'Oh, my grandma is sick and I got to go see her before I go to training camp with the Boston Celtics. That's why I need the money.' He told the kid, 'When Kevin comes home, he'll pay you back. Just ask him.' You know, when this kid isn't on drugs, he's the nicest kid in the world. But, at times like that, when he is, he isn't worth knowing."

Finally, Kevin kicked him out of the house and didn't let him back.

"You know," Tom Rome said, thinking about it, "I don't understand the attractions that lead someone away from success. Kids like Lloyd still respect that success, that NBA success, but they refuse to do what is needed to achieve it when it is right there in front of them.

"It's the existentialist dilemma," he said. "It's a bizarre combination of skills and non-skills, refinements and non-refinements. I equate basketball to a high form of dance. It's art. And yet, a guy like Lloyd is artless when it comes to figuring out how to stay on a team, how to stick with a program. There has got to be a root cause. Maybe, it's that kids like him are not encouraged to develop responsibility. Maybe, it's the environment. Maybe, it's that they expect the world owes them a living. I don't know.

"It's the Lloyd Daniels Mystery. We don't want him to be the next Fly Williams. But it could be that he'd rather be 'Lloyd Daniels, The Playground Legend' instead of 'Lloyd Daniels, The NBA Legend.' "

19 · Back in the 'Ville

The building is brown outside now, but despite a fresh coat of paint the old apartment on Jersey Avenue still fails to make much of an appearance. Maybe it is the wrought-iron gates needed to protect the remaining windows from unwanted late-night visitors, or maybe the broken building door which, without a doorknob, blows open and rattles on its hinges in the brisk mid-winter breeze. Maybe it is the skewed, hand-painted number—Number 508, New Jersey—that adorns the arch over the door.

It still looks unclean. Looks worn, looks used. Litter clings to the low fence surrounding the unkempt front yard. The neighborhood, well, it still looks like a scene from an old war movie—a dog lies dead in the vacant lot behind the building; an old, abandoned fire truck lies overturned amid the rubble in the lot a block over. A few little kids played in the postage-stamp sized playground across the street, still too young not to remain impervious to the elements, their time still to come.

"Mrs. Sargeant!" Ronnie yelled, as he stood near the door. "Mrs. Sargeant!" Above him, in the second-floor window, eyes peeked from behind a drawn curtain. "Mrs. Sargeant!" Ronnie yelled, again. Still, there was no answer.

Uneasily, Ronnie pushed open the unlocked front door to the building and stepped into the hall. It was a hideous color orange, dark and unlit. Bare wires hung from a broken fixture overhead. Nearby, a pipe leaked its contents, one drop at a time, onto the floor, which seemed to disintegrate beneath his feet. In front of him, the stairs also seemed to crumble as they reached toward the second floor landing.

Ronnie knocked on the first-floor door and, as he did, a noise startled him. "Mrs. Sargeant?" he asked. No, he decided, the noise was from behind him, footsteps, then the voice of a man who was coming down those rickety old stairs. "Who you lookin' for?" the man said, matter-of-fact.

"I was looking for Mrs. Sargeant," Ronnie said. "I'm a coach. I used to coach her grandson, Lloyd Daniels. I heard he was around here."

"The tall kid who played basketball?" the man said, changing his tone.

"Yeah," Ronnie said. "That's him."

"Saw him yesterday, I think," the man said. "Haven't seen him today. He might have gone to the YMCA to shoot around a bit. Mrs. Sargeant, though, she ain't here. She went to stay with her daughter, I think."

"Do you know where?" Ronnie asked.

"No," said the man. "But, if I see him, who'd I tell him was lookin'?"

"Tell him Ron," Ronnie said. "He'll know. Tell him to call Ron."

Lloyd had been home for a few weeks now, ever since he had left Moline, Illinois, where he had lived the previous three months. He had gone there, just five months after he recovered from the shooting, to play for the Quad City Thunder in the Continental Basketball Association. He had done all he could there, too—attended a rehabilitation program at the United Medical Center of Davenport, Iowa, submitted to regular testing, pissed clean—and he had made the team. "We were all a bit skeptical," Thunder coach Mauro Panaggio said at the time, "but he has been very positive, very cooperative. His biggest problem seems to be that he was one of those individuals who learned how to run before he learned how to walk. Somewhere along the line, that catches up to you. It is obvious the talent is there. But it still needs to be educated, still needs to be refined. It's up to him."

Things being what they were, Panaggio and his staff were not about to wait long for that to happen. This was professional basketball. Lloyd had lasted just four games with the Thunder. The ironic part was, for once in his life, he had managed to remain clean. It was just that Quad City had a chance to acquire George Gervin, the former ABA and NBA All-Star, who was making a comeback at age thirty-seven. Gervin, a player Lloyd had often been compared to, played the same position. With a choice between a has-been who still had some marquee value and a never-was who was still not in game shape and who could find trouble at any corner in town, Quad City made its decision. Lloyd got cut.

Back in New York, Lloyd had seemingly disappeared into the streets. A few old friends, a few dealers who he had grown up with, the few that still were around, had heard from him. But Lloyd seemed to move through the neighborhood like the night wind, elusive. He would be one place one day, then gone the next. His grandmother, Lulia, had not heard from him. Neither had Kevin. Neither had Ronnie. So, Ronnie had taken to the neighborhood in an attempt to find him. He wanted to make sure he at least was alive.

After stopping by New Jersey Avenue, Ronnie checked the schoolyards. He went to 192 Park, went to P.S. 202. He stopped by the YMCA on Jamaica Avenue near the cemetery, but folks there said they had not seen Lloyd. He checked the projects, where he met a few B-Boys from the Brownsville Crew. But, no one had seen Lloyd. Ronnie took one last run over to Jersey Avenue. At least, he figured, he could leave a note for Annie Sargeant.

But when Ronnie opened the door to the building, a man was standing there—his coat on, a dirtied ski hat on his head, cigarette in hand. He looked haggard. "I'm Lloyd's uncle," the man said. "You lookin' for Lloyd?"

Ronnie looked at him, dumbfounded. "Yeah," he said.

"Well," the man said. "I could take you to him. He's in the projects. It wouldn't be no trouble." He paused for a moment. "A few bucks," he said, "should take care of it. That wouldn't be no trouble, right?"

"Yeah, whatever," Ronnie said, with a sly chuckle.

"Good," said Lloyd's uncle, who demanded $10. "Let's go."

Lloyd was stretched out under the covers in the bottom of a low bunk bed, his face buried in an open bottle of Vick's Vapo-rub, when Ronnie walked in. "Yo, Ron man," Lloyd said without moving from the bed, when he saw Ronnie. "What you doin' here? I ain't seen you in a while."

"What do you mean, what brings me by here?" Ronnie said, almost in disbelief. "What are you, sick or something?"

"Yeah, man. I got me a cold."

"No," Ronnie said. "I mean, what are you sick? I came by because no one's heard from you. Everyone thinks you're dead."

"Well, I ain't dead," he said.

"Yeah," Ronnie said, snidely. "You ain't dead."

The television was turned on. The Chicago Bulls were playing someone on national TV. "Go Michael J.," Lloyd yelled, as Michael Jordan went in for a jam. On the wall over the bed hung three posters. One of Jordan, one of Magic Johnson and the one of Lloyd. "You know," Lloyd said. "Someday . . ."

Ronnie cut him off. "Aw, shut the fuck up, someday. You know, you used to be all right. Notice how I said, 'Used to.' "

"What you mean, all right?" Lloyd said. "What you mean, 'Used to been?' "

"Like I said . . ."

"I told you, man, I'm sick. You know, I think that's 'cause my girl might be pregnant. Know how the men, theys sometimes get sick when they girls get pregnant? Ain't that right? Well, I think my girl's pregnant, 'cause I been sick a bit lately, like in the mornin's. But I still been playin' ball all the time. I still got it. I do. I mean it. I still got a chance. I know I do."

Ronnie shook his head.

At the foot of the bed Lloyd's cousin, Randy Stephens, sat laughing. "Ah, Lloyd," he said. "The man's doggin' you. Doggin' you big-time."

Stephens was fourteen. And, like a fifteen-year-old half-brother that Lloyd had named Jermaine, whom he never saw but who lived in Charlotte, North Carolina, and was reputed to be both a good player and a good student, already Stephens had a rep as a player who could make things happen. Better, he was a good student. "I've got a ninety-four average," he said. "I go to school all the time." Around the room, which belonged to him, hung certificates—some for his "excellent attendance record," some for his work in school and some for his "good citizenship."

"The kid's all right, Ron," Lloyd said. "He got a good game. He's goin' to be better than me. He even goes to school. He ain't like me."

"Someone here got brains, then," Ronnie said.

For an hour, Ronnie and Lloyd went back and forth. Ronnie getting in his digs, Lloyd trying to explain how he still had a chance, Randy laughing every time Ronnie scored with a shot. At one point, Randy switched the channel and found a game with Nevada-Las Vegas. Moses Scurry was in. So were Stacey Augmon and Larry Johnson.

"I guess it's a good thing you weren't on that team," Ronnie said to Lloyd, who would have been a senior on that team. "I don't know if you could handle being the second-best player behind Larry Johnson, which is what you'd have been."

"You know that ain't true, Ron," Lloyd said.

"If it ain't," Ronnie said, "when are you ever going to prove it?" Lloyd looked away, grabbed the bottle of Vick's and took another sniff.

Out in the hall that led to the living room, Annie Sargeant stood with her daughter, Barbara Stephens, Randy's mother. "You think Lloyd's ever goin' to make it?" she said. "He keeps sayin' he will, that some teams is interested in him. I think he could. He could, right? What you think? I think he could go somewhere—Europe, they say theys got some ball teams in Europe that likes him—and do good. I think he just needs one more chance."

"Yeah," she was told. "Yeah, sure."

It was a shame, because Lloyd would have fit in well with the Nevada-Las Vegas team that won the 1990 NCAA Championship. One, he could play. Even Jerry Tarkanian would have been hard-pressed to claim Lloyd wouldn't have started at one of the guard positions. And, based on some of the situations the team got into, it seemed Lloyd would not have been out of place.

Not only did this Rebels team talk real trash to its opponents—one Loyola-Marymount University player said, "On the court, other teams go, 'Where's your jumpshot?' These guys go, 'Where's your mother?' and, before you can answer, they go, 'In my hotel room' "—but it also did things like run up its phone bills. In fact, during the season six players were suspended for one game each for failure to pay their hotel phone bills. One of them was Moses Scurry. Of course, earlier in the season, Scurry had been academically ineligible for several games. The 6-foot-8, 205-pound forward had also been suspended for another game—for punching Utah State University coach Kohn Smith during a scuffle.

"How was I supposed to know he was the coach?" Scurry asked, in the aftermath of the incident. "He had a sweater on. I thought coaches wear suits and ties."

Despite his run-ins, Scurry was still playing well and by the end of the season even graced the cover of *Sports Illustrated*—pictured in action from the NCAA Championship Game, where Nevada-Las Vegas routed Duke.

Still, during the 1989-90 season no one in America really was on top of his game as much as Kenny Anderson. Just a freshman, Anderson had come into Georgia Tech and become an instant success. As the season neared the end, he was leading the Atlantic Coast Conference in assists, was a shoo-in for NCAA Division I Rookie of the Year and had become part of a new collegiate legend—something called "Lethal Weapon 3," the nickname awarded the three-guard offense of him, Brian Oliver and Dennis Scott.

"I'm not going crazy or nothing," Anderson said near the end of the season, which saw Georgia Tech earn a berth in the 1990 NCAA Final Four in Denver. "But I feel like I was touched this year, you know, touched by God or something. I mean, my year has gone so well that I don't know what else to think. All this happening to me has been incredible. It feels like a repeat of my freshman year in high school, it really does."

Lloyd was remembering the old days, too, as he sat in a booth at an Italian restaurant in Flatlands near Mill Basin talking about his life and where it had gone wrong. He had ordered his food and, unable to read the menu, had reached his decision on what to eat after he asked everyone else at the table what they were going to order. He was drinking a beer. "You know," he said, as he thought about his past, "I've had a fucked up life. People wanted to see me make it. But people couldn't be with me all the time, so I was fuckin' up. If I could do it all over, I'll put my hand on the Bible, I would do it different. You don't know how hard it is comin' up in a rough life.

"People made it easy for me, so I ain't goin' to use it as no excuse," he said, between bites of chicken. "I ain't goin' to use that as an excuse, you know, cryin' my head off sayin', 'That's why Lloyd didn't made it.' But you look, you probably couldn't have made it, comin' from my background. You see where I live. Don't I live all over? Do I got one steady home? Tell me I'm wrong. Do I have one steady home? Look at New Jersey Avenue. It's fucked up over there. My grandmother don't even stay there no more. You see how fucked up it is. Did you go inside? Rats be all in there, roaches be all over. I'm tellin' you straight up, as a man, a lot of people couldn't come up in my life. I ain't got to use that as no excuse, 'cause I had that basketball ability to take my grandmother and my family out of that. But I never learned how to do things like nobody else. I never had no one to show me. I needed somebody hard on me. I didn't have that."

As he sat there, it was easy to feel compassion for him, for all that he had missed in life, for his bad beginning, for the rough times. But he was twenty-two now, old enough to know better, old enough to be responsible for himself. After all, though some had tried to use him, exploit him for his basketball talent, many along the way had tried to help him make a better life, had tried to steer him clear of trouble, show him the right path.

But Lloyd had always just refused to listen. He had refused to listen to the advice of teachers, who wanted to help him in school. He had refused to listen to all the coaches who tried to teach him self-discipline, who knew what he could do if he only put his mind to it. He had refused to listen to friends, who were looking out for him. And, he had refused to listen to those who only wanted to see him make the simple effort that was needed to enable him to find success. So, wasn't he to blame, too?

"I could still make some camp," he said, as he finished the last drops of his third beer. He motioned for the waitress, who brought another, spilling it on the table. "Okay," she said, trying to make a joke of it. "Who's the alkie?"

"What'd she say?" Lloyd said, with a chuckle. "She call me an alkie?"

Told yes, he turned to her and said, "Well, then I guess you should get me another one."

It was as if, despite all he had been through, he just couldn't comprehend that he had done this to himself, that he remained the difference between success and failure, that he needed to change things if he wanted them to change. After all these years, Lloyd still knew the right things to say—but not how to act on them.

The con man had conned himself.

"Like I said, I could make a veteran camp," he said. "I ain't braggin' or nothin', but I killed some rookies last summer. I killed some rookies. If I'm straight, man, I can play with anybody. Ain't no one can play with me, you know that. I still got the 30-footer. I think my 'J' is better now, even. I just got to get back humble, I got to get back humble now, man, 'cause I still got it. I just got to get clean. I'm tryin' to work hard. I'm playin' ball every day. I swear to God, I'm playin' ball, man. I be in the parks, just shootin' around. Remember how I used to do? I'm workin' hard, just keep my skills up there. I'm tryin' to get back, no one ain't got to lead me. I'm doin' it now. For once in my life, I'm not bullshittin' myself. The man's tryin' to do somethin'. If I don't make it, if I can't make it big-time, then somethin's wrong, hear me?"

"The kid's a goner," Ronnie said, later, as he sat behind the wheel of his car, the engine running. "He's gone."

It was 10 p.m. It was pitch black outside. And here, on a sidestreet in the heart of East New York, Lloyd had asked Ronnie to stop the car, so he could take a piss on the side of a van parked in front of some row houses. "I got to take Herbie Love Puppy out for a walk," he said, as he hopped out. "This ain't goin' to be in the book, is it? You ain't goin' to put this in the book?"

Now, as Lloyd stood outside under the winter night sky, two teenage girls came down the block and, seeing him, one covered her eyes and the other walked around the far side of the van. "Hey, ladies," Lloyd said as he smiled, still taking his piss. "Herbie wants to say hello. Say hello to Herbie."

"You're sick," Ronnie said, when Lloyd got back in the car. "Just sick." He was laughing hard, now.

"Ain't goin' in the book, right?" Lloyd said. "No one wants to read 'bout Swee'pea takin' a piss, right?"

"Not unless it's clean piss," Ronnie said, as he stopped the car a few blocks away to drop Lloyd off where his cousin lived. "Not if it isn't clean."

"I'm tellin' you, man," Lloyd said as he stepped out of the car and back into the cold night air. "This time it'll be different, Ron. I mean it. This time, I'm goin' to make it, man. I am. I tell you, I am."

"He's a goner," Ronnie said, again, as he pulled away, leaving Lloyd standing there, alone in the night. "That's it, I think."

He shook his head. "He's gone."

The power lift moved across the floor dragging its cargo with it and it wasn't until after he had stacked the cartons on the floor that Lloyd Daniels, Sr., stopped it and sat for a moment. He was forty-two years old, a five-day-a-week stock man in the basement of Pergament's in Lake Success, New York. He was lean, in good shape and his face still looked young, though perhaps just a bit tired of all this. On each of his leather work gloves was written "Pops." He was, after all, about twenty years older than all of his co-workers here in stock.

"I don't really want to talk 'bout Lloyd," he said. "You wonder when the kid will ever realize what he's done to himself. You wonder when he'll ever get it together. The thing is, you can't tell these kids nothin' nowadays. They have to learn it all for themselves. That's just the way it is with them. That's all I can say. I can't say nothin' more 'bout it. 'Bout nothin'."

Then the man, who had never spent more than five minutes with his son since he had abandoned him, took his gloves, put them back on, dismissed himself from the conversation and went back to work.

It was strange, because the words echoed almost in an exact fashion what Lulia Hendley had said about her eldest son. That you couldn't tell him anything, that he had to learn it all for himself.

"Maybe that's just kids," she had said. "You just hope theys learned it right before it's too late."

Lulia was seated in her living room. Behind her were portraits of all the family members. In the next room, her grandchildren screamed as they ran back and forth across the floor. "You know," she said, "I had a son, died at twenty-six. Got shot. Shot three times with a .38 in the back. He had been connin' peoples at card games and God knows what else. Then one mornin', a Saturday mornin' I think, right down on Jamaica Avenue in front of the Blue Chips, somebody shot him three times in the back. His name was Hollis, Hollis Daniels. Junior's uncle. I had to go out there and identify him. It wasn't real pretty. But he had been hangin' out with his crew. It was what he wanted from life. You couldn't tell him nothin', either."

She was asked what this all had to do with her grandson. She said it had everything. She had heard all the stories, now. She said she felt it was hopeless, the situation. Where she used to laugh and joke with people about Lloyd—"Junior's goin' to make me an old man," she'd once said—now she became serious, quite serious. She had not seen Lloyd since he had been shot. She was not sure, in fact, if she would ever see him again.

"I don't know," she said, her voice now barely audible above the din from the other room. "Junior's a lost cause. I think he's lost in the mist now. He's twenty-two years old and he's not listenin' to nobody. And, you see what's goin' to make it bad for Lloyd is, number one, he doesn't have the education. See, if he had an education, it wouldn't be bad if he didn't make it. He could go out and get him a job. But what, what he's goin' to do? Tell me, what's he goin' to do? He don't know how to do nothin' else but basketball. That's it."

She looked down. There was a tear in the corner of her eye. Generations had passed in her family, as they had passed on the streets and in the parks, and still little had changed. Folks were still making the same mistakes. Folks were still finding the same trouble. And, in all honesty, Lulia could hardly see if they would ever get better, ever work out.

"Sooner or later," she said, "he'll kill hisself with drugs or booze or get killed hangin' out in the wrong place. I hate to say it, but that's my gut feelin'. He'll die a young man. If he don't convince himself he has a problem, then he'll die a young man. He's going in the wrong direction not to die a young man." Then, that strong-willed woman began to cry.

Index

About the Authors

John Valenti III, was born in 1960 in Brooklyn, NY and was raised in a variety of places. A 1982 graduate of Hofstra University, he has worked at *New York Newsday* since 1981. In 1987, he was part of a two-man investigative team that, stemming from a look into the college recruitment of Lloyd Daniels, documented alleged abuses in the recruitment of basketball players at the University of Nevada-Las Vegas. This series sparked an NCAA investigation of the school and garnered an award from the Associated Press Sports Editors Association as one of the best investigative stories of the year. He was also honored by *The Sporting News* in "Best Sports Stories: The Anthology that Honors 1989's Top Sports Writing and Photography," for a newspaper feature he wrote on the tragic fall of former Nevada-Las Vegas basketball star Richie Adams.

A former contributor to *Sport Magazine* and *The Sporting News*, Valenti covers a variety of college and pro sports for *New York Newsday*, though his favorite sport remains playground basketball. He and his wife Judy Lee, and son Jarek live in West Islip, NY.

Ronald E. Naclerio, born in 1958, is no stranger to sports. A former baseball prospect at St. John's University, he played the outfield on a team that went to the 1978 NCAA College World Series and later roomed with New York Mets relief ace John Franco. Known for his speed, in 1979 Naclerio led the NCAA in stolen bases and then did the same in the New York-Penn League, where he played in the White Sox organization before injuries cut short his career. Naclerio then returned to Cardozo High School in Bayside, Queens, his alma mater, to become a basketball coach.

A 1979 graduate of St. Johns, Naclerio received his Master of Science degree in 1987 and currently is the Dean of Special Education at J.H.S. 8 in Jamaica, Queens. He is the New York City Area Editor for *The Hoop Scoop*, a monthly basketball publication, and there isn't a player or playground in New York City that he hasn't heard of or visited. Naclerio is single and resides in Bayside, NY.

Knight Foundation
2 S. Biscayne Blvd
Miami, Fla
33131